"Chad Hoggan and Tetyana Hoggan-Klout ⁄⁄⁄⁄⁄ mitted researchers from various parts of Eure ⁄⁄⁄⁄⁄ write about one of the most urgent challenges our societies cope with today. This has resulted into a set of highly imaginative papers, reflecting on practices and theories of education, learning, dialogue, empowerment, trauma alleviation and story-telling. The book meets an urgent need in the field of adult education and beyond, where practitioners, activists and researchers continually engage themselves to create humane conditions of encounter and growth for people who desperately hope for a new beginning, respect and opportunities in a world that confronts them with many unforeseen challenges. Education professionals and practitioners will find much inspiration in this collection of captivating contributions."

Danny Wildermeersch, Professor Emeritus of Social and Cultural Pedagogy, Katholieke Universiteit Leuven, Leuven, Flanders, Belgium

"*Adult Learning in a Migration Society* is a timely and welcome contribution to the field of adult education. Authors from eleven countries in Europe and North America explore the role adult education plays in the development of migration societies. Chapters address not only the nature of the learning that takes place both at the individual and societal levels, but the tensions inherent in this learning such as integration versus indoctrination, adaptation versus resistance, the benefits and challenges of receiving societies. Woven throughout the chapters is the notion that such adult learning is transformative in nature as both the individual migrant and the migration society are continuously engaged in making meaning of the migrant experience. This volume robustly captures the importance of adult learning, and transformative learning in particular, in grappling with one of the more contentious issues in today's world."

Sharan Merriam, Professor Emerita of Adult and Continuing Education (co-author of *Learning in Adulthood*, 2020), The University of Georgia, Athens, GA

"In *Adult Learning in a Migration Society*, the reader is brought into the experiences of migrants, volunteer workers, counselors as well as researchers across different geographical locations. With a specific emphasis on the experiences and meaning making of migrants, the book provides thoughtful insights on what it means to be forced to flee one's own home, enter a new country, and the struggle to make a new home. The chapters together provide well needed food for thought for all those who are interested in issues pertaining to migration and learning."

Andreas Fejes, Professor and Chair of Adult Education Research, Linköping University, Linköping, Sweden

"A very timely book that reinforces the historical narrative that every member of society is a product of migration, a global phenomenon occurring since the beginning of recorded history. Yet, the backlash that confronts today's immigrants must be brought to the forefront of education, particularly adult education, where advocacy for diversity and inclusion form the bedrock of the scholarship and practice of the profession. This book profiles the works of international scholars who share perspectives and experiences of migrants as they transition from their beloved homeland to find 'home' in foreign lands. Highlighted in the discourse are persistent challenges, current practices, governmental responses, and the resilience of a people in transition. An important text from which to educate on the challenges and promises of migration in global contexts."

Mary V. Alfred, Professor of Adult Education, Texas A&M University, USA

ADULT LEARNING IN A MIGRATION SOCIETY

Migration is an old, perhaps perpetual, phenomenon. Currently, it is an urgent challenge involving huge numbers of people who leave their home in search of a better life. Differences in language, customs, and norms are often joined by specific manifestations of xenophobia born of particular differences between host countries and their current influx of migrants. In a pronounced way, then, migration reveals important societal questions—of solidarity, of identity, of transition and transformation, of human rights and obligations.

The explorations in this collection highlight individual stories of migrants, showcase innovative research methods, and explore concepts and theories that might be usefully applied toward learning needs in a migration society. Including insights from scholars across 14 different countries, this book offers an international perspective on the role of adult education in addressing migration. Such international comparisons hold great potential for seeing new possibilities in any single country, whether in Europe, North America, or across the world.

Chad Hoggan is an Associate Professor of Adult & Lifelong Education at North Carolina State University and co-editor of the Journal of Transformative Education. His research addresses the learning involved during major life changes and has included migrants, military veterans, and historically underserved college students.

Tetyana Hoggan-Kloubert is on the faculty at the University of Augsburg. Having migrated from Ukraine to Germany, she researches adult and civic education in diverse migration societies and in post-totalitarian contexts. She received her Ph.D. and habilitation from the University of Augsburg (Germany), focusing on the topics of indoctrination, propaganda, and democracy.

AMERICAN ASSOCIATION FOR ADULT AND CONTINUING EDUCATION CO-PUBLICATIONS

Adult Learning in a Migration Society
Eds. Chad Hoggan and Tetyana Hoggan-Kloubert

ADULT LEARNING IN A MIGRATION SOCIETY

*Edited by Chad Hoggan and
Tetyana Hoggan-Kloubert*

NEW YORK AND LONDON

Cover image: Photo by Dr. Michael Schirner

First published 2022
by Routledge
605 Third Avenue, New York, NY 10158

and by Routledge
2 Park Square, Milton Park, Abingdon, Oxon OX14 4RN

Routledge is an imprint of the Taylor & Francis Group, an informa business

Library of Congress Cataloging-in-Publication Data
Names: Hoggan, Chad, 1971- editor. | Hoggan-Kloubert, Tetyana, 1981-editor.
Title: Adult learning in a migration society / edited by Chad Hoggan, Tetyana Hoggan-Kloubert.
Description: New York, NY : Routledge, 2022. |
Series: Series on adult education | Includes bibliographical references and index.
Identifiers: LCCN 2021032363 (print) | LCCN 2021032364 (ebook) |
ISBN 9780367644109 (hardback) | ISBN 9780367644116 (paperback) |
ISBN 9781003124412 (ebook)
Subjects: LCSH: Immigrants--Education--Case studies. | Adult education--Case studies.
Classification: LCC LC3715 .A38 2022 (print) | LCC LC3715 (ebook) |
DDC 371.826/912--dc23
LC record available at https://lccn.loc.gov/2021032363
LC ebook record available at https://lccn.loc.gov/2021032364

ISBN: 978-0-367-64410-9 (hbk)
ISBN: 978-0-367-64411-6 (pbk)
ISBN: 978-1-003-12441-2 (ebk)

DOI: 10.4324/9781003124412

Typeset in Bembo
by Taylor & Francis Books

CONTENTS

ILLUSTRATIONS

Figures

Tables

SERIES EDITOR INTRODUCTION

On behalf of the American Association of Adult and Continuing Education, I am very excited to see the inaugural publication of our Series on Adult Education. This series was designed to offer innovative and imaginative approaches to issues in adult and continuing education. We also hope that this new series will build a confluence of identity and strength, providing a central place for new research on adult continuing education. Drawing attention to the field will help with further understanding the ways that adult education and lifelong learning impact learning organizations and institutions, and how policy decisions can affect the provision of services.

This first publication is emblematic of the kinds of works that this series was developed to publish. Edited by Chad Hoggan and Tetyana Hoggan-Kloubert, *Adult Learning in a Migration Society* examines the multiple ways that migrants and those who work with migrants learn and ultimately work to transform themselves and their environments. Understanding the experience of migration is an issue of the utmost importance because it affects so many societies in our present world. While we in the United States have faced this issue explicitly for centuries, the debate continues. This book, which is international in focus, looks at the migration experience in Europe. Its thoughtful and timely explication of transformative learning in the lives of those affected by migration serves as a useful template for thinking about adult learning in its broadest context. It also adds to the theoretical basis for understanding migrants and working with them and as such is a welcome addition to the vast literature on migration. The emphasis on transformative learning offers a unique window for furthering our understanding of the migration experience. It emphasizes both the unique and generalized issues that migrants around the world face.

This book is a wonderful first publication for our new series and is of great importance to the field. As we look to the future, it is my hope that the series will become essential reading for those interested in and concerned about adult and continuing education.

I would like to thank the editors and the contributing authors for their hard work and insight in this endeavor. I would also like to thank the Publications Committee for their work in developing this series and my predecessors in the AAACE Presidency, Larry Martin and Mary Alfred, who initially envisioned this project.

Thomas D. Cox, E.D.
President, AAACE (2020–2021)

FOREWORD

Paul Mecheril

Movements of people across borders have taken place almost everywhere and in every historical era. Migration is a universal human activity. Even if it is not an exclusively modern phenomenon, it is nonetheless characterized by specifically modern conditions. Perhaps at no point in history were so many people worldwide *prepared* to migrate, *compelled* to migrate due to environmental disasters, (civil) wars, and other threats, and *able* to shift their location of work and daily life across great distances thanks to technological changes that mitigate the limits of space and time. Accordingly, in recent times, cross-border movements of people have taken on particular significance for individuals and societies worldwide.

The world is drawing closer together in terms of communication and transportation technologies, and local events are giving rise to trans-local effects. The nation-state is thus no longer the unquestioned point of reference for individual and collective ways of life. This becomes particularly clear when looking at the deep economic, ecological, medial, toxicological, social, political, technological, and cultural entanglements of the various regions, nation-states and continents of the world. The process of transnationalizing the world is progressing not solely, but also, due to intensive migration movements.

Migration, in a very basic sense, can be understood as the attempt to take charge of one's own life with regards to geographical, ecological, political, and cultural circumstances. Against this backdrop, transnational and transcontinental migration is an attempt to influence one's own life in a fundamental sense and is therefore representative of a prototype of the modern, self-determined lifestyle—with all its ambivalences, illusions and dubious consequences. "Be brave, use your reason and free yourself from the position that was forced upon you by the geopolitical order." Drawing on a reference to Immanuel Kant, this is the credo of the new transnational modernity that is formed and formulated by migrants without an intention or a program necessarily underlying it.

Migration is a specific form of bodily border-crossing. The consequences of movements across borders can be examined and understood as a phenomenon in which new knowledges, experiences, languages, and perspectives are introduced into existing social constellations, and as a result are rearranged and inevitably changed. The border-crossing movement of people, the movement of their ways of life and their languages, hopes, desires, stories, and memories, mobilizes the function of borders, but also raises the question of their functionality and challenges the registers of the symbolic, legal, and moral legitimacy of borders.

Migration phenomena challenge, unsettle, and disrupt the legitimacy and functionality of the (natio-racial-culturally coded) "Us." They also question the legitimacy and functionality of institutional routines such as linguistic practices or practices of collective memory. Lastly, migration as the movement of people across borders, as well as a discourse that shapes new knowledge about belonging and citizenship, troubles culturally dominant views and opinions about the legitimacy and functionality of individual privileges, for example the privilege to not only expect but also to claim that one's own language is also the language of the other.

As Ezra Park pointed out over 90 years ago in the *American Journal of Sociology*, the effect of mobility and migration is the secularization of relationships that were once sacred. At the same time, many political, discursive and cultural reactions to migration phenomena aim to intensify the sacral nimbus of institutions, such as the nation-state, which is based on a certain way of constructing space as territory, and of constructing people who have referential links as a nationally-ethnically-culturally encoded "Us."

Under the current conditions, which are also shaped by transnational migration, the understanding and practices of the nation-state are in a deep and fundamental crisis both in terms of practical functionality and legitimacy. In the foreword to the German edition of his book on nations and nationalism first published in 1990, Eric Hobsbawm writes that the process that allowed farmers to be turned into Frenchmen and immigrants into American citizens is currently being reversed, and he closes the foreword with the question of what, if anything, will replace the general model of the relationship between a state and its people in the 21st century. His response: We don't know.

In contrast to what the predominant semantics of crises suggest, we are currently dealing not so much with a migration or refugee crisis as with a crisis of legitimacy and functionality of the nation-state, a crisis that is intensified not only, but certainly also, by transnational migration. Transnational migration can be understood and studied as a phenomenon dealt with in political and public discourses that problematizes the limits of the given order and thus unsettles this order.

In this sense, the central socio-theoretical hallmark of migration is its ability to unsettle social relations and regulations, which can be interpreted politically from two different perspectives when presented as a "crisis"—either as a threat or as an opportunity. In medical terms the word crisis connotes a state of uncertainty or limbo that is moving towards a turning point. Since early modernity, the medical definition of crisis has been carried over and applied to the realm of the social. In line with this analogy, societal and political conditions are occasionally compared to a feverish, and as such critical, condition that for its continuity depends on a decisive change one way or the other.

Throughout this book, I read the contributions as a commitment to reflecting on the problematization of the natio-ethno-cultural boundary between "Us" and "the Others" in European contexts as an opportunity to expand the realm of what Hoggan-Kloubert and Hoggan call "human dignity." And perhaps this is precisely the task of responsible migration research, whose first goal is not to contribute to the stabilization of the given institutions, but to strive to identify and describe conditions for the possibility of dignified life in the migration society.

Above all, the attempts to sacralize the "Us," based on and mobilizing racist ways of thinking and feeling, as we can observe worldwide and not at least in Europe, point to the importance of this orientation. Racism is a doubly modern order. The cataloguing of humanity in the spirit of the awakening natural sciences is a distinctive moment in the assertion of racial division. Observed individual characteristics are inserted and arranged and "tamed" and "conquered" by incorporation into an order. At the beginning of racial thinking, the medium for the "conquest of the human" is the color of skin: it becomes an important instrument for the selection and classification of human beings into different races. Here coloration is not so much an "objective point of reference" for the attributes of human beings as it is the result of cultural processes of definition. The fundamental question of racism, how human life is understood and which characteristics assign individual groups their place in the social structure, and the way racism answers this question, must be considered in the context of other (world) societal phenomena: racism serves as an ideology of justification to legitimize colonial expansions and slavery and, currently, orders of belonging with their material and symbolic boundaries that distribute the right to lead dignified, secure lives differently.

A particular type of affect and affective way of speaking, for example, in the European public sphere is tied to racist differentiations between a natio-racial-culturally coded "Us" and the dangerous, backward "Them" (Not-Us), which furthermore serves to strengthen this differentiation, and can be described and understood as a practice of Othering and Selfing with recourse to threat scenarios (and scenes). The racist demonization of migrants serves to maintain a hegemonic order of belonging with which self-determination rights of "the Others" are warded off. Thus, we are dealing with two sides of a coin: the imagination of the Other and the process of securing material and symbolic privileges.

An increase in the transnational movement of people can be observed due to the shrinking global space, a phenomenon which is in part due to (the advance of) communication and transport technology. This gives rise to two principles: either to recognize the movement or to intensify practices of symbolic and material border security and the use and development of corresponding technologies, thereby increasing the costs of border security. I believe that these costs cannot be morally justified. I am not speaking primarily about the economic costs of border security, although these are certainly significant. The global regulation of migration is not only financially expensive as well as illusionary because its efficacy is limited, but it also incurs a high cost in terms of human lives and human suffering. Here we are talking about the moral costs of preventing the global right to self-determination as a result of global patterns of movement where, for example, according to the United Nations High Commissioner for Refugees, more than 2200 refugees died in the Mediterranean Sea in 2018. Racist patterns of thought and feeling serve to legitimize this practice.

Nation-states distinguish between those who belong to the particular societal context and those who do not. They accomplish this using natio-racial-culturally coded patterns in a highly complex, often contradictory, and ever-changing context. The education system and educational approaches play an important role in the affirmation and reproduction of these patterns of distinction in part due to the institutionalization of a special form of social work involving "work with migrants," or because schools may employ the mechanisms of institutional discrimination, or because adult education in the migration society is guided by the need to compensate for the supposed competence deficits on the part of migrants. But, pedagogy also has the potential and possibilities to reflect upon these patterns and the practices that confirm them, as well as to consider and promote emancipatory alternatives. Those interested in such alternatives will gain diverse perspectives and differentiated suggestions through the chapters of the present book.

Emancipatory pedagogy can never simply refer affirmatively to given societal conditions. Consequently, the contributions of *Adult Learning in a Migration Society* are committed to the paradigm of transformative learning, i.e., learning that does not represent a mere gain of knowledge or information, but transforms in a reflexive figure the socially learned and appropriated patterns in which learning takes place. Transformative learning and transformative adult education in the migration society aim, as the contributions to this book make very stimulatingly clear, to critically reflect upon particular forms of life that deny those who are considered as "Others" in the migration society the right to a dignified life. In this sense, transformative learning positively aims at creating and enabling learning processes that contribute to forms of sociability and solidarity.

With reference to conditions in migration societies, solidarity can be understood as a generally appropriate goal of transformative learning processes. However, as the explanations in the book chapters illustrate thoughtfully, this cannot be about the narrow solidarity that only allows solidarity within the limited framework of a particular "Us."

Under societal conditions of plurality and (super)diversity, solidarity among the unfamiliar and foreign gains in importance. The reference to the unfamiliarity and strangeness of others with whom one is not "familiar," but who are nevertheless pragmatically relevant (e.g., on a political or ecological dimension) and to whom the motif of solidarity refers, sets itself apart from models that tie solidarity exclusively to lifeworld and emotional proximity.

This book aims to recognize and shape practical connections that link people beyond the sole reference to the "village," the "nation," the "people," and beyond the sole solidary reference to other "villagers" or "compatriots." The understanding of solidarity, which is significant in the context of transformative learning in the migration society, thus refers to social relations of a commitment to a counterpart who may be "unfamiliar," but with whom the individual actor stands in practical connection in the context of the global migration society. Here, solidarity is borne by reference to others, which (in turn) only becomes solidarity as an action or willingness to act. In this respect, solidarity is something different and something more than mere compassion, than indignation, or than a moral statement. Solidarity in the migration society is a commitment to changing and preventing conditions in which social cooperation partners, both foreign to me or familiar, cannot develop and evolve dignified forms of life.

Adult Learning in a Migration Society aims to expand the realm in which what people do, feel and think is entitled to dignity. The chapters of this book are committed to this emancipatory learning principle and offer diverse intellectual impulses to anyone interested in questions of learning in a migration society that sees itself as democratic.

CONTRIBUTORS

Chad Hoggan is an Associate Professor of Adult and Lifelong Education at North Carolina State University, USA, and Co-editor of the Journal of Transformative Education. His research addresses learning experiences that dramatically affect how people see themselves and the world around them. He has studied this with a wide range of research participants, including immigrants, breast cancer survivors, military veterans, and historically underserved college students. His books include *Creative Expression in Transformative Learning* and *Transformational Learning in Community Colleges,* which won the Cyril O. Houle Award for Outstanding Literature in Adult Education from the American Association for Adult & Continuing Education (AAACE) in 2020.

Tetyana Hoggan-Kloubert is 'akademische Rätin' (Associate Professor) at the University of Augsburg, Germany. Having migrated from Ukraine to Germany in 2001, she researches migration, civic education (and indoctrination) in Eastern Europe, Western Europe and the United States. As a visiting researcher, she conducted research at various U.S. universities (Harvard University, Tufts University). Since 2015 she has been annually co-organizing the Summer Institute of Civic Studies, which focuses on how citizens can be supported in their efforts to co-create their worlds.

Stefan Alexa is an educator, researcher and writer, with an active interest in fiction and auto/ biography. He completed his Doctorate in Education at Canterbury Christ Church University, UK, with a thesis that appraised the concept of 'terrorist learning' within a narratively imagined space where 'pilgrimages', 'clowns', 'masks' and—not least—his own 'nomadic' journeys out and back to Bukovina, a meaningful borderland in Eastern Europe, were invited to work together in auto/

biographic ways. He is currently a Senior Lecturer at Bath Spa University and Anglia Ruskin University, UK and a Founding Fellow of the Chartered College of Teaching, UK.

Georgia Barkoglou is a PhD student at the Open University of Cyprus. Her doctoral research investigates life transitions and transformation of adult migrant learners' identities through their biographical experiences. She holds a Master's degree in Educational Studies that investigated teachers' needs and perspectives on the education of Muslim students in Thrace, Greece. She is currently working as a Greek Literature teacher. She is also a volunteer adult educator at the Solidarity School of Odysseus in Thessaloniki.

Elisabeth Beck is a Research Associate at the Center for Flight and Migration at the University of Eichstätt-Ingolstadt, Germany. She was a research associate at the Chair of Pedagogy for Adult and Further Education and the Chair of Pedagogy for Comparative Educational Research at the University of Augsburg. She also worked as a coordinator for educational offerings for refugees and migrants. Her research focuses on educational processes in the context of heterogeneity and Holocaust education in a migration society.

Carmel Borg is Associate Professor and Head of the Department of Arts, Open Communities and Adult Education, at the Faculty of Education, University of Malta. His scholarship foregrounds the relationship between education, democracy and social justice. For six years, Professor Borg acted as an external expert for the European Commission's education agency, advising on matters ranging from compulsory education to adult, continuing and higher education. He is also involved in a number of community-based projects focusing on critical literacy and active citizenship. Professor Borg is the founding editor of the Malta Review of Educational Research (MRER).

Maria Brown lectures in Adult and Community-based Education within the Department of Arts, Open Communities and Adult Education at the Faculty of Education, University of Malta. Her research interests include sociology of education, adult education, community development, sustainable development, social inequality, vulnerable groups, subcultures, research methods and social policy. She is active in the European Cooperation in Science and Technology (COST) and is a founding member of the Malta Sociological Association.

Fergal Finnegan is an Assistant Professor at Maynooth University, Ireland, where he co-directs the Doctorate in Higher and Adult Education and the PhD in Adult and Community Education programs. Before becoming an academic, he was a community adult educator and literacy worker, which included work with migrants and refugees. He is a co-convenor of the ESREA network on Active Democratic Citizenship and Adult Learning, as well as Co-editor of the Journal of

Transformative Education. Fergal's research interests include biographical methods, social class, access and equality in higher education, popular education and social movements, as well as critical realism and Pierre Bourdieu.

Laura Formenti is a Full Professor at Milano-Bicocca University, Italy, where her teaching includes Adult Education, Family Pedagogy, Counselling and Career Guidance, and Gender Violence. She is Chair of the Italian University Network for Lifelong Learning and member of the Steering Committee of ESREA (European Society for Research on the Education of Adults). She does research on the complexity of human systems, using aesthetic, narrative and cooperative methods to make a difference in adult lives and learning, as well as communities and organizations. Her book, *Transforming Perspectives in Lifelong Learning and Adult Education*, written with Linden West, won the prestigious Cyril O. Houle Award for Outstanding Literature in Adult Education from the American Association for Adult & Continuing Education (AAACE) in 2019.

Lea Gelardi is a Research Associate at the Center for Flight and Migration, an inter-disciplinary institution for research and education at the Catholic University of Eich-stätt-Ingolstadt, Germany. She studied sociology and political science in Germany and Italy. Her research interests include refugee camps, border and boundary studies, migration and asylum regimes, and integration discourses. She also holds seminars within the Department of Sociology and the Department of Refugee and Migration Studies at the Catholic University of Eichstätt-Ingolstadt.

Maria N. Gravani is Associate Professor in Adult & Continuing Education at the Open University of Cyprus (OUC), where she is Academic Coordinator of the Master's in Continuing Education and Lifelong Learning, and the International Master's in Adult Education for Social Change (Erasmus Mundus). She is an elected Member of the ESREA Presidium (2017–present) and co-convenor of the ESREA network on Adult Educators, Trainers and their Professional Development. Maria's research interests include the teaching and learning of adults across a variety of contexts (distance education, higher education, second chance education, education for migrants) for individual empowerment and social change, as well as the training and professionalization of adult educators. Before moving to the OUC, Maria has worked as a researcher in the UK (Bristol University), Ireland (Trinity College Dublin) and Greece (University of Peloponnese).

Larissa Jõgi is a Professor of Andragogy at Tallinn University, Estonia. She is a member of the ESREA and one of the conveners of the ESREA network 'Adult Educator, Trainer Professional Development.' She has been involved in many international and national research projects and has edited journals and books. Her research focuses on learning during the course of life, learning and migration, teaching in universities, the professional identity of university teachers, learning during the course of life, professionalization of adult educators and methodologies of qualitative research.

Brigitte Kukovetz is post-doctoral university assistant at the University of Graz, Austria, Department Migration—Diversity—Education. Her research focuses on adult education in migration societies, civic learning and political education. Recent topics include: the hindering and fostering conditions for professionals with migration experiences within adult education, the construction and deconstruction of differences within social work, and the potential of volunteering and active citizenship for political education in migration societies.

Silvia Luraschi is an educator, Feldenkrais method practitioner, and researcher in adult education at the Università degli Studi di Milano-Bicocca, Italy. Her research interests embrace embodied narratives, aesthetic practices, and walking methodologies. She was recently involved in "Unexpected subjects: a sensobiographic and participatory research on the movements of young adult migrants" (Grant ALSOS), where the walking experience is a dialogic practice for both migrant and native young adults.

Małgorzata Malec Rawiński is Associate Professor in the Department of Education at Stockholm University, Sweden, before which she worked for many years (2006–2017) at the University of Wrocław, Poland. Her research interests include adult education, older adults' learning, social and critical educational gerontology, lifelong learning, biographical approaches, local community, education of social exclusion-risk adults. In recent years, Małgorzata's interest and research work has focused on socio-cultural and biographical perspectives on migration.

Annette Sprung is Professor of Migration and Education at the University of Graz/Austria. Her research focuses on (adult) education in migration societies, active citizenship education and further topics around migration, racism, diversity, and social inequality. She explores transdisciplinary spaces and alternative methodological approaches, such as participatory and arts-based research. Annette holds the position of co-convenor for the Network on Migration, Transnationalism and Racisms of ESREA. She is currently working on active urban citizenship in migration societies.

Meril Ümarik is an Associate Professor of educational research and a Senior Research Fellow at the School of Educational Sciences, Tallinn University, Estonia. Her research interests involve educational reforms (in vocational education and higher education) and adoption of reform policies, teachers' professionalism, professional identities of academics, and adaptation of adult new immigrants. Her methodological expertise lies in qualitative research methods.

Linden West is Professor of Education at Christ Canterbury Church University, England. He is widely published in adult education and has jointly coordinated the ESREA Life History and Biography and Transformative Processes in Learning and Education Networks over many years. His books include *Distress in the City, Racism,*

Fundamentalism and a Democratic Education and most recently, *Transforming Perspectives in Lifelong Learning and Adult Education,* with Laura Formenti, which won the 2019 Cyril O. Houle Award for Outstanding Literature in Adult Education award from the American Association for Adult & Continuing Education (AAACE). He was inducted into the International Adult and Continuing Education Hall of Fame in 2020. He also works as a psychoanalytic psychotherapist.

1

"WE ALL ARE MIGRANTS"

Migration and the Learning Needs of Society

Chad Hoggan and Tetyana Hoggan-Kloubert

Migration has been an integral part of all, except perhaps the most remote, societies throughout history, and it is an integral and (likely) permanent characteristic of the modern world. In the best of cases, migrants leave their home country in search of better economic opportunities or novel experiences. In more difficult situations, they flee from poverty, genocide, or civil war; seeking the possibility of a life for themselves and their families free from terror or suffering. With an estimated 270 million people crossing national borders each year (World Migration Report, 2020), migration is exposing an urgent need for societies to re-think notions of 'us' and 'others,' and what it means to treat people first and foremost as human beings, regardless of their accidents of birth. To this end, this book is an exploration into new possibilities, especially as they relate to learning, change, and even transformation in a migration society.

The explorations in this collection highlight individual stories of migrants, showcase innovative research methods, and explore concepts and theories that might be usefully applied toward learning needs in a migration society. Through this multiplicity of per-spectives, we wanted to create an international perspective on the role of adult education in addressing migration. Countries represented in this book are: Austria, Cyprus, Esto-nia, Germany, Greece, Ireland, Italy, Malta, Sweden, United Kingdom, and USA. While reflecting on the particularities of migration in specific societies, there is a focus on common challenges and questions, current practices, and unresolved problems. We believe such international comparisons hold great potential for seeing new possibilities in any single country, whether in Europe, North America, or across the world.

Migration and Its Challenges

Countries which are (currently) relatively stable and prosperous, and which are therefore on the receiving end of migration, face legitimate concerns about how to

DOI: 10.4324/9781003124412-1

accommodate large inflows of people, with possibilities for employment, and in some cases with support during a transition period, perhaps with housing, clothing, and/or food.[1] We do not dismiss these practical realities. However, we see them as an issue of 'how' rather than an issue of 'whether.' We refer to the famous quotation of German writer Martin Walser: "Dem Gehenden schiebt sich der Weg unter die Füße" ("The path moves itself under the feet of the walker"). To us, it seems that the issue is not that migration challenges are insurmountable, but rather that there needs to be a commitment to addressing them. Society's values are manifest in their priorities, in the questions, goals, and tasks to which they devote themselves. The challenges arising from migration are difficult, but surely not so onerous as, for instance, the obstacles overcome in developing nuclear weapons, space travel, or vaccines against deadly diseases. If the general population saw a benefit to an influx of migrants, the attendant practical considerations would probably be overcome very quickly.

And in fact, people should; the OECD consistently reports on the economic benefits of immigration (see for example, OECD, 2014). But one should not have to provide an argument that migration benefits the receiving society. There exists, we believe, a moral obligation to help those in need. If we aspire to be more than a dog-eat-dog world, then it is incumbent on people to support others who are in vulnerable situations, who are suffering, who are fleeing from terror or poverty. Legitimate concerns about society's ability to provide space and opportunity for migrants are often conflated with what we believe are falsely-based apprehensions, such as a dilution of the culture, values, norms, and social/legal achievements of the receiving country. In each epoch and locale, migration is connected with specific manifestations of xenophobia or, in more general terms, tribalism; caring only for those perceived to be in one's circle of social kinship. The particular brand of challenges arising currently in Europe and the U.S. highlights the juxtaposition between their lofty espoused values (e.g., "unity in diversity," "all men are created equal … with certain unalienable rights … life, liberty, and the pursuit of happiness"), and the fears and prejudices born of particular differences between receiving countries and their current influx of migrants. In a pronounced way, then, migration is revealing and highlighting important societal questions: of solidarity, of identity, of transition and transformation, of human rights and obligations.

Migration and Adult Education

It would be difficult to find a living person who is *not* a product of migration at some point (and likely many points) of their family history. The prevalence of migration means that any given society is constantly being influenced by the blending of cultures, traditions, and norms. And, given that migration has been a constant phenomenon since at least the beginning of recorded history, there never has been such a thing as a static, homogenous society. Societies have always been in a state of flux, of development, often transformation.

Adult Education has traditionally been a companion and promoter of social change and societal developments, providing assistance and facilitation in times of crisis and transition, helping people accommodate to new social, economic, and political phenomena; in short, posing questions and offering possible answers to socially urgent challenges (see e.g., N.F.S. Grundtvig, Jane Addams, Anna J. Cooper, Albert Mansbridge, Myles Horton, Paulo Freire). Migration is such a socially urgent challenge, and adult education can aid in this broader work of helping society develop adequate responses to it. This book therefore seeks to explore concepts, theories, and approaches with which to think about, discuss, and shape the societal processes of 'dealing with' the challenges, real and imagined, arising from migration. Addressing the topic of migration also offers an opportunity to re-think and re-negotiate old and established assumptions and to push forward in search of new, if tentative, answers.

Migration is ubiquitous. At any given moment, society is being influenced by the blending of cultures, traditions, and norms. Both new arrivals and the longer-settled members of society are (at least potentially) lifelong learners who constantly develop and improve the capacities necessary to better understand the complexities of their social worlds (in order to function better in them), and to co-shape their shared society. Adult education, as an aid to lifelong learning, therefore holds the potential to help facilitate the development of migration societies—at the individual and collective level. The role that adult education might play in such development is the central theme of this book, which is based on a series of underlying premises and possible resulting tensions that we briefly mention here.

First, we assert that adult education is committed to the ideals and principles of democracy, and its core task is to foster, promote, and develop a democratic society. In addressing the challenges of migration, adult education may find itself between two demands. There is the demand to make educational processes effective and efficient in pursuit of learning objectives, which seek to integrate migrants into the receiving society. However, an overemphasis on this leads to an imposition of certain principles and values onto migrants (which verges on indoctrination rather than education), and there exists an ethical demand to respect adults' autonomy and right to self-determination. On the other hand, too much emphasis on self-determination can be problematic, for instance, when learners' principles and values contradict the ethical norms or legal standards of society. Recognizing and negotiating this tension is essential.

Second, promoting democracy requires a nurturing of social solidarity, which includes the strengthening of social cohesion and a sense of belonging to communities. In the case of migration, this can easily translate into a false or forced 'homogenization' of society. We see here a tension between fostering cohesion of different groups into a 'whole,' and a commitment to honoring individuality, subjectivity, and difference. There is a balance that must be negotiated between the goal of social cohesion and a respect for dissimilarities and divergences (and, yes, potential conflicts), which requires cultivating social, collective engagement by enhancing the capacities to participate in the various contexts in which an individual lives.

Although we argue that society needs to learn, develop, and possibly transform in the wake of migration, we do not advocate for using a sledgehammer to crack a nut, to destroy all the established principles and values (of the receiving society, but also of migrants) in order to re-negotiate them anew. The tension here involves the norms and (ethical) achievements of one's society that are non-negotiable, even in the course of societal change brought about by the mixing of cultures. What are the foundations of our society that we must keep (e.g., human rights)? Alternatively, which norms are merely idiosyncratic cultural products that can coexist or co-mingle with the idiosyncratic products from other cultures (e.g., festivals)? And, what might need to be discussed and collaboratively developed by a new diverse 'we' in our societies (e.g., legal holidays)?

This question could be connected to the German debate about the benefits and dangers of the so called 'Leitkultur'—the guiding culture or value systems considered as an intersubjective agreement on the rules and practices of a society's coexistence. Leitkultur can be seen as requiring a set of common basic values, shared by all citizens and newcomers. It can become problematic, however, when it is (either explicitly or implicitly) shortened to the thesis that newcomers must adapt to the majority culture. This insistence on homogeneity implies a devaluation of the person in their uniqueness and undermines a culture of respect and recognition.

The authors in this book problematize these and similar tensions in a variety of ways and seek a balance for adult education between consent and dissent; between adaptation and resistance; between personal integration and societal transformation; and between uncritical embeddedness in and overcritical distancing from one's social milieu. Learning in the wake of migration certainly includes individual qualifications and competencies, but also goes beyond these requirements. If we take the commitment of adult education to democracy seriously, then co-shaping a pluralistic, heterogeneous society means not only individual work and participation, but also interpersonal cooperation and collaboration, joint actions, and deliberation in a public sphere.

In different forms, with multiple arguments and examples, the authors in this book argue that learning in a migration society necessarily includes social change. The corresponding educational efforts emphasize the need for mutual recognition and a plurality of views, in order to develop collaborative possibilities for present and future interaction. Only in this way can citizens (with or without a recent migration experience) take part in the processes of critical discussion, on which depend the quality and legitimacy of a democracy.

Transformative Learning

A key premise of this book is that the learning required in a migration society is transformational in nature. Life in migration societies requires an ability to re-orient oneself in new contexts, to become acquainted with differing perspectives and ways of life, and to think beyond personal and established frames. This explicit distinction of the 'transformative dimensions of learning' was first articulated by Mezirow (1978, 1991). From this perspective, humans are continuously engaged in a process of making meaning of their experiences, using mental frameworks to shape how they perceive themselves and the world around them. Important for our discussion in this book are the two types of mental frameworks. The first is a 'meaning scheme,' which is a "constellation of concept, belief, judgment, and feelings which shapes a particular interpretation" (1991, p. 223). An example of a meaning scheme might be a person's views, biases, and feelings toward migrant groups from a particular country or of a certain religion. These meaning schemes are deep-seated and habitual, but at least they are relatively easy to become aware of. It is possible, for instance, through meeting and getting to know a migrant from a particular background, to realize one's inaccurate and unfair biases, and then to critique and change them.

In contrast to meaning schemes are 'meaning perspectives,' which are broad, orienting predispositions; these operate behind the metaphorical scenes of our meaning making. And, when possible to be noticed, they often seem like common sense. Meaning perspectives are therefore exceedingly difficult to truly assess. They might include, for instance, that *of course* there is a significant difference between national and, say, state or city borders, and that these national borders create (again, '*of course*') an important distinction between 'us' and 'others.' They might also include an acceptance of tribalism, that *of course* a person is justified in caring primarily for those in their own social circle, and not particularly feeling a kinship with those outside of that group.

Sometimes in our lives, these meaning perspectives are contradicted and shown to be inadequate to explain what we are experiencing. Mezirow called this a 'disorienting dilemma.' Such dilemmas can cause us to take a closer look at the frameworks we are using to understand the world. In essence, he argued that the real task of adulthood is to examine our meaning schemes and perspectives that were developed during our formative years, and to decide for ourselves what we think they should be in order to have a better understanding of ourselves and the world.

> Adulthood is the time for reassessing the assumptions of our formative years that have often resulted in distorted views of reality. ... Changing social norms can make it much easier to encounter, entertain, and sustain changes in alternative perspectives. ...
>
> Perspective transformation may be individual, ... group, ... or collective. ... (It) is the process of becoming critically aware of how and why our presuppositions have come to constrain the way we perceive, understand, and feel about our world; of reformulating these assumptions to permit a more inclusive, discriminating, permeable, and integrative perspectives, and of making decisions or otherwise acting upon these new understandings. ... Meaning perspectives that permit us to deal with a broader range of experience, to be more discriminating, to be more open to other perspectives, and to better integrate our experiences are superior perspectives. (Mezirow, 1991, p. 13–14)

In the decades since Mezirow introduced his theory, many scholars expanded on his work, emphasizing how the process of transformation can take many forms. Based on this larger scholarship, Hoggan and Browning (2019) describe six facets of meaning perspectives described in the literature. These are one's:

- Worldview (e.g., assumptions, beliefs, values, expectations);
- Self (e.g., identity, personal knowledge, personal narrative, personality);
- Epistemology (i.e., habits related to knowledge, how one determines what they know);
- Ontology (e.g., dispositions, tendencies, felt experience of life);
- Behaviors; and
- Capacities (e.g., cognitive complexity, spiritual connectedness).

Learning is transformative when some combination of these facets of the meaning-making process are sufficiently different from previous ways that they "result in significant and irreversible changes in the way a person experiences, conceptualizes, and interacts with the world" (Hoggan, 2016, p. 71).

The process of transformation is understandably difficult. It involves, inter alia, intense emotions, imagining new possibilities, and 'trying on' new societal roles (Mezirow, 1978). Acknowledging the difficulty, we nevertheless assert that this is exactly the type of learning that is being prompted by and is necessary for a migration society. And, although not every chapter in this book explicitly draws on this theory, they all are consistent in their underlying messages that individuals and societies need to engage in the difficult task of questioning their deep-seated meaning perspectives about what is normal, good, and right, especially when it comes to situations such as migration that often involve human vulnerability, suffering, and exploitation.

Migration Society, Postmigrant Society, and Superdiversity

The book is a response to the inducement to learn caused by the experience of migration, for migrating individuals, but especially for the larger society. There is a need for scholarship that provides new concepts; that names and reframes phenomena in order to challenge problematic (individual and societal) meaning perspectives. The scholarship in this book draws from and builds upon existing concepts and analytic lenses. Several terms are used throughout the chapters to describe society in the wake of migration, including: 'migration society,' 'postmigrant society,' and 'superdiversity.' In the following, we provide a short introduction of these terms and their related contexts.

To describe society today, most of the authors refer to the term 'migration society.' According to Mecheril (2016), this term indicates the various aspects, structures, and processes of a dynamic, mutually constitutive social reality, such as the emergence of transnational spaces, new and multiple affiliations, and the hybridization of ways and concepts of living. It promotes dialogue about such notions as foreignness, alterity, racism, belonging, prejudices, and attributions. *Migration society* points to old and new phenomena that are developing through interaction between different individuals and groups, and those phenomena are relevant for migrants, as well as for the receiving society.

Some authors in this book use the term 'post-migrant society,' which primarily indicates a certain research perspective, namely a post-structural or post-colonial[2] lens that criticizes and renounces the hegemonic 'integration paradigm' and refuses to accept existing power relations as given and unchangeable. A post-migrant perspective also means including marginalized stories into the research and discourse, telling the story of migration anew, and radically rethinking the entire field, going beyond the so-called hegemonic discourse (Yildiz, 2015).

'Superdiversity' as a term emphasizes the extensive heterogeneity and complex social patterns within modern societies due to migration and other factors. Expanding traditional categories of diversity, superdiversity acknowledges social class, societal status, health and disability, gender, age, aesthetic preferences, and so forth; with emphasis on issues of inequality, prejudice, and power relationships (Vertovec, 2007). Superdiversity describes recent societal transformations which occurred in the course of global migration processes, characterized by phenomena such as diversity not only between migrants and their receiving countries, but also increasing diversity amongst migrants themselves. This diversification includes, for instance, multiple types of migrant (e.g., refugee, undocumented migrant, secondary migrant), new and varying legal statuses for migrants, and different patterns of migration itself (e.g., from more countries, with continued connections by migrants between their receiving and home countries). The term *superdiversity* became so popular that Vertovec (2019) updated it with a typology of its various usages in the research literature. He found the term used to indicate:

- Very much diversity (synonymous with diversity, but emphasizing the expansion of different categories);
- Backdrop to a study (used to describe scene-setting, such as superdiverse places, superdiverse times or circumstances, and 'digital superdiversity');
- Methodological reassessment (combined with an intersectional approach to offer a new interdisciplinary lens to research);
- More ethnicity (emphasizing that the current migration has brought more ethnic groups to the host societies than has been the case in the past);
- Multidimensional reconfiguration of various social norms (emphasizing the need to take multiple variables into account when trying to measure diversity and calling attention to how variables and attributes are combined);
- Beyond the focus on ethnicity (highlighting that ethnicity must be cross-tabulated with other categories to develop better analyses of current diversity); and
- New or other complexities (referring to 'liquid' migration, non-linearity of migration processes, blurring of distinction, formation of new hierarchies and powers with migrant groups).

In this book, while describing and analyzing the complex and entangled contexts of migration, the authors use the term 'superdiversity' in one or several ways of this typology.

Genesis of Book and Themes Explored

This book is the result of a focused effort by a group of researchers to reflect on their work involving migrants and migration. In the fall of 2019, we reached out to a number of scholars across Europe who might be interested in exploring with us the connection between transformative learning and migration. We were (originally) interested in the learning that is required of migrants; learning that is transformational in nature. So, we invited scholars to participate in a two-day symposium. The idea was that everyone would write a paper on this subject (the connection between migration and transformative learning); we would all read each other's papers prior to the symposium; and then we would spend our time together in discussion of the various ideas, interconnections, and implications. The symposium was planned for March 2020, and therefore after all the planning, logistics, hotel reservations, purchasing of plane tickets, and so forth, the emergence of covid-19 required us to cancel all plans to meet together face-to-face. Instead, we met virtually for a series of four 3-hour meetings spread over a weekend. An initial insight explored was that all of us are migrants—if not in our own lifetime, then at least sometime in our family line. What began as an exploration into the learning needs of migrants, quickly expanded also into meta-reflection about our combined experience of research, about the ways that our implicit assumptions and the resulting research designs influence the outcomes, about the theoretical lenses used in and currently lacking for migration research.

Another evolution was our focus on where the most important learning was required. People in the process of migration will certainly always need to learn, in both cumulative and transformative ways. However, the more important learning is almost certainly that of society. How are we (as societies) thinking about our cultural identities and how they are 'threatened' by newcomers? How do we develop new senses of home and belonging? How do we categorize people between 'us' and 'others,' and how might we begin thinking in terms of all people as deserving of human dignity regardless of where they are born? The conversations were so intriguing, the insights so rich, that we decided to meet again for more discussions, and thus began our Migration Research Consortium. In this collection are some tentative responses to the questions raised during this research we conducted with each other.

Several themes arose during these conversations, which the authors have explored in various ways. First, we noted that the discourse around migration and adult education often portrays migrants in terms of their (very legitimate) needs. They seek support for acquiring new skills and competencies (which are required in the new society) and/or aid during their process of transition. In these cases, migrants are presented as people who need help, who are receivers of our support.

This situation is representative, however, of only a brief amount of time in the lives of people who migrate (Jõgi & Ümarik, Chapter 7; Gravani & Barkoglou, Chapter 5). Chapters in this book illustrate ways that even well-intentioned efforts by those seeking to help migrants can manifest power (Beck & Gelardi, Chapter 3) and paternalism (Kukovetz & Sprung, Chapter 11), and that migrants' lives are defined by more than just their temporary experience of migration (West, Chapter 4; Malec Rawiński, Chapter 6).

Another theme was the role of adult education as being more than addressing immediate learning needs, such as learning a language or a new profession. It extends also into developing capacities for participation in the broader social and public sphere (Hoggan-Kloubert & Hoggan, Chapter 9). Chapters speak of the need for opportunities to voice divergent critical positions in the public realm (Finnegan, Chapter 2), as well as the role of adult education in the process of emancipation and decolonization (Brown, Gravani & Borg, Chapter 8).

A third theme was the importance of creating dialogue, venues for contact and exchange, spaces of encounter and recognition in our societies, where individual life-trajectories, stories, images, and worldviews can be shared and valued (West, Chapter 4). The challenge is to arrange opportunities for learning from others, especially across difference. Examples include learning that occurs: *en passant* while taking a hike (Formenti & Luraschi, Chapter 10), through the sharing of pictures and images (Alexa & West, Chapter 13; Luraschi & Finnegan, Chapter 14), by analyzing life paths and breaks (Malec Rawiński, Chapter 6; Gravani & Barkoglou, Chapter 5; Jõgi & Ümarik, Chapter 7), and by discussing historic trauma and collective memories (Beck, Chapter 12).

Overview of Parts and Chapters

What resulted from the collaboration among our Migration Research Consortium were explicit attempts to name the 'so-what' of the research and/or theorizing that each of us had done. These insights took different forms, which we use here to organize the various chapters. We begin in Part One with theories and concepts to better understand learning in a migration society, to re-think and re-negotiate 'old' and established assumptions of our disciplines, and to push forward in the search for new (if tentative) answers. In "Migration and Transformative Adult Education: Reflections on Complexity, Criticality, and Counter-Publics in the Age of Super-diversity," Fergal Finnegan explores the interconnections between migration education and social learning processes. Weaving together concepts from several critical theorists, this chapter provides a 'reconstructive critique' of transformative learning theory in ways useful to envisioning what an emancipatory adult education might look like.

Next is "Entangled Narratives: On the (Un)Learning about Migration and Integration in a Post-Migrant Society," by Elisabeth Beck and Lea Gelardi. Using German educational requirements for migrants as a touchstone, this chapter uses a post-migrant and postcolonial perspective to problematize the focus on integration of newcomers into society. Concluding this section is "Migration, Learning and Its Enemies: 'Us,' 'Them' and the Possibilities of Cosmopolitan Learning," by Linden West. This chapter employs an 'interdisciplinary psychosocial framing' to explore some of the traumas inherent in migration. From this, West presents a vision for adult education as a space of sharing stories, conviviality, generosity, appreciation of a shared humanity, and thereby also a mutual collaborative learning.

Part Two explores the learning that migrants experience. Education in a migration society is based on the notion of multiple identities and commitments, as well as different but overlapping circles of belonging. Contrasting different experiences of migration, these chapters provide valuable comparative analyses in order to shed light on the varying ways that migrants learn, change, and adapt to their new environments. This section begins with "Exploring Adult Migrants' Learning Needs Using an Empowerment-Critical Approach: A Biographical Research" by Georgia Barkoglou and Maria Gravani. These authors demonstrate the 'heterogeneity and a non-linearity in transformation' through the life stories of four adult migrants. Similarly, in "The Constant Negotiation of Belonging: Experiences of Aging Polish Migrants in Sweden" by Małgorzata Malec Rawiński, the life stories of two older Polish migrants are shared, providing insights into the reality for migrants of living between two cultures, and the distinction between one's place of living and place of belonging.

In "Seeking Hope, Safety and New Perspectives: Learning and Adapting for Adult Migrants," Larissa Jõgi and Meril Ümarik present the stories and analysis of two migrants to Estonia. These cases present contrasting life trajectories and personal narratives, in which there can be seen a complex interplay of individual agency and contextual factors (including the role of education) in shaping migrants' adaptation as a transformative learning process. In "Adult Migrant Education as a Mediator of Democratic Citizenship in Postcolonial Contexts: Inferences from Adult Migrant Language Programs in Malta and Cyprus," Maria Brown, Maria Gravani, and Carmel Borg conduct a cross-case analysis of language learning programs for migrants in Malta and Cyprus. The initial development of tolerance and differentiated thinking they observed in these courses contrasts sharply with common populist mis-representations of migrants in both countries, but it did not necessarily develop into decolonizing and emancipating practices.

Part Three focuses on the learning of members of the societies on the receiving end of migration. No modern society can be accurately described without taking into account the process, development, and consequences of different migration movements. Adult education in a migration society not only has the task of supporting migrants in their integration process, but also of developing a vision of a new inclusive social model, grounded in diversity and multiple belongings.

In Chapter 9: "Embracing Transformation: Migration and Human Dignity," Tetyana Hoggan-Kloubert and Chad Hoggan argue that there is a fundamental requirement of respect for human dignity of everyone in the society, regardless of where they were born. This chapter illustrates what educational programs based on this premise might entail. Next is "Building the 'Here' and 'There' in Different Sensescapes: Embodied Dialogues among Refugees and Natives" by Laura Formenti and Silvia Luraschi. This chapter demonstrates the use of an innovative research method, the sensobiographic walk, an educational and social intervention designed to foster understanding and inclusion between new migrants and members of the local community.

In "Transformative Civic Learning within Volunteering in Refugee Relief," Brigitte Kukovetz and Annette Sprung explore the transformative effects of civic engagement in Austria. They illustrate how a 'disorienting dilemma' can arise from migrants' stories of trauma, as well as from volunteers' own experiences with restrictive migration policies and practices. The section concludes with "Learning Beyond the Obvious: Holocaust Education, Historical Education, and Remembrance in a Plural Society." In this chapter, Elisabeth Beck offers a vision of historical education that both honors and benefits from heterogeneity. By including multiple stories, histories, and memories, such as those of migrant populations, education can go 'beyond the obvious' of simply trying to assimilate migrants into their new society, and in so doing promote broader perceptions of different past(s) and diverse peoples.

Part Four highlights reflections occurring through dialogue between different researchers. This is an untraditional form of scholarship (see Formenti & West, 2018), but one that we feel is helpful for exploring insights, especially those arising from interconnections between scholars' work and their own family histories and personal experiences. This section begins with "Where is home? Migration, Trauma, and Adult Education: A Dialogue" by Stefan Alexa and Linden West. This chapter is not only a dialogue, but also an experiment in the use of fiction to explore complexities that are difficult to convey. The authors reflect on issues they have seen and experienced relative to the difficulties and traumas of migration, and what that might mean for adult education. The book concludes with "A Dialogue on Migration, Critical Auto/Biographical Research and Transformative Education" by Silvia Luraschi and Fergal Finnegan. This chapter is a conversation between two researchers about their experiences with biography: using biographical research methods, as well as exploring auto-biographical reflections of their own families' experiences with migration.

Concluding Remarks

This book is about our origins and our paths—the arbitrariness of our places of birth and the choices that we make in our lives, about the ways:

—we leave and arrive,
—we tell stories and remain silent,
—we listen and ignore.

On these paths, we cross physical and mental borders; marking different frontiers, limitations, and divisions. Learning in the context of migration is necessary because of—and possible in spite of—these borders. It holds the potential to help overcome alienation from the old and accustomed that has been left behind, as well as estrangement from the new and unusual that we encounter.

There are no set or easy answers to the challenges that arise from migration. However, as we have tried to make clear, we believe an important first step is for society to reflect on these challenges and differentiate between those which are real and those which are largely the result of faulty assumptions and biases. How might we think differently about migrants and migration? How might we become more inclusive in our differentiation between 'us' and 'others'? How might adult education more effectively facilitate learning in a migration society? To engage meaningfully in such a reflection will require explorations into new possibilities. The writing of this book was a *Bildungsreise*, an educational journey through such explorations. We hope for readers it will be the same.

Notes

1 Another possibility is to share responsibility, where appropriate, for living conditions in countries of emigration. This is a separate and complex issue that cannot be addressed adequately here.
2 The term 'post-colonialism' does not imply that colonialism has ended, but rather a shift of focus in analyzing the world; namely, effects of certain [colonial] ways of structuring the world are de-legitimized, and the internalization of patterns of thinking and behavior are problematized (Hall, 1996).

References

Citizenpath (2020). 5 Countries with the Most Immigrants. December 2020. https://citi zenpath.com/countries-with-the-most-immigrants/.

Formenti, L., & West, L. (2018) *Transforming Perspectives in Lifelong Learning and Adult Education: A Dialogue*. Palgrave Macmillan.

Hall, S. (1996). When was? Thinking at the Limit. In: Iain Chambers & Lidia Curti (Eds.): *The Post-Colonial Question. Common Skies, Divided Horizons*, Routledge, pp. 242–260.

Hoggan, C. D., & Browning, B. (2019). *Transformational Learning in Community Colleges: Charting a Course for Academic and Personal Success*. Harvard Education Press.

Mecheril, P. (2016). Migrationspädagogik: ein Projekt. In: P. Mecheril (Hg.). *Handbuch: Migrationspädagogik*. (S.8–31). Beltz.

Mezirow, J. (1978). "Education for Perspective Transformation. Women's Re-Entry Programs in Community Colleges."

Mezirow, J. (1991). *Transformative Dimensions of Adult Learning*. Jossey-Bass.

OECD (2014). OECD Migration Policy Debates: Is Immigration Good for the Economy? https://www.oecd.org/migration/OECD%20Migration%20Policy%20Debates%20Num ero%202.pdf.

UN (United Nations). (2017). International migration report. https://www.un.org/en/ development/desa/population/migration/publications/migrationreport/index.asp.

Vertovec, S. (2007). "Super-Diversity and Its Implications." *Ethnic and Racial Studies*, 30(6): 1024–1054.

Vertovec, S. (2019). "Talking around super-diversity." *Ethnic and Racial Studies*, 42(1): 125–139.

Yıldız, E. (2015) Postmigrantische Perspektiven. Aufbruch in eine neue Geschichtlichkeit. In: Erol Yıldız & Marc Hill (Hg.): *Postmigrantische Perspektiven jenseits der Parallelgesellschaft*. Bielefeld, pp. 19–36.

PART I

Developing Theories and Concepts Relevant to Learning in a Migration Society

2

MIGRATION AND TRANSFORMATIVE ADULT EDUCATION

Reflections on Complexity, Criticality, and Counter-publics in the Age of Superdiversity

Fergal Finnegan

In this chapter, I want to explore the topic of migration in relation to adult education taking a critical realist approach to transformative learning. My approach (see Finnegan, 2011, 2014, 2016, 2019; Hoggan et al., 2017; Fleming et al., 2019) is strongly influenced by the work of Mezirow (1991, 2000, 2007), a central figure in adult education theory and research. The position I have elaborated and the arguments made in the chapter are underpinned by the conviction that Mezirow's account of transformative learning (TL) is theoretically and practically very rich, but also uneven in certain important respects. These gaps can be addressed by bringing TL into dialogue with strands of critical theory and relational sociology, which are typically either overlooked or are relatively marginal in TL scholarship.

What Mezirow has to say about adult education and rational, critical reflection and action in a complex world is, I believe, very pertinent to the education related to migration. I will frame and critique Mezirow's arguments through the work of a number of contemporary critical theorists, with a particular focus on the work of Oskar Negt and Alexander Kluge. The influence of critical theory goes beyond the use of specific concepts, but also informs the structure and purpose of this chapter. As Fraser and Jaeggi (2018, p. 5) note, "the original idea of critical theory [was] as an interdisciplinary project aimed at grasping society as a totality [.] linking normative questions to the analysis of societal tendencies and to a diagnosis of the times." While I make no claims to offer any substantive 'diagnosis of the times' here, I am convinced that to understand the tasks required for adult education in relation to migration, we need to develop a broad political analysis and pay close attention to where there is any emancipatory potential in the current conjuncture. In particular, the social analysis offered here wishes to explore how material practices, institutions, and social relations relate to the "semiotic systems that shape lived experience in a complex world" (Sum & Jessop, 2013, p. 26).

DOI: 10.4324/9781003124411-3

The chapter is divided into four sections. The first section sketches out a systemic perspective on migration and how this relates to wider tendencies and dynamics within contemporary capitalism, as well as recent political changes based on critical theory and cultural political economy. I turn in the second section to discuss and critique a number of key ideas in the work of Mezirow and relate these to migration and adult education. In the third section I explore this further by looking at Mezirow's notion of democratic learning and the sources on which it is based, especially as it relates to the public sphere. This is then critically reworked through a discussion of Negt and Kluge's analysis of counter-publics. Finally, in the fourth section, I draw these strands together in a brief discussion of transformative pedagogy and the role of politics in the classroom in connection with the topic of migration.

Contextualising Migration: Capitalism and a World of Flows

Migration has been a feature of human life throughout history, but it is now happening on a new scale and with unprecedented velocity. Data on global migration is incomplete but, based on available figures, the UN (2019) estimates 272 million people live outside their country of birth (3.5% of the world population). The increase in the number of migrants globally over the past generation is noteworthy (there were 153 million people living outside their country of birth in 1990).

Drawing on critical theory, we can argue the increased movement of people across borders is best analyzed as one element of a more general set of processes linked to the logic of accumulation and expansion of capitalism as a world system (Fraser & Jaeggi, 2018). The production, exchange, and circulation of commodities relies on ceaseless movement: on the flow of money and finance, on the flow of goods and services, on the flow of information, images, and symbols, and of course the controlled flow of human beings—laboring bodies with required knowledges and competencies—across territories and spaces. These flows have increased in velocity and intensity in the neoliberal and financialized phase of capitalism, which began with experiments in free market reform in the 1970s and became a global phenomenon in the 1980s and 1990s (Fraser & Jaeggi, 2018), albeit following diverse and variegated pathways in different regions and countries (Brenner et al., 2010). In this sense, neoliberal capitalism marks a new phase in the ongoing acceleration of modern life (Rose, 2015).

Scale and velocity are, of course, only part of the story of contemporary migration. There are also significant patterns in direction, which are also linked to the geographies of the accumulation and concentration of wealth. If you review the data and explore some of the available mapping tools[1] used to capture the nature of migratory flows, there is—as one might anticipate—a significant amount of migration into countries in the G7 and rich Gulf states (approximately half of recorded migration is to ten such countries). In other words, a consideration of migration in broad terms not only leads us to consider the way we organize the tasks of production and social reproduction on a global scale, but also prompts questions about access to, and the just and proper use of, resources.

It is obvious but important to note that whether through displacement or through choice, different groups of migrants deal with very varied social, legal, and working conditions in destination countries. As Standing (2014) argues, the basic conditions of life are often remarkably different for citizens and denizens, and between members of the 'precariat' and elite workers. The experience of say, a U. S. born hedge fund manager resident in London or a Russian oligarch living in Cyprus is obviously very different from a Ukrainian doing care work in Austria or a domestic servant from Bangladesh in Saudi Arabia; let alone migrants without papers or those who are forced to flee existential threats. The thin, stretched category of migrant hides a multiplicity of worlds.

Social and Cultural Complexity and the Politics of Migration

Host societies and the societies which are left by migrants are not static things, and migration has become a major factor in wider processes of cultural emergence. This is a highly dynamic and layered set of processes as Appadurai (2013, pp. 62–63) notes:

> the complexity of global cultural flows has had deep effects on what I once called the 'production of locality' and the production of local subjectivity. These flows and networks confound older models of acculturation, cultural contact and mixture since they also brought new materials for the construction of subjectivity.

This leads to new forms of interaction and ways of being, which have been characterized by some researchers as a type of 'superdiversity' (Vandenabeele & Debruyne, 2020) that is unprecedented and is changing the texture of everyday life, work, education, and politics.

Globally, we are at a very early stage in developing forms of public discourse, institutional practices, and educational terms of reference that are commensurable with these new shared realities. In fact, in many places, the role of migration in an accelerated world is mystified, and the emergence of superdiversity is treated as a threat. As we are well aware, migration has taken on enormous and even explosive political and social significance internationally. As a number of researchers (Fekete, 2018; Neiwert, 2018; Titley, 2020) have noted, a great deal of contemporary political discourse in Europe and America—what we might usefully describe here as largely created by semiotic flows—is based on radical and even brutal simplifications, and the conscious or unconscious conflation of a very diverse set of social challenges with the 'issue' of migration. In much of the global north (Israel, USA, UK, Sweden, Finland, Poland, Slovakia, Italy, Austria, etc.) politics have veered strongly towards the right over the past decade, and in many places the political 'center' has adopted to varying degrees aspects of far-right rhetoric and policy ideas through scaremongering about migration (Mudde, 2019). Fekete (2018) discerns in recent years 'a cultural revolution' in which the far right has sought to recast social norms, "through culture wars and patriot games with the ultimate goal of trans-forming the way race, race relations and human rights are discussed" (p. 55). Nativist, fascist, quasi-fascist, authoritarian, so-called populist, and right-wing lib-ertarian parties and groups have all seized on migration as a way of pursuing a wider political agenda.

In this way, migration has become a cipher for an accelerated world and is used to simplify and misdescribe the deeper causes and dynamics of social change. The destabilizing effects of neoliberal globalization—deepening inequalities, unrespon-sive elites, increasing precarity and diminishing welfare rights, the passing away of established lifeworlds, and fears about the future—are yoked together with migra-tion by the far right and sections of the right. Migration is used as both a signifier and 'explanation' of crisis and deemed a key factor behind the scarcity of resources and perceived social degeneration.

To summarize, contemporary migration cannot be discussed in isolation from an analysis of the intended and unintended consequences of trends and tendencies of modern capitalism, and in particular the long-term effects, and partial unravelling, of the project of neoliberalism. The increased flows of people, ideas, practices, and culture across national boundaries have given rise to processes of cultural emer-gence, including a type of 'superdiversity' which we need to be able to respond to as citizens and educators. In a very profound sense, this calls for a general social learning process. However, over the past decade, the issue of migration has been successfully used by the right to advance a wider political agenda that creates major obstacles to advancing this general learning process.

Migration, Mezirow's Theory of Transformative Learning, and the Tasks of Adult Education

I now want to explore some of the implications of this critical socio-historical ana-lysis of migration for adult education. To do this, I will turn to Jack Mezirow and offer a reconstructive critique of his theory of transformative learning (TL) drawing on critical theory. I will highlight three things which I believe are especially important 'departure points' for transformative adult education in relation to migration using TL. They are: 1) the importance of deep critical reflection and the role of acknowledging, valuing, and working through complexity in adult educa-tion; 2) that transformative adult education needs to be envisaged in terms of a general social learning process across society, whilst also having a bearing on specific educational initiatives for migrants; and 3) that emancipatory values need to be strongly reaffirmed as central to transformative education in the present conjuncture.

Critical Reflection and Responding to Complexity

An adequate educational response has to begin with an acknowledgement of the full complexity of migration and processes of cultural emergence. It is directly pertinent then, that Mezirow's (1991, 2000, 2007) work, and much of the research that has built upon his work within the field of TL, are predicated upon the idea of a complex world, which is fluid and changing, and in which the making of the self is ongoing and always unfinished. These are common and well-established tropes in the social sciences and popular culture—to the point of being a cliché—but what is especially noteworthy about Mezirow's work is that it is focused on how to *generatively* respond as adult educators to these circumstances. Mezirow's work can be described as a theory of reflexive agency for adult education, which presumes learners, communities, and societies *need* to be able to deal with high levels of complexity, as well as develop a tolerance for ambiguity. Related to this, Mezirow (1991, 2007) argues certain practices and ideas, and certain modes of relating to self and others allow us to respond to flux and complexity in a way that leads to deep, even transformative modes of learning.

This is worth unpacking. Mezirow (1991) says the need to make meaning of our circumstances is a basic feature of human life. Meaning making is bounded by our assumptive worlds, what he calls 'meaning perspectives' (1991, 2000). Through individual and social change processes, perspectives which previously functioned well stop working. Or, due to the patterns of socialization and/or the effects of ideological distortion, we may have never fully understood important facets of personal and social experience. In these various ways, we can become 'stuck' in how we make sense of things. Mezirow (1991) describes learning as a routine and constant feature of our lives and argues that problems and dilemmas that we encounter prompt us to reflect at varying levels of depth. For Mezirow (1991), critical reflection on our assumptions—deep critical reflection—is especially salient in adult education, as this form of critical reflection has enormous potential and power which can lead to the development of more integrated, inclusive, open, and critical perspectives.

According to Mezirow (1991, 2007), the world is complex and changeable, and our interpretations of it are contingent and fallible, and deep critical reflection in these circumstances allows us to develop more accurate and discriminating modes of thought. Acknowledging the way things are—the reality principle if you like—through rational intersubjective deliberation, creates the opportunity for acting in new ways. Deep forms of critical reflection thus involve grasping the contingent and multi-perspectival nature of reality and nurturing an epistemological orientation that questions the givenness of our assumptions.

Mezirow (2000) sees critical reflection as strengthening our capacity for autonomy and agency, and therefore both personally developmental and politically significant. Education, which encourages us to examine and reframe our assumptions, also requires that we foster critical, rational, collaborative, and democratic modes of thinking in individuals, groups, and society as a whole. To summarize, TL offers a way of thinking about education which is, above all, focused on the emergent power to act in one's own interests in a critically informed and rational way (Finnegan, 2019), and this in turn is vital for elaborating a fully democratic culture.

A General Learning Process and the Dynamic Relationship Between General and Particular Needs

Thus far, I have made the case that migration is best understood in relation to a wider set of economic, political, and cultural processes within late accelerated capitalism, and that Mezirow offers a way of thinking about critical, reflexive agency in response to the complexities of contemporary life which is very useful. In this, and the subsection that follows, I want to make something more explicit that was only mentioned briefly earlier; namely, the proposition that the present era is not only defined by increasing complexity, but also the experience of recurring crises of various sorts (e.g., financial, ecological, social, democratic, educational, health) (Douzinas, 2013). The experience of polycrisis alongside increasing complexity can lead to

> a crisis that you might name an erosion of the culturally given. A crisis situation that people cannot meet in habitual ways, i.e. on the basis of what they have learned, and further do not know exactly what stable orientations are.
>
> *(Negt cited in Zeuner, 2013, p. 144)*

One common response to crisis and a lack of stability is to take refuge in simplistic explanations for why this is occurring, and this—to reiterate a key contention of this chapter—has influenced the way migration is approached. To meet the specific challenges of migration and general challenges of accelerated capitalism in a transformative way, it obviously calls for multistranded learning processes across society involving multiple actors. This needs to be framed as part of a general social learning process, with the aim of grasping the tendencies and direction of contemporary society and creating space to explore how this relates to one's assumptive world. The key point here is that we cannot treat the educational response to migration in a complex world of flows as the sole or primary responsibility of migrants.

Nonetheless, there is also a need for transformative programs designed specifically for migrants. What can be said about these specific needs? As noted earlier, migration is a highly differentiated phenomenon, and my seven years of experience in community education programs aimed specifically at migrants and subsequent research with migrants (Finnegan et al., 2014), makes me very circumspect when talking about migrants' educational needs in a general way. Of course, educators working with migrant groups should be aware of some practical and existential challenges that come with being located 'between' places and cultures, and have a good understanding of the practical and legal realities faced by migrants. But beyond this though, I do not think we can discuss migrant needs, let alone desires or interests, without reference to a given group of migrants in a specific place in a particular time. Migrants needs and desires are multiple, diverse, and context dependent, and the goal of education should be, in large part, to explore these in an open way. Furthermore, it follows from what was said about Mezirow above, that within transformative forms of education we should anticipate that needs and desires are not static and will be altered through the process of critical reflection.

Reaffirming and Strengthening the Centrality of Emancipatory Values

Analyzing the relationship between particular needs and general needs is a political matter, which is intrinsically value laden (Sayer, 2011) and requires that I now say something more about the normative foundations and goals of transformative adult education and how this has a bearing on how we might approach migration.

As we have seen, Mezirow proposes that deep critical reflection has specific qualities and is also bound to certain values. In fact, Mezirow could not be more explicit, that fostering transformative learning depends on creating collaborative democratic learning spaces in which participants act as equals. Mezirow argues:

> Full development of the human potential for transformative learning depends on values such as freedom, equality, tolerance, social justice, civic responsibility, and education. It assumes that these values are basic to our human need to constructively use the experience of others to understand, or make more dependable, the meaning of our experience.
>
> *(2000, p. 16)*

While Mezirow (1991, 2000, 2007) is consistent and clear about the core values he holds as central (equality and freedom in support of democracy), he tends to sketch this out as a normative 'background,' which will be readily understood by readers and practitioners, rather than systematically explicating what he means. Arguably, this did not present a problem in a historical period in which there was still a relatively stable social consensus that promoting both equality and freedom were important values, albeit understood in very divergent and even conflicting ways (i.e., liberal, radical). This has changed dramatically. As noted earlier, we have witnessed a significant discursive and political shift in Europe and the U.S. in relation to the triad of co-constituting values of equality, freedom, and democracy, which are central to Mezirow's theory of transformative learning.

This has a direct link to how migration is discussed and framed. Mudde (2019), a Dutch political scientist, notes that the mainstreaming of far-right ideas means that equality—as a principle—is now under sustained attack. This attack on equality is defended and even advanced through a particularistic notion of freedom, and that rights are something held by particular groups (defined by citizenship of a nation state and/or ethnicity). Mudde regards the attack on the principle of equality as corrosive and potentially threatening to democracy. In a fascinating account of the rise of populism, Revelli (2019, p. 18) takes up these themes and describes the current situation in the following terms:

> We face a crisis of democracy (of representation, of legitimation, of sovereignty)—without doubt—much more serious than we are usually prepared to

admit [...] we need to contend with the underlying social crisis, the real hypocentre—a point of deep rupture—of the earthquake that is shaking our political order.

In these circumstances, strongly reaffirming the centrality of equality, freedom, and democracy in transformative education has become more urgent and requires that we are sharper and more explicit about the meaning given to these principles— both in general terms and in relation to specific phenomena. With this in mind, I want to supplement what Mezirow says about emancipatory values—with other critical theorists—and make the case that a commitment to equality entails seeking equality in and through dialogue in a classroom, but also seeking equality beyond the classroom in social conditions in terms of wealth, legal protections, and access to valued social practices (Baker et al., 2009). This conception of equality is only ethically and intellectually coherent when applied to all human beings, regardless of accidents of birth and citizenship. From this perspective, when we speak of the needs of migrants in relation to transformative learning, it is both a pedagogic orientation and a wider political vision that seeks social change to overcome unnecessary suffering caused by maldistribution, misrecognition, and by restrictions on participation in specific institutions and society as a whole (Fraser, 2013). Freedom is understood as the movement from unwanted to wanted determinations in support of a flourishing life, which is achieved through individual and collective 'projects of autonomy' realized through rational, reflexive agency. In this sense, freedom and equality are co-constituting values and demand an experimental and deliberative form of democracy (I will expand further on this below; see also Finnegan, 2016, 2019). This is the goal of both the general learning process and educational initiatives for migrants.

Transformative Learning, the Public Sphere and Counter-Publics

A more detailed map of social space is needed to adequately describe the nexus between general social learning processes and particular forms of migrant education. To do this, I will say something about how Mezirow (1991, 2000) envisages the relationship between educational spaces and social space as a whole, and elaborate on this idea through a critique of Mezirow based on the work of Negt and Kluge on 'counter-publics.'

The Public Sphere, Deliberative Democracy and Reflective Learning

It is well-known that Mezirow draws heavily on Jürgen Habermas' version of critical theory, especially the ideas from the *Theory of Communicative Action* (1984, 1987) and *Knowledge and Human Interests* (1978)—this is central to his arguments about the importance of collaborative, critical discourse in transformative education (Fleming, 2002). Less explicitly, but just as importantly, it informs how Mezirow views the role of education and learning in relation to the public sphere and democracy. In this model, transformative learning is linked to the democratic social participation and discursive will formation more generally, and this envisages an experimental and participatory form of democracy across all areas of society.

It is not said often enough, though, that Mezirow offers a particular and selective interpretation of Habermas (Eschenbacher, 2019; Fleming et al., 2019). Knowledge, learning, and communication are foregrounded, and the politics of praxis and the systemic force that 'colonize the lifeworld' are left largely aside. It is also weakly historical. This is understandable—Mezirow wishes to highlight change through adult learning—but this means a powerful and potentially radical idea of deliberative democracy based on ongoing critical reflection 'floats' a little. The classroom and learning space is real; the learner is center stage, but the institutional and social nature of democratic processes and limits they encounter are fuzzy. This is a relatively 'flat' and smooth description of adult education for democracy and as such, is easily reduced to a, "liberal model of public space [which] transforms the public dialogue of empowerment far too quickly into a judicial discourse about basic rights and liberties" (Benhabib, 1992, p. 113.).

There is a large volume of historical and theoretical scholarship which has expanded and problematized Habermas' conception of the public sphere, and which points to the fact that a deeper engagement with Habermas alone will not be sufficient (e.g.; Benhabib, 1992; Fraser, 2013 *inter alia*). I want to turn here to one single strand of this scholarship—the fascinating and challenging theoretical-historical work of the German critical theorists Negt and Kluge (2016).

Counter-publics

Negt and Kluge's (2016) elusive and layered study[2] offers a number of propositions which I think are relevant for refining an understanding of the public sphere in the age of migration for TL researchers and practitioners. In their account, the key focus is on the relationship and conflicts between the dominant public sphere and multiple counter-publics created from 'below.' In confronting the ideas and practices of the dominant public, these counter-publics seek to overcome inequality, subordination, and alienation, as well as to articulate unmet and actively blocked social needs and desires. Further, this activity has the potential to remake the horizon in which we understand our social experience and enhance subordinated groups' capacity for emancipatory reflexive agency. This book is also helpful in thinking about the value of educational and political initiatives that build on social experiences which are largely hidden in the public sphere. They argue while the dominant public sphere represents itself as universal, and as expression of the general will, counter-publics assert the importance of the particularity of social experiences.

Negt and Kluge's (2016) main empirical and historical points of reference here are the workers' and radical students' movements, but this of course can be easily extended to the activity of anti-colonial, feminist, anti-racist, and ecological movements which also have created counter-publics. Further, they note that the nature of such oppositional counter-publics is often hidden and weakly institutionalized, and do not leave the same signs and traces of their activity as efforts in the dominant public sphere. These counter-publics also necessarily have a very different relationship with the state. They are, to adapt Anderson's (1988) evocative phrase, very distinct types of 'imagined communities,' which are typically not bound to the nation state and often self-consciously internationalist.

I think this conception of the counter-publics within and against the dominant public sphere, involving multiple actors with very asymmetric powers and conflicting interests, is useful in developing Mezirow/Habermas' arguments about learning and democracy as it pertains to migration. Counter-publics create space to explore the subjective experience of subordinated groups and to reflect and act for equality and freedom. The proposition here is that deliberative democracy can only be constructed by actively discovering the limits to democratic participation in the dominant public sphere as currently constituted. Counter-publics are, in this sense, movements of transformative learning of a particular sort which seek to change political and cultural assumptions. My suggestion is that educators interested in emancipatory TL therefore need to seek out such counter-publics and orientate themselves towards them. In terms of migration, it means connecting with migrant-led and anti-racist counter-publics and trying to understand and explore how this might inform the general social learning processes on migration[3].

Responding to Changes in the Public Sphere

Any attempt to think through these issues—to orientate oneself in a period of accelerated crisis—has to take some account of the changing nature of the public sphere. Hanse (2016, p. xiii) describes how transnational media of various sorts have created a global public sphere and a "process of deterritorialization, [in which] we witness the emergence of new highly ambivalent forms of particularity and universality." The use of social media and the incessant flow of images, ideas, and information across borders is currently reconfiguring this transnational public sphere in highly unpredictable ways. We know that these flows are being partially channeled and manipulated by corporate interests and nation states (Zuboff, 2019). The 'local' is reified and made spectacular, while global processes are hidden or mystified (Hanse, 2016); phenomena are violently yoked together to create distorted conceptions of the social whole; false reports and half-truths go viral (Neiwert, 2018; Titley, 2020). As one media analyst who focuses on migration, racism, and the public sphere notes:

> a cultural attachment to critically vacuous abstractions about free speech has become more pronounced even as the communicative landscape becomes more complex, and the forms of politics it amplifies become more marked in social and political life. In contemporary media debates freedom of speech is regularly invoked in absolutist terms, shorn of its complex intersections with competing rights and interests.
>
> *(Titley, 2020, p. 9)*

The strategic and tendentious invocation of the right to free speech has been remarkably successful in skewing public discourse *away* from substantive questions of freedom, equality, and democracy (i.e., how do structural and institutional relations and the distribution of resources enable or constrain participation in valued social practices and institutions).

In a recent book, History and Obstinancy, Kluge and Negt (2014) helpfully remind us that the emergence of the idea of critique was "a defensive reaction to a tsunami of printed texts" (p. 195) following the invention of the printing press. In the face of digital excess, a key task of counter-publics and educators is to support people to deselect and differentiate between discursive flows which mediate, occlude, and instrumentalize human needs, and those which articulate real and emancipatory needs. This—along with the use of social media to bear witness to hidden suffering (Trilling, 2018) and mobilize counter-publics (Appardurai, 2013)—creates a wide range of possibilities for transformative education.

Transformative Pedagogy and Politics in the Classroom

Mezirow and other colleagues (Mezirow et al., 2000; Taylor, 2000) make the case for responsive, dialogical programs and pedagogies which tap into the lived experience of students and foster critical reflection. As is evident from what I have said already, developing such initiatives linked to the phenomenon of migration also calls for careful consideration of social trends and tendencies of the wider cultural political economy, and an analysis of the affordances and limits of the public sphere and counter-publics.

I now want to briefly summarize and synthesize the points made above and then link this to the specificities of the classroom as a space. There is, from this perspective, a pedagogical and political imperative to facilitate groups of migrants to speak to their own needs. While transformative education should seek to have such needs explored in their particularity, it cannot be thought of separately from social needs more generally. I have argued that to adequately frame and act upon the needs of specific groups of migrants in a transformative way, we need to build on the emphasis in TL of how specific learning encounters are situated in social relations, and to pay due regard to complexity, deep critical reflection, and emancipatory values. I believe transformative educators need to actively look outwards and pay attention to, and where possible, collaborate with counter-publics. This also means thinking carefully about how the public sphere is being changed through the use of social media and to develop educational strategies that respond to this in ways which are critically reflexive. For this sort of work to be sustainable and effective in the medium-term, calls for international collaboration between educators, researchers, and counter-publics in creating transnational curricula (Mayo, 2013), which express and explore the experience of superdiversity and hone the ability to read between the local and global in an informed and critical way. In broad terms, the implications of this approach are clear enough. On an immediate level, there are nonetheless subtleties, contradictions, and challenges in pursuing such an approach that should not be overlooked.

To highlight just one example, the precise way we bring critical social analysis to bear on everyday encounters with students needs care and consideration. Like Mezirow (1991), I think classrooms of transformative education are distinct forms of social space in their own right. I have argued it is important to view them as connected to, even feeding and being fed by, counter-publics, but they cannot serve as simply as a 'node' of these counter-publics. A counter-public is defined by oppositional normative and political claims, which often give rise to reflexivity. Transformative educational spaces are designed, above all, to be reflexive and only secondarily to make claims beyond that space (Mezirow, 1991, 2000). This is a very significant difference. Educational dialogue needs to open and cannot be entirely predefined by ideological goals or values (Holzkamp, 2013), but depends on flexibility, co-investigation, and maintaining a spirit of open inquiry. Openness means allowing people to speak as they see things on their terms, and it follows from this that there will be dissensus and conflict in the classroom, including between migrant students and non-migrant students. This is perhaps especially acute when students come from different communities that have been silenced in different ways. West (2016) has made precisely these points in his fascinating account of the growth of racism and fundamentalism in Stoke, in the U.K. On this basis, West makes a persuasive argument that openness to difference, and that the exploration of real and perceived differences is foundational, both for transformative adult education and for a living democracy.

Working with these conflicts and contradictions pedagogically is hardly straightforward and cannot be discussed out of context. For example, there have been occasions in my experience where racist slurs have been made directly or students have shared material which is badly informed, tendentious, and even hateful. Here, one's pedagogical role is, I believe, to create a boundary that does not normalize racism or treat racism as just another 'point of view.' But I have also been in situations where xenophobic or even racist remarks have provided opportunities to disentangle issues and misunderstandings, and have provoked useful dialogue. Assessing this depends on careful situated judgement and sustained sociopolitical analysis, including clarity about key values and principles.

These reflections are offered as potential departure points for developing modes of transformative learning and institutions of transformative education which are adequate to our times and can explore migration with individuals, groups, communities, and societies in critically reflective, democratic, and emancipatory ways. They are broad but offered modestly—they are hardly sufficient except as an invitation to further discussion—but with the firm conviction that we need to be politically bold and ambitious to meet the challenges we face.

Notes

1 See for example https://migrationdataportal.org/?i=stock_abs_&t=2019
2 The book is ambitious, if a bit lopsided, but it is immensely rich because it is an engagement with rather than an easy refutation of Habermas, and the authors bring extensive experience in adult education and social movements to bear on the questions they explore.

3 I want to note an issue which is not fully addressed by Kluge, Negt, Habermas or Mezirow: the existence of unnecessary human suffering which hardly registers in the public sphere (Bourdieu et al, 1999) but also remains outside the awareness of counter-publics. Some of the hidden suffering of specific groups of migrants is captured very well in Trilling's (2018) evocative and moving account of migrants with papers and asylum seekers at the borders of Europe. The book illustrates that although migration is a highly mediated and much discussed issue within policy circles and civil society (Kukovetz & Sprung, 2020), and has created and informed counter-publics, the full extent and significance of these experiences has yet to fully register in any form of public, be they dominant or oppositional.

References

Anderson, B. (1988). *Imagined Communities: Reflections on the Origin and Spread of Nationalism.* Verso.

Appadurai, A. (2013). *The Future as a Cultural Fact: Essays on the Global Condition.* Verso.

Baker, J., Lynch, K., Cantillon, S., & Walsh, J. (2009). *Equality: From Theory to Action* (2nd ed.). Palgrave Macmillan.

Benhabib, S. (1992). *Situating the Self: Gender, Community and Postmodernism in Contemporary Ethics.* Routledge.

Bourdieu, P.*et al.* (1999). *The Weight of the World: Social Suffering in Contemporary Society.* Polity.

Brenner, N., Peck, J., & Theodore, N. (2010). Variegated Neoliberalization: Geographies, Modalities, Pathways. *Global Networks,* 10, 182–222. https://doi.org/10.1111/j.1471-0374.2009.00277.x.

Douzinas, C. (2013). *Philosophy and Resistance in the Crisis.* Polity.

Eschenbacher, S. (2019). *Regaining balance: Transformative learning theory between individual transformation and social action.* Paper presented at ESREA 9th Triennial European Research Conference, Adult education research and practice between the welfare state and neoliberalism, 20th September, Belgrade University.

Fekete, L. (2018). *Europe's Fault Lines: Racism and the Rise of the Right.* Verso.

Finnegan, F. (2011). *Learning as transformation or adaptation? Thinking with and against Mezirow and Bourdieu.* Paper presented at Transformative Learning Conference: In a Time of Crisis: Individual and Collective Challenges, 28th May, Athens.

Finnegan, F. (2014). Embodied experience, transformative learning and the production of space. In A. Nicolaides & D. Holt (Eds.), *Spaces of Transformation and Transformation of Space. Proceedings of the 11th International Transformative Learning Conference.* Teachers College Columbia University.

Finnegan, F. (2016). The future is unwritten: Democratic adult education against and beyond neoliberalism. *The Adult Learner,* 46–58.

Finnegan, F. (2019) 'Freedom is a very fine thing': Individual and collective forms of emancipation in transformative learning. In T. Fleming, A. Kokkos, & F. Finnegan (Eds.), *European Perspectives on Transformation Theory.* Palgrave Macmillan.

Fleming, T. (2002). Habermas on civil society, lifeworld and system: Unearthing the social in Transformation Theory. *Teachers College Record,* 1–17.

Fleming, T., Kokkos, A., & Finnegan, F. (Eds.) (2019). *European Perspectives on Transformation Theory.* Palgrave Macmillan.

Fraser, N. (2013). *Fortunes of Feminism: From State-managed Capitalism to Neoliberal Crisis.* Verso.

Fraser, N., & Jaeggi, R. (2018). *Capitalism: A Conversation in Critical Theory.* Polity.

Habermas, J. (1978). *Knowledge and Human Interests.* Heinemann.

Habermas, J. (1984). *The Theory of Communicative Action.* Vol. 1, *Reason and the Rationalization of Society.* Heinemann Education.

Habermas, J. (1987). *The Theory of Communicative Action.* Vol 2. Polity.

Hanse, M. (2016). Introduction: On new public spheres. In O. Negt & A. Kluge (Eds.), *Public Sphere and Experience: Towards an Analysis of Bourgeois and Proletarian Public Sphere* (pp ix–xlii). Verso.

Hoggan, C., Mälkki, K., & Finnegan, F. (2017). Developing the theory of perspective transformation: Continuity, intersubjectivity, and emancipatory praxis. *Adult Education Quarterly,* 67(1), 48–64.

Holzkamp, K. (2013). *Psychology from the Standpoint of the Subject: Selected Writings of Klaus Holzkamp.* Palgrave Macmillan.

Kluge, A. & Negt, O. (2014). *History and Obstinacy.* Zone Books.

Kukovetz, B., & Sprung, A. (2020). Questioning power relations: Learning processes through solidarity with refugees. In F. Finnegan & B. Grummell (Eds.), *Power and Possibility: Adult Education in a Diverse and Complex World* (pp. 131–142). SENSE/Brill.

Mayo, P. (2013). *Echoes from Freire for a Critically Engaged Pedagogy.* Bloomsbury.

Mezirow, J. (1991). *Transformative Dimensions of Adult Learning.* Jossey-Bass.

Mezirow, J. (2000). Learning to think like an adult. In J. Mezirow & Associates (Eds.), *Learning as Transformation: Critical Perspectives on a Theory in Progress* (pp. 3–33). Jossey-Bass.

Mezirow, J. (2007). Adult education and empowerment for individual and community development. In B. Connolly, T. Fleming, D. McCormack, & A. Ryan (Eds.), *Radical learning for liberation 2* (pp. 10–17). MACE.

Mudde, C. (2019). *The Far Right Today.* Polity.

Negt, O., & Kluge, A. (2016). *Public Sphere and Experience: Towards an Analysis of Bourgeois and Proletarian Public Sphere.* Verso.

Neiwert, D. (2018). *Alt-America: The Rise of the Radical Right in the Age of Trump.* Verso.

Revelli, M. (2019). *The New Populism: Democracy Stares into the Abyss.* Verso.

Rose, N. (2015). *Social Acceleration: A New Theory of Modernity* (New directions in critical theory). Columbia University Press.

Sayer, R. A. (2011). *Why Things Matter to People: Social Science, Values and Ethical Life.* Cambridge University Press.

Standing, G. (2014). *A Precariat Charter: From Denizens to Citizens.* Bloomsbury Academic.

Sum, N., & Jessop, B. (2013). *Towards a Cultural Political Economy: Putting Culture in its Place in Political Economy.* Edward Elgar.

Taylor, E. (2000). Fostering Mezirow's transformative learning theory in the adult education classroom: A critical review. *Canadian Journal for the Study of Adult Education,* 14(2), 1–28. https://cjsae.library.dal.ca/index.php/cjsae/article/view/1929.

Titley, G. (2020). *Is Free Speech Racist?* Polity.

Trilling, D. (2018). *Lights in the Distance: Exile and Refuge at the Borders of Europe.* Picador.

UN. (2019). *Global Migration Report.* UN.

Vandenabeele, J., & Debruyne, P. A. (2020). Nurturing solidarity in diversity: The superdiverse shopfloor of Tower Automotive in Ghent. In F. Finnegan & B. Grummell (Eds.), *Power and Possibility: Adult Education in a Diverse and Complex World* (pp. 155–166). SENSE/Brill.

West, L. (2016). *Distress in the City: Racism, Fundamentalism and Democratic Education.* Trentham Books.

Zeuner, C. (2013). From workers education to societal competencies: Approaches to a critical, emancipatory education for democracy. *European Journal for Research on the Education and Learning of Adults,* 4(2), 139–152. DOI: doi:10.3384/rela.2000-7426.rela9011.

Zuboff, S. (2019). *The Age of Surveillance Capitalism: The Fight for a Human Future at the New Frontier of Power.* Profile Books.

3

ENTANGLED NARRATIVES

On the (Un)Learning about Migration and Integration in a Post-Migrant Society

Elisabeth Beck and Lea Gelardi

Learning has always been and will continue to be both a challenging and enriching process for every individual. It appears even more necessary in modern societies that have become extremely divided, polarized, and shaped by critical societal conditions; including international border and migration regimes, global social inequalities, racism, the development and intensified reemergence of populism and nationalism, hegemonic power relations, and global capitalism. At the same time, ongoing protest movements for democratic principles and against racism, climate change, and political repression proceed. These supposedly contradictory developments are not a paradox; they rather provide a picture of a transforming social balance of power (see Foroutan et al., 2018, p. 14). Therein, the possibilities and places for social participation are unequally distributed (see Foroutan & İkiz, 2016, p. 140). Educational organizations are embedded in these conditions of a changing heterogeneous society where negotiations of exclusion, inclusion, normalization, and belonging are carried out. These processes are questioned, irritated, and deconstructed, but also reproduced in education and learning, which—especially in the context of migration—creates opportunities and barriers for participation.

Education can be both emancipatory and, at the same time, disciplinary and exclusionary. This is of particular relevance because educational practice is always confronted with differences and inequality. The discussion of difference usually starts by setting a—sometimes implicit—standard, a norm, and examining what irritates it or deviates from it. This often occurs by using different markers and differentiating lines, such as race, class, gender, and origin. In educational institutions and settings, stereotypical images of the unknown, inequalities, and hierarchies due to origin are observable—these can lead to disadvantages and discrimination. The educational system can, therefore, be described as a space of producing and manifesting symbolic orders[1] (see Bourdieu, 2005).

DOI: 10.4324/9781003124412-4

Inequalities and disadvantages regarding the level of education among adults with a so-called 'migration background' are shown in different surveys, such as PIAAC (OECD, 2013) and AES-Migra (BMBF, 2018). In Germany, the difference in proficiency scores between adults—with and without a migration background—is especially high. The explanation of the root causes varies dependent on perspectives, pointing to structural and institutional discrimination (see for example, Sprung, 2011; Gomolla & Radtke, 2007) or the personal responsibility of the migrants. The latter perspective is connected to specific educational obligations and expected efforts from migrants, their imputed unwillingness to participate in (adult) education, and can be seen, for example, in the Bavarian Integration Law.

Bavaria is one of the 16 states of the Federal Republic of Germany and is considered one of the most conservative (generally, and concerning migration and integration, particularly). Education is considered the key to successful 'integration' (see BayIntG, 2016, article 3, paragraph 1). This statement is essential, as the federal states are each responsible for the design and implementation of education. Especially in the Bavarian state, the terms and concepts of education, migration, and 'integration' are strongly entangled, which leads to the narrative that migrants must integrate primarily through education. In this narrative, associated assumptions and expectations are not critically questioned. If we, therefore, take a deeper look at the educational system as a place that fights *and* (re)produces inequality, the following questions arise. First, which understanding of migrants, migration, and 'integration' is negotiated and (re)produced in the interwoven discourse? And second, which (educational) approaches are needed to address the challenges in education in a highly diverse society?

This chapter aims to discover which notions of migration and 'integration' are frequently discussed and manifested in the educational context within a plural society. Therefore, the contribution of this research gives insights into contemporary theoretical approaches about education and learning from a post-migrant and postcolonial perspective. This paper examines political and scientific negotiations of migration and 'integration' in the educational system. In doing so, the question arises of how education can be thought of and conceptualized in a new and critically reflective way within a modern society. The purpose is to use a post-migrant and postcolonial perspective to irritate and criticize predominant thinking and acting patterns. After outlining the issue in the following chapter, by using examples from the 'integration courses' promoted by the German government and the Bavarian Integration Law, the container concept of 'person with a migration background' will be critically reflected in the light of earlier sociological migration theories, in which a continuous (re)production of 'strangers' can be identified. Following this, the post-migrant perspective will be introduced as a proposal for social analysis and to get beyond such reproductions. Next, a brief presentation of postcolonial theory and its relevance for today's understanding of education and the educational system is given. The paper concludes by formulating impulses for education that take into account the plurality of society.

(Assimilating) Integration through Education?

Talking about migration is almost always talking about 'integration.' In the early years of the 2000s, the independent commission on immigration (so-called Süssmuth Commission) convened by the German government—at least rhetorically—declared Germany an immigration country, and the resulting Immigration Law came into force. Since then, promoting 'integration' became an official governmental task (Süssmuth, 2015). 'Integration' became, and is still, one of the most dominating discourses connected with migration, and part of a meritocratic policy in which those are rewarded who make an effort. This political understanding of 'integration' should also become visible in integration politics.

The core component of the governmental integration policies became the integration courses provided by the German Federal Office for Migration and Refugees (BAMF). The courses are intended to convey German language skills and knowledge necessary for *orientation* in the German society. The course concept reflects the current integration policy principle 'to promote and to demand' (*Fördern und Fordern*), including the promotion of 'integration,' as well as demanded efforts and duties of 'integration' by the migrants themselves (see BayIntG, 2016, article 1). Although a contribution of the society to 'integration' processes is included here, the focus lies on the efforts and obligations to be rendered by migrants, not the state or the imagined majority society (see BayIntG, 2016, article 3, paragraph 2; Castro Varela, 2013, p. 8).

The effort is primarily expected to be made in educational programs, first and foremost, in the integration courses "as a central government measure to promote integration" (Lochner, 2018). Learning the language of the so-called 'receiving country,' entering the labor market, and adopting culture and values are the central objectives; the non- or not-yet-integrated migrants should or must achieve them through education. The impartment of 'basic skills' should lead to a successful 'integration,' especially in the area of language, since assimilation is explicitly expected and legally fixed: "Only those who speak German can fully integrate into public life and work. It is therefore in the migrants' own best interest to be committed to language acquisition" (BayIntG, 2016, article 4, paragraph 1). Here, the predominance of a 'monolingual habitus' is still evident—this exclusively defines the 'receiving' country's official and common language as legitimate (Gogolin, 2008). Instead of acknowledging the potential of bilingualism or multilingualism, language assimilation is proclaimed to be necessary for 'integration' (see Esser, 2000; Heckmann, 2005).

Furthermore, the integration courses' overall goal is "to promote the integration of migrants in terms of social participation and equal opportunities" (BAMF, 2015, p. 6). 'Integration' in this sense refers to a non-belonging, which causes an assumed necessity of regulation in the form of adaptation to societal conditions through education. Migrants are addressed as deficient regarding specific expected standards of values and norms related to a 'lead culture' (*Leitkultur*)[2] (BayIntG, 2016, article 1, paragraph 4). They are marked as an 'integration problem' (Karakayali &

Mecheril, 2018, p. 231) or members of a specific group that requires special education and training. Their deficits and 'educational gaps' (BayIntG, 2016, article 1, paragraph 1) are to be equalized in order to ensure the objectives of participation, equal opportunities, and therefore, 'integration.'

In this design, migrants can then 'successfully integrate,' 'refuse,' or 'fail' to integrate, which in the latter leads to sanction and exclusion. 'Integration' is understood exclusively as a task in the context of migration and for migrants, and not more comprehensively in the sense of a functioning integrative society in general, in which all forms of social inclusion are possible and recognized. The selected groups of possible and obligated participants in integration courses are defined as: people 'with a migration background,' foreigners, asylum seekers, refugees, and those who do not speak sufficient German or who are particularly in need of 'integration' (see BAMF, n.d.). People are identified by their country of origin. Other aspects of diversity, for example, gender or age, are not considered or problematized in the same intensive and controversial way—unless they are linked to the marker 'migration background,' (e.g., represented in the image of the 'young male migrant').

Because of politically predetermined groups of addressees, no space remains for negotiations about self-positioning and external attributions. While self-positioning enables migrants to define their identity and position in the social structure, or at least to set them subjectively for themselves, external attributions lead to migrants being ascribed certain characteristics according to an assumed group belonging. The construction of migrants as a large subgroup of society, deviating from an assumed standard and 'in need of integration,' particular education, or training, can be seen in the German term 'with a migration background.' Within this container concept, highly diverse people are constructed as a homogenous group of 'foreigners' or "people in particular need of integration" (BayIntG, 2016, article 2; BAMF, n.d.). Nevertheless, differentiation and graduations of an assumed 'integration necessity' are made, for example, in accordance with the country of origin (EU/non-EU, global North/global South). To protect the supposedly 'normal' from the deviant, the latter must adapt to the former (i.e., the 'foreigners' to the 'locals'). This demand is implicitly reflected in various educational offerings. Furthermore, specific educational programs, including the integration courses, are explicitly developed to maintain the idea of imagined homogeneity. Interestingly, the capability of those already considered 'German' (presumably from a non-migration background) to 'integrate' in society or feel committed to its constitution and legal norms, is not put into question. They are seen as already or sufficiently 'integrated.' For them, the question of deficits in their democratic attitude, for example, does not arise.

In summary, this type of integration policy in the form of the integration courses can be described as regimes of normalization and disciplining (see Castro Varela, 2013, p. 33). The purpose is primarily an assimilation rather than significant emancipation. Although assimilation can be valuable because of necessary adaptions to new circumstances in life, for plural and democratic societies, emancipatory learning is essential. Emancipation is necessary to strengthen the capacity to reflect, judge, act, and criticize. These competencies are fundamental in and for a democratic society (see Anders et al., 2020). A democracy thrives on its active and reflective civil society, in which all people—regardless of migration experiences—develop the ability to critically analyze, question society, and initiate societal change. Nevertheless, integration politics usually aim for 'integration,' meaning assimilation by migrants; deviations and irregularities are problematized and sanctioned. Accordingly, it implies a primarily personal rather than political and societal obligation.

The Stranger in Crisis

The integration policy's focus on assimilation, closely linked to education, has a long theoretical tradition and can be found in many migration sociology theories. Several theorists especially emphasize language and passing through the educational system of the 'receiving' society as one of the essential components for successful 'integration' (Eisenstadt, 1954; Gordon, 1964; Park & Burgess, 1969; Heckmann, 2005; Esser, 2000).

The sociological theories of Simmel, Schütz, and Park are known for their perspectives on assimilation. The naming of integration mechanisms stays implicit, even though they focus on daily interactions as well as assimilation processes of 'the stranger' (Simmel, 1908), 'the immigrant' (Schütz, 1944, 1972), or 'the marginal man' (Park, 1928, 1969), in the 'new' existing culture. Missing, or not yet finished assimilation (and therefore also 'integration'), goes along with vagueness and non-affiliation, which is why the stranger is usually in crisis.

Schütz (1972) describes this passing from one culture to another as mainly crisis-prone and focuses on the process of approaching (p. 54), rather than adaption or assimilation. This crisis is the case because the stranger does not share the same cultural patterns, lacking implicit knowledge regarding the new 'ingroup.' Instruction manuals or prescriptions (e.g., folk wisdom, customs, traditions) the stranger could rely on in his home country do not function well in the new environment, and new 'guidelines' (ibid., p. 57) are missing. The loss of established patterns of thinking and acting leads to disorientation. For Park (1928), the stranger's or *marginal man's* crisis is permanent (p. 893). In his view, assimilation and amalgamation are needed to overcome the crisis. He describes the marginal man as a 'cultural hybrid' (ibid., p. 892): old habits are discarded, but new ones are not yet developed. The passing comes along with a 'moral dichotomy' (p. 893). The marginal man lives between two worlds, not entirely belonging to either (p. 893). The process ends, or has to end, in reflecting only the social order of the receiving society. For Park (1928) and Schütz (1972, p. 69), the encounter ends in assimilation, which solves 'the problem' or the crisis, and the stranger will no longer be strange.

Beyond the (Re)Production of the 'Stranger(s)'

In the described theories, an essentialist understanding of origin and culture is dominant. This also becomes visible terminologically. Schütz (1944, 1972) develops his theory around 'the stranger' by describing an 'ingroup,' an 'outsider,' and the social situation of the immigrant, as a prototype for his analysis (see Schütz, 1972, p. 53). He assumes that

> [a]ny member born or reared within the group accepts the ready-made standardized scheme of the cultural pattern handed down to him by ancestors, teachers, and authorities as an unquestioned and unquestionable guide in all the situations which normally occur within the social world.
>
> *(Schütz, 1944, p. 501)*

Schütz creates here an image of groups and cultural patterns as fixed containers with permanent boundaries within a social world. Such a dichotomous way of thinking of strangers and locals allows the construction of the group of outsiders invading the state or, in this context, the 'culture'—this is considered as a danger to the "homogeneity of the state, the society, and the political body" (Bigo, 2010, p. 45). Moreover, even though Park (1928) uses a more procedural terminology like 'cultural hybrid,' he remains committed to dualistic ideas of culture and belonging. Thus, the mentioned approaches do not reach beyond a constant reproduction of the 'strangers.'

By considering the global pluralization processes mentioned in the beginning, the question emerges of whether such dualistic ideas of 'culture' and belonging—such 'either-or' concepts—can adequately meet the complexity of a current world society that is highly influenced by various mobility forms. The risk of such descriptions of migration and society lies in the reproduction of cultural patterns, generalizing stereotypes, and the idea that 'culture' or ethnic groups are associated with specific characteristics. Therefore, it is necessary to overcome the inadmissible equation of nation, ethnicity, and 'culture' in a pluralized world—because it hides stereotypical attributions and promotes essentialism.

Furthermore, to interrupt set orders of belonging, there is a need to go beyond 'methodological nationalism'—"the assumption that the nation/state/society is the natural social and political form of the modern world" (Wimmer & Glick Schiller, 2002, p. 301). The nation-state is a comparatively young concept and is by no means a natural order of membership. Migration—considered the deviation from normalized settledness in a nation-state—challenges the so-called national-racial-culturally coded belonging (Mecheril, 2018). Mecheril suggests this particular term of belonging to draw attention to the blurring of the boundaries between nation, ethnicity, and 'culture,' by criticizing it at the same time.

Migration is identified as the cause of increasing pluralization because the diversity it brings appears more evident than, say, in existing diversity in terms of age, gender, sexual orientation, social class, and so forth. There are desires for clarity and categorizations in society and politics, especially from those unsettled by ambiguity (see Bauman, 2016). Clearly defined groups of 'insiders' and 'outsiders' promise orientation in an ever-changing society. Younger perspectives on migration and society call such clarities into question. Migration does not explain alterity;

it is not the only explanation for crisis and societal conflicts. Rather, according to Foroutan (2018, p. 270), the question can be asked, how does a plural democracy fulfill its promise of equality of rights and possibilities for all, regardless of—among other things—origin, gender, sexual orientation, or religion? "The core conflict of heterogeneous societies is not about migration, but about the negotiation and acknowledgment of equality as a central promise of modern democracies that refer to plurality and parity as their principle" (p. 271).

The struggle to recognize equality in the context of diversity is related to specific ideas of (non)belonging and difference. The negotiation of difference mostly occurs in the discussion about 'the other,' 'the alien,' and 'the stranger,' due to migration. Castro Varela and Mecheril (2010) point out that 'migration' often does not refer to migrating in the sense of a mobility process, but is interchangeably used with an attributed "deviation from notions of normality regarding biography, identity, and habitus" (p. 38). Differences do not emerge solely from nature, but they are also constructed, produced, and can be, therefore, analyzed in their complex and powerful interplay as socially significant relations of dominance and oppression (Riegel, 2016, p. 8). This becomes clear in the concept of 'with a migration background.' This attribution continually confirms foreignness and 'strangers,' which have to be integrated. Özdemir (2020) calls the construct of 'migration background' a "stress factor in the hamster wheel of integration debates" and pleads for the abolition of this categorization, because it "has become an expression of exclusion" and continuously reproduces borders between assumed 'locals' and 'strangers.' The strangers remain 'migration-others' (Mecheril, 2013), strange minorities 'on the margin' (Park, 1928, p. 887). Again, the power of language becomes evident here because terms enable or prevent affiliations for both 'the stranger' and the one 'with a migration background.'

Consequently, recognizing society's plurality and the associated social changes, new approaches in understanding and explaining migration, 'integration' society—and in this context also education—are required. The post-migrant approach opens the possibility of shifting the perspective on how to look at migration and 'integration' by acknowledging that both mobility and migration, as well as multiple belongings, are social and historical normality (see Foroutan et al., 2014). In this sense, the concept of post-migrant society does not imply a finished, completed, or coherent theory. It is rather a theoretical work in progress, which provides a range of various scientific approaches to analyze and understand the social complexity.

Migration and 'Integration' Revisited: A Critical Examination of Social Power Relations

The Post-Migrant Perspective: A New Approach for Social Analysis

The post-migrant perspective creates an opportunity to exceed the binary attributions outlined above. Therefore, social questions should be looked at through the 'lens of migration' (Espahangizi, 2018, p. 49). Migration has to be considered a society-forming and -constructing force. Instead of deviation or exception, migration is part of social reality and normality, because society has always been pervaded by migration. By shedding light on external ascriptions and exclusion processes, it becomes explicit that migration as a social reality receives neither widespread scientific nor social recognition. This is why using a post-migrant perspective means recognizing plurality as a starting point of any social analyses. In a post-migrant country, migration cannot (or no longer can) be considered a deviation or exception. The one-dimensional, assimilating orientation of language and 'lead culture' acquisition should be put into question. In this sense, terms like 'migration background' manifest one-dimensional thinking. 'Being German,' 'being Italian,' or 'being Nigerian' should not be seen as something natural, essentialist, or exclusive, but compatible with a multitude of affiliations. With terms like 'hybridity' (Yildiz, 2018, p. 21) and 'transtopies' (p. 25) presumed clarity, and the classical image of identity and 'culture' as homogenous forces can be irritated. By questioning certain notions, it becomes possible to break with the dualistic logic of differentiating categories, such as 'insiders' and 'outsiders,' 'ingroups' and 'outgroups,' 'locals' and 'foreigners.' Conflicting and ambiguous terms like 'integration' do not necessarily need to be eliminated, but rather put into question (What is meant by them in the respective context?). In this sense, it should also be considered to what extent specific categories or labels exclusively consist of external ascriptions, or if there are also possibilities for self-categorizations and self-descriptions.

At this point, the fundamental distinction to Park's *marginal* man at the margins of society (as mentioned above) becomes explicit. While Park positions the stranger at the margins, the post-migrant perspective centralizes migration in the analysis of highly diverse societies. In this context, it is essential to recognize the heterogeneity of narratives, stories, and experiences of migrants and their descendants, by avoiding the (re)production of images of 'the (migrant) other' in which individual stories are used as blueprints for experiences of an assumed migrant collective. Stories *about* migrants also risk constructing "white, national, settled non-migrants" (Römhild, 2015, p. 39). The realization of migration as a matter of fact does not mean to analyze 'the others' in the sense of a 'migrantology' (Römhild, 2018, p. 70). Education and the study of societies in general require a 'migrantization' (p. 71). In the framework of education, migrantization means that educational institutions need to be 'de-migrantizised,' in a sense that there is no special focus on 'the migrants.' Similarly, research on society needs to be 'migrantizised,' which means migration must always be considered as an omnipresent, cross-sectional, and interdisciplinary topic. Additionally, the term post-migrant addresses society as a whole. The fact that Germany can be analyzed as a post-migrant society does not necessarily mean political inclusion or positive acceptance. Therefore, it can be fruitful to see this recognition as a realization and transformation process in society. This process is conflictual and also implies counter-reactions, controversies, and refusal. Consequently, it is crucial to shed light on these negotiation processes and social battles in post-migrant societies (see Espahangizi, 2018, p. 40).

A post-migrant perspective promotes a shift of view on migration, 'integration,' and society towards a critical examination of social power relations. This is why connections and parallels can be identified between post-migrant and postcolonial perspectives. Postcolonial approaches reflect an orientation towards a counter-hegemonic knowledge production, too, which offers the possibility to tell the history of migration differently—voicing the unspoken, invisible, and unnoticed. Similar to the post-migrant perspective, the postcolonial approach offers possibilities to bring alternative connections, histories, pasts, fractures, and marginalized points of view into awareness (see Yildiz, 2018, p. 20).

The Postcolonial Perspective: A Form of Resistance against Colonial Domination and Its (Educational) Consequences

Postcolonial studies are critical interventions in social sciences and humanities (see Castro Varela, 2016, p. 152). They are based on the assumption that discourses about migration and 'integration' emerge from neo-colonial ideas and thoughts. Postcolonial studies offer a set of different—sometimes ambiguous—theoretical approaches rather than representing a consistent theory. They try to investigate the processes and consequences of colonial domination and their social and intellectual impacts (p. 153). However, the term 'postcolonial' is intensely discussed and imprecisely defined. The term postcolonialism refers to 'entangled histories' (Conrad & Randeria, 2002, p. 17) (i.e., to the relation between the histories of a constructed 'West' and colonialized countries) of a global South and a global North. As with the term post-migrant, the prefix 'post' in postcolonialism can sometimes be misleading (see Mecheril, 2014). It is not a temporal marker; it does not only mean looking at a time or period *after* migration, colonialism, decolonization processes, or the accomplished acceptance of migration as normality. Such a chronological reading is problematic because colonial relations and imaginations still exist. Postcolonialism can instead be understood as a form of resistance against colonial domination and its consequences. The 'post' describes a critical perspective—postcolonial critique aims to deconstruct and overcome the colonial discourses' central assumptions (see Conrad, 2012). It challenges, criticizes, refracts, subverts, and offers alternatives to colonial world orders (see Bartels et al., 2019, p. 2). It looks at complexities and ambiguities in historical processes, and demands a change of view on history and politics (Castro Varela & Dhawan, 2020, p. 24). As diverse as histories are, decolonizing processes are highly complicated, ambiguous, and ongoing. Consequently, "there are many—not necessarily compatible—postcolonialisms, each seeking energetically to intervene in the unfinished history of modern world" (Huggan, 2013b, p. 20).

A postcolonial discourse and critical migration research can enrich each other mutually. At their interface, relevant questions can be negotiated, for example, on particular ways and traditions of knowing and interpreting the world, and how they have led to marginalization, ignorance, and exclusion of others. Additionally, a postcolonial perspective criticizes the synonymous use of terms such as nation, race, ethnicity, and culture. It considers the relation between power and knowledge, and provincializes Europe (see Chakrabarty, 2000) by challenging the European privilege of being the only legitimate location of knowledge production (see Bartels et al., 2019, p. 1). Thereby, the idea of *harmless* knowledge and knowledge production—especially knowledge about history—is challenged and deconstructed; knowledge always serves to maintain existing domination and power relations (see Foucault, 1978). Due to imperialistic invasions, European knowledge was brought to former colonies, and pre-colonial knowledge was also destroyed.

The question of how knowledge is produced and what purpose it serves is particularly relevant in the context of education. This has a massive impact on the meaning of education and what needs to be taught and learned in society. The humanistic values of the Enlightenment highly influence today's understanding of education. During this era, on the one hand, philosophers developed and formulated ideas about the universal rights of 'man' (see critically, for example, Scherschel, 2006), and on the other hand, humanistic education was elitist, exclusive, and disciplining. The promises of humanism were not the same for everyone (see Vater, 2020). Humanism, in which "the personality … was an elitist, conservative subjectivity, which was not accessible to everyone, but was nevertheless represented as nature" (ibid., p. 3) can be described as a Eurocentric illusion. Humanistic education stood for freedom, openness, emancipation, equality, justice, democracy, and enlightenment. However, these were never open and accessible to everyone (see Spivak, 2012). Possibilities, dispositions, and resources to participate and contribute to society were lacking for the marginalized. Marginalized people are not heard. Instead, they are told what to learn to live in a society that is still based on colonial logic, marginalization, and racism (see Spivak, 2008). It is relevant to look at the mechanisms that influence which knowledge, for example about 'the' past, is valuable enough to be taught. It is also essential to understand which ideas shape the image of migration, which is strongly connected to the colonial past: "Which images of migration dominate in global and local discourses, and who decides which modes of migration are a 'problem' and which are not?" (Bartels et al., 2019, p. 1). Postcolonial and post-migrant discourses open the view for alternative negotiation and possibilities of migration.

Postcolonial migration does not happen coincidentally—it follows the historical paths of former colonial forces in the opposite direction. In many ways, migration is connected to colonial experiences and results in progressing diversification and pluralization of a society that still imagines itself as homogenous. In education, imperialism, neo-colonialism, failed decolonization processes, and their relevance for the still prevailing orders of power are insufficiently dealt with. Although its reception—particularly in Germany—began late, postcolonial theory is an established critical discourse (see Dhawan & Castro Varela, 2019, p. 304), especially with the multitude of European and international studies on this topic (see Huggan, 2013a). Core concepts deal with processes of 'othering' (see Said, 1999) and 'epistemic violence' (Spivak, 2008). The concept of 'othering' addresses questions of representation and intervention in hegemonic images of 'culture' and identity in European discourse. The identification and deconstruction of 'othering' processes can help analyze inequalities, disadvantages, discrimination, and racism in education due to differences. For Spivak, colonialism practices 'epistemic violence.' It undermines and declines pre-colonial knowledge systems and proclaims 'Western' knowledge—regardless of what—as the only 'truth.' Again, when taking a closer look at the integration course, only one 'truth' about the society, values, norms, and traditions is presented; only one particular perspective on 'the' past is provided.

There are hardly any opportunities to bring in different positions and views in the tightly woven curriculum. Even when there is room for dialogue, this is often at risk of remaining in and reproducing the dichotomy of 'us' and 'the others' (see Heinemann, 2017; Kloubert, 2020). "This results in a denial of the possibility of self-representation for the 'subaltern,' a term derived from Antonio Gramsci and referring to the marginalized who are subject to a ruling hegemonic elite" (Bartels et al., 2019, p. 153). Consequently, the 'subaltern' and their knowledge are silenced and essentialized. The analysis of epistemic violence can contribute to deconstructing dominant forms of knowledge production, and at the same time, revealing and reinforcing alternative pasts, histories, narratives, and perspectives, which are indeed an integral part of modern and democratic societies.

Discovering 'other' knowledge and perspectives on assumed 'truths' and certainties can lead not only to relearning but also unlearning. The power of unlearning (see Spivak, 1996) not only lies in the ability to focus on one's limitations, disadvantages, assumptions, and privileges in life generally and education particularly, but also in the willingness to give them up.

> Unlearning means to imagine ourselves as subjects that have been historically made, that are part of social relations and hold distinct positions within these relations. ... The concept of unlearning draws our attention to the complexity of learning processes, but also to the intertwining of learning and education with power and domination.
>
> *(Castro Varela, 2017)*

Unlearning means the relocation of routined, established, but excluding, patterns of interpretation and action (see Haug, 2003). Hence, in general, education must be, first and foremost, critical and emancipatory, especially in the particular context of the discourse on migration and 'integration.'

(Re)Production of (In)Equalities: Education, Power, and Domination

Inequalities appear particularly relevant at the interface of education and migration. Education—more precisely the school—on the one hand, plays a central role because of its allocative function. By opening or closing access to education, qualifications, and training, social positions are assigned based on social, economic, cultural, and symbolic capital (Bourdieu, 1985). On the other hand, the educational system plays a core role in promoting equality (i.e., equal rights, access to, participation in, and contribution to society). Consequently, education can be exclusionary and disciplining by assigning a social place, and at the same time, it can be emancipatory by opening possibilities and strengthening capabilities for involvement and participation. Nevertheless, social inequalities, differences, and power relations—particularly in education—become visible (see, for example, Atali-Zimmer & Mecheril, 2018; El-Mafaalani, 2012). Education (re)produces racist and hegemonic discourses, and is therefore a powerful instrument in stabilizing inequalities and hegemonic conditions. In the educational system, inequalities are reinforced and fixed, and thus 'integration through education' can repeatedly be claimed. Hence, it is not only that education enables 'integration.' The continuing demand for integrative educational offerings for 'the migrants in need' generates a market (i.e., a so-called 'integration industry'), which forms migrants and people 'with a migration background' into 'integration products' (Özdemir, 2020). In the sense of the underlying logic, the education system benefits from the constant request for education aiming at 'integration.' Deviations from an assumed standard learner are still considered challenging and unwanted. In educational settings, various perspectives, stories, experiences (with inclusion and exclusion, normalization and alienation), and languages come together in one space. (Adult) educators have to deal with and shape educational processes within the reality of diversity. The so-called migration pedagogy—primarily formulated by Mecheril (2016)—indicates an approach that deals with the central concepts in the field of learning, education, and pedagogy in a diverse society. In this view, migration pedagogy is not a target group-pedagogy, nor is it a pedagogy of foreigners or integration whose primary goal is the (assimilative) change of migrants. This approach is about recognizing the power of institutional and discursive orders. The social diversity of society is de facto reflected in education. Consequently, struggles of external attribution and self-positioning, as well as negotiation processes, are necessary and can lead to resistance and conflicts (El-Mafaalani, 2012, p. 17). This requires constant reflections and search movements by the discipline, educators, and other actors who must continuously reflect upon their own theoretical orientation and foundation (Mecheril, 2016).

(Un)Learning of 'Truths' and Certainties

The educational system and its institutions can be described as places of emancipation and democratization, and at the same time, these places hold power and domination where struggles for belonging, membership, effectiveness, and solidarity are fought (Mecheril, 2016, p. 17). They are connected to certain notions of migration and 'integration.' However, according to Terkessidis (2010), "variety is not an annoying imported problem, but simply the initial status" around which education should be designed (p. 12). This chapter, therefore, sought to address the need for alternative approaches to the challenges of learning in a highly diverse society.

A still ongoing (re)production of 'strangers' can be seen in the construct of 'with a migration background.' The contribution indicated that the 'stranger' (the migrant) is imagined as persistently in need of 'integration'—this could be achieved through education. Newer perspectives on the interwoven field of migration, 'integration,' and education try to reach beyond the (re)production of 'strangers' and challenge the assumed clarities of constructed categories of 'insiders' and 'outsiders.' Therefore, the approaches of the post-migrant and postcolonial perspective were introduced. The post-migrant perspective offers alternative possibilities for analyzing society. The perspective is based on the assumption that migration is a central part of human history. The study of education particularly, and society generally, requires a 'migrantization' (Römhild, 2018, p. 71), meaning that migration must always be considered an omnipresent cross-sectional and interdisciplinary topic, without focusing on 'the migrants' as a specific group of particular needs. The postcolonial perspective focuses on the critical examination of social power relations. It can be understood as a form of critique of (still prevailing) colonial domination and its consequences. This perspective offers a look at complexities and ambiguities in historical processes and demands a change of view on how to think and talk about migration, 'integration,' education, history, and (integration) politics. The postcolonial perspective can be valuable for educational contexts because it can reveal mechanisms that influence which knowledge, stories, narratives, and histories are considered relevant and therefore taught in education. These two approaches for understanding and analyzing society correspond—which was finally shown—with the approach of migration pedagogy.

In summary, by acknowledging society's diversity and the fact that migration is part of social reality and normality, new ways of thinking about migration and 'integration' can be negotiated in education. The concepts of post-migration and postcolonialism can help to make such a shift of perspective. Migration processes can always be challenging and stressful—crises occur, and disorientation complicates coping with unknown situations. However, such crises—or as Mezirow (1978) states, 'disorienting dilemmas'—hold unique opportunities for fundamental transformation through (un)learning, and therefore individual and collective growth and development (Hoggan-Kloubert & Hoggan, Chapter 9, this volume). A critical perspective on the negotiation of migration and 'integration' in education also pleads for making marginalized and subaltern perspectives, stories, pasts, and knowledge, visible and audible. From a post-migrant and postcolonial perspective, this can mean counteracting migrant knowledge's delegitimization and promoting an epistemic change in society.

Notes

1 The term 'symbolic orders' is mainly used in gender studies, as Bourdieu developed it to expose and deconstruct the invisible mechanisms of male domination. He distinguishes between places of production and manifestation of symbolic orders (see Arslan & Bozay, 2019, p. 2).

2 Despite the frequent use of the term *Leitkultur*, it does not get explicitly defined in the Bavarian Integration Law. Within the Law, *Leitkultur* is connected to an assumed certain native culture and economic and social system (BayIntG, 2016, article 3, paragraph 4). Since the debate on the new Immigration Law, the term is controversially discussed. There are ongoing debates about the necessity and meaning of the term, e.g., prominently in the context of the publication of Thilo Sarrazin's book *Deutschland schafft sich ab* (2010) and lately in the course of Thomas de Maizière's (former German interior minister) '10-points-plan' for a German *Leitkultur* in 2017 (ZEIT ONLINE, 2017). For a general overview regarding the debate on German *Leitkultur* see Rohgalf 2016.

References

Anders, Y., Daniel, H. D., Hannover, B., Köller, O., Lenzen, D., McElvany, N., Roßbach, H.-G., Seidel, T., Tippelt, R., & Wößmann, L. (Eds.) (2020). *Bildung zu demokratischer Kompetenz. Gutachten.* Waxmann. https://www.pedocs.de/volltexte/2020/20224/pdf/vbw_2020_Bildung_zu_demokratischer_Kompetenz.pdf.

Arslan, E., & Bozay, K. (2019). Einleitung. In E. Arslan & K. Bozay (Eds.), *Symbolische Ordnung und Flüchtlingsbewegungen in der Einwanderungsgesellschaft* (pp. 1–7). Springer VS.

Atali-Timmer, F., & Mecheril, P. (2018). Die subtile Wirksamkeit von Rassekonstruktionen in Bildungsräumen. Empirische Spuren. In C. Bünger, A. Czejkowska, M. Durst, S. Kluge, A. Liesner, I. Lohmann, D. Salomon, J.-M. Springer, S. Spieker, G. Steffens, & A. Wischmann (Eds.), *Jahrbuch für Pädagogik 2017. Pädagogik in Zeiten von Krieg und Terror* (pp. 195–207). Peter Lang.

[BAMF] Bundesamt für Migration und Flüchtlinge. (n.d.). *Teilnahme und Kosten.* https://www.bamf.de/DE/Themen/Integration/ZugewanderteTeilnehmende/Integrationskurse/TeilnahmeKosten/teilnahmekosten-node.html.

[BAMF] Bundesamt für Migration und Flüchtlinge. (2015). *Konzept für einen bundesweiten Integrationskurs.* Überarbeitete Neuauflage. https://www.bamf.de/SharedDocs/Anlagen/DE/Integration/Integrationskurse/Kurstraeger/KonzepteLeitfaeden/konz-f-bundesw-integrationskurs.pdf?__blob=publicationFile&v=8.

Bartels, A., Eckstein, L., Waller, N., & Wiemann, D. (2019). *Postcolonial Literatures in English. An Introduction.* J. B. Metzler.

Bauman, Z. (2016). *Die Angst vor den anderen. Ein Essay über Migration und Panikmache.* Suhrkamp.

[BayIntG] Bayerisches Integrationsgesetz. (2016). Bayerisches Integrationsgesetz. https://www.gesetze-bayern.de/Content/Document/BayIntG.

Bigo, D. (2010). Sicherheit und Immigration. Zu einer Kritik der Gouvernementalität des Unbehagens. In M. Misselwitz & K. Schlichte (Eds.), *Politik der Unentschiedenheit. Die internationale Politik und ihr Umgang mit Kriegsflüchtlingen* (pp. 39–75). Transcript.

[BMBF] Bundesministerium für Bildung und Forschung. (2018). *Weiterbildungsverhalten von Personen mit Migrationshintergrund. Ergebnisse der erweiterten Erhebung des Adult Education Survey (AES-Migra 2016).* https://www.bmbf.de/upload_filestore/pub/Weiterbildungsverhalten_von_Personen_mit_Migrationshintergrund.pdf.

Bourdieu, P. (1985). The social space and the genesis of groups. *Theory and Society, 14*(6), 723–744.

Bourdieu, P. (2005). *Die männliche Herrschaft.* 1. Auflage. Suhrkamp.

Castro Varela, M. d. M. (2013). *Ist Integration nötig? Eine Streitschrift von María do Mar Castro Varela.* Verlag des Deutschen Vereins für öffentliche und private Fürsorge e.V.

Castro Varela, M. d. M. (2016). Postkolonialität. In P. Mecheril (Ed.), *Handbuch Migrationspädagogik* (pp. 152–166). Beltz.

Castro Varela, M. d. M. (2017). (Un-)Wissen. Verlernen als komplexer Lernprozess. *Migrazine*. http://www.migrazine.at/artikel/un-wissen-verlernen-als-komplexer-lernprozess.

Castro Varela, M. d. M., & Dhawan, N. (2020). *Postkoloniale Theorie. Eine kritische Einführung*. 3rd edition. Transcript.

Castro Varela, M. d. M., & Mecheril, P. (2010). Grenze und Bewegung. Migrationswissenschaftliche Klärungen. In P. Mecheril (Ed.), *Migrationspädagogik* (pp. 23–53). Beltz.

Chakrabarty, D. (2000). *Provincializing Europe: Postcolonial Thought and Historical Difference*. Princeton University Press.

Conrad, S. (2012). *Kolonialismus und Postkolonialismus: Schlüsselbegriffe der aktuellen Debatte*. https://www.bpb.de/apuz/146971/kolonialismus-und-postkolonialismus?p=all.

Conrad, S., & Randeria, S. (2002). Einleitung. Geteilte Geschichten—Europa in einer Postkolonialen Welt. In S. Conrad & S. Randeria (Eds.), *Jenseits des Eurozentrismus. Postkoloniale Perspektiven in den Geschichts- und Kulturwissenschaften* (pp. 9–50). Campus.

Dhawan, N., & Castro Varela, M. d. M. (2019). Kulturkolonialismus und postkoloniale Kritik: Perspektiven der Geschlechterforschung. In B. Kortendiek, B. Regraf, & K. Sabisch (Eds.), *Handbuch interdisziplinäre Geschlechterforschung* (pp. 303–312). Springer VS.

Eisenstadt, S. N. (1954). *The Absorption of Immigrants*. Routledge.

El-Mafaalani, A. (2012). *BildungsaufsteigerInnen aus benachteiligten Milieus. Habitustransformation und soziale Mobilität bei Einheimischen und Türkeistämmigen*. Springer VS.

Espahangizi, K. M. (2018). Ab wann sind Gesellschaften postmigrantisch? In N. Foroutan, J. Karakayali, & R. Spielhaus (Eds.), *Postmigrantische Perspektiven. Ordnungssysteme, Repräsentationen, Kritik* (pp. 35–55). Campus Verlag.

Esser, H. (2000). *Soziologie. Spezielle Grundlagen, Band 2: Die Konstruktion der Gesellschaft*. Campus Verlag.

Foroutan, N. (2018). Was will eine postmigrantische Gesellschaftsanalyse? In N. Foroutan, J. Karakayali, & R. Spielhaus (Eds.), *Postmigrantische Perspektiven. Ordnungssysteme, Repräsentationen, Kritik* (pp. 269–299). Campus Verlag.

Foroutan, N., Canan, C., Arnold, S., Schwarze, B., Beigang, S., & Kalkum, D. (2014). *Deutschland postmigrantisch I. Gesellschaft, Religion, Identität. Erste Ergebnisse*. Berliner Institut für empirische Integrations- und Migrationsforschung (BIM).

Foroutan, N., & İkiz, D. (2016). Migrationsgesellschaft. In P. Mecheril (Ed.), *Handbuch Migrationspädagogik* (pp. 138–151). Beltz.

Foroutan, N., Karakayali, J., & Spielhaus, R. (2018). Einleitung: Kritische Wissensproduktion zur postmigrantischen Gesellschaft. In N. Foroutan, J. Karakayali, & R. Spielhaus (Eds.), *Postmigrantische Perspektiven. Ordnungssysteme, Repräsentationen, Kritik* (pp. 9–16). Campus Verlag.

Foucault, M. (1978). *Dispositive der Macht. Über Sexualität, Wissen und Wahrheit*. Merve.

Gogolin, I. (2008). *Der monolinguale Habitus der multilingualen Schule*. (2nd unrevised edition). Waxmann.

Gomolla, M., & Radtke, F.-O. (2007). *Institutionelle Diskriminierung. Die Herstellung ethnischer Differenz in der Schule* (3rd ed.). VS Verlag für Sozialwissenschaften.

Gordon, M. M. (1964). *Assimilation in American Life: The Role of Race, Religion, and National Origin*. Oxford University Press.

Haug, F. (2003). *Lernverhältnisse. Selbstbewegungen und Selbstblockierungen*. Argument Verlag.

Heckmann, F. (2005). *Bedingungen erfolgreicher Integration. Bayerisches Integrationsforum Integration im Dialog—Migranten in Bayern*. Europäisches Forum für Migrationsstudien.

Heinemann, A. M. B. (2017). The making of good citizens. German courses for migrants and refugees. *Studies in the Education of Adults*, 49(2), 177–195.

Huggan, G. (Ed.). (2013a). *The Oxford Handbook of Postcolonial Studies*. Oxford University Press.

Huggan, G. (2013b). General introduction. In G. Huggan (Ed.), *The Oxford Handbook of Postcolonial Studies* (pp. 1–26). Oxford University Press.

Karakayali, J., & Mecheril, P. (2018). Umkämpfte Krisen: Migrationsregime als Analyseperspektive migrationsgesellschaftlicher Gegenwart. In N. Foroutan, J. Karakayali, & R. Spielhaus (Eds.), *Postmigrantische Perspektiven. Ordnungssysteme, Repräsentationen, Kritik* (pp. 225–235). Campus Verlag.

Kloubert, T. (2020). Democracy education in the context of German "Orientation Courses" for migrants. In T. Kloubert (Ed.), *Erwachsenenbildung und Migration. Internationale Kontexte und historische Bezüge* (pp. 115–132). Springer VS.

Lochner, S. (2018). *Integrationskurse als Motor für gesellschaftlichen Zusammenhalt?*https://www.bpb.de/gesellschaft/migration/kurzdossiers/264011/integrationskurse-als-motor-fuer-gesellschaftlichen-zusammenhalt.

Mecheril, P. (2013). *Prekäre Verhältnisse. Über natio-ethno-kulturelle (Mehrfach-) Zugehörigkeit.* Waxmann.

Mecheril, P. (2014). Was ist das X im Postmigrantischen? *Zeitschrift für kritische Stadtforschung,* 2014(3), 107–112.

Mecheril, P. (2016). Migrationspädagogik—ein Projekt. In P. Mecheril (Ed.), *Handbuch Migrationspädagogik* (pp. 8–30). Beltz.

Mecheril, P. (2018). Orders of belonging and education. Migration pedagogy as criticism. In D. Bachmann-Medick & J. Kugele (Eds.), *Migration: Changing Concepts, Critical Approaches* (pp. 121–138). de Gruyter.

Mezirow, J. (1978). Perspective transformation. *Adult Education Quarterly,* 28(2), 100–110.

OECD. (2013). *Skilled for life? Key findings from the survey of adult skills.* https://www.oecd.org/skills/piaac/SkillsOutlook_2013_ebook.pdf.

Özdemir, A. K. (2020). Ein Plädoyer: Migrationserbe statt 'Migrationshintergrund.'https://www.migazin.de/2020/07/13/migrationserbe-statt-migrationshintergrund/.

Park, R. E. (1928). Human migration and the marginal man. *American Journal of Sociology,* 33(6), 881–893.

Park, R. E., & Burgess, E. W. (1969). *Introduction to the Science of Sociology. Including an Index to Basic Sociological Concepts.* The University of Chicago Press.

Riegel, C. (2016). *Intersektionalität – Bildung – Othering. Pädagogisches Handeln in widersprüchlichen Verhältnissen.* Transcript.

Rohgalf, J. (2016). Kollektive Identität als Mauer: Versuch über die Leitkultur. In L. Ludmila Lutz-Auras & P. Gottschlich (Eds.), *Menschen, Macht und Mauern. Fallbeispiele und Perspektiven* (pp. 277–298). Springer VS.

Römhild, R. (2015). Jenseits ethnischer Grenzen. Für eine postmigrantische Kultur- und Gesellschaftsforschung. In E. Yildiz & M. Hill (Eds.), *Nach der Migration. Postmigrantische Perspektiven jenseits der Parallelgesellschaft* (pp. 37–48). Transcript.

Römhild, R. (2018). Europa post-migrantisch: Entdeckungen jenseits ethnischer, nationaler und kolonialer Grenzen. In N. Foroutan, J. Karakayali, & R. Spielhaus (Eds.), *Postmigrantische Perspektiven. Ordnungssysteme, Repräsentationen, Kritik* (pp. 69–81). Campus Verlag.

Said, E. (1999). Die Konstruktion des 'Anderen'. In C. Burgmer (Ed.), *Rassismus in der Diskussion* (pp. 27–44). Elefanten Press.

Sarrazin, T. (2010). *Deutschland schafft sich ab.* DVA.

Scherschel, K. (2006). Aufgeklärtes Denken und Abwertung ethnisch Anderer—historische und aktuelle Aspekte. *Zeitschrift für Genozidforschung,* 7(1), 49–71.

Schütz, A. (1944). The stranger. An essay in social psychology. *American Journal of Sociology,* 49(6), 499–507.

Schütz, A. (1972). Der Fremde. In A. Brodersen (Ed.), *Gesammelte Aufsätze II. Studien zur soziologischen Theorie* (pp. 53–69). Martinus Nijhoff.

Simmel, G. (1908). Exkurs über den Fremden. In O. Rammstedt (Ed.), *Soziologie. Untersuchungen über die Formen der Vergesellschaftung. Gesammelte Ausgabe, Bd.* 11 (pp. 764–771). Suhrkamp.

Spivak, G. C. (1996). The Spivak reader. In D. Landry & G. MacLean (Eds.), *Selected Works of Gayatri Chakravorty Spivak*. Routledge.

Spivak, G. C. (2008). *Can the Subaltern Speak? Postkolonialität und subalterne Artikulation*. Turia + Kant.

Spivak, G. C. (2012). *An Aesthetic Education in the Era of Globalization*. Harvard University Press.

Sprung, A. (2011). *Zwischen Diskriminierung und Anerkennung. Weiterbildung in der Migrationsgesellschaft*. Waxmann.

Süssmuth, R. (2015). 15 Jahre Zuwanderungskommission. "Wir brauchen ein Einwanderungsgesetz." https://mediendienst-integration.de/artikel/15-jahre-zuwanderungskommission-rita-suessmuth-einwanderungsgesetz.html.

Terkessidis, M. (2010). *Interkultur*. Suhrkamp.

Vater, S. (2020). Bildung eine Anpassungsleistung. Neoliberalismus, die Engführung von Bildung und eine mögliche humanistische Alternative. Magazin erwachsenenbildung.at. Das Fachmedium für Forschung, Praxis und Diskurs. https://erwachsenenbildung.at/magazin/20-39/meb20-39.pdf.

Wimmer, A., & Glick Schiller, N. (2002). Methodological nationalism and beyond. *Global Networks, 2*(4), 301–334.

Yildiz, E. (2018). Ideen zum Postmigrantischen. In N. Foroutan, J. Karakayali, & R. Spielhaus (Eds.), *Postmigrantische Perspektiven. Ordnungssysteme, Repräsentationen, Kritik* (pp. 19–34). Campus Verlag.

ZEIT ONLINE. (2017). "Wir sind nicht Burka": Innenminister will deutsche Leitkultur. https://www.zeit.de/politik/deutschland/2017-04/thomas-demaiziere-innenminister-leitkultur/seite-2.

4

MIGRATION, LEARNING, AND ITS ENEMIES

'Us,' 'Them,' and the Possibilities of Cosmopolitan Learning

Linden West

Migration, as noted early in this book, is an old phenomenon. It can provide respite from tyranny and disturbing, dangerous events. It can represent relief and constitute a quest, no less, for something better and safer for self and family; a new home and all that represents (see Chapter 11, present volume). The journey is often dangerous, however: traversing unpredictable oceans, barbed wire and imposing walls, where paying smugglers seems the only way across. And the process of arrival may further traumatize the already traumatized, in the abuse and hate they encounter. Journeys generate complex feelings of loss, uncertainty, ambivalence, alongside hope that all will eventually be worthwhile. Forced migration brings especial suffering to body, mind, psyche, and soul: abandoning loved ones, perhaps, cherished homes, maybe, or at least the known and familiar, in exchange for uncertainty, anxiety, and what may seem, at times, precarious hope. The trauma, I suggest, of departure, journey, and eventual arrival is rarely fully processed, and can become the stuff of family nightmare. Trauma continues to play out in cultural, social, political, familial, and psychic life among migrants, as well as many of those they encounter. Migrants often find themselves living in marginalized communities which have suffered their own economic, social, and political traumas. But there can still be room for hope and optimism: many good people seek to welcome, listen, and care, while adult education provides, as we will see, precious space between migrants and their hosts, where self and other meet in creative spaces, for dialogue and cosmopolitan learning. I define the latter as an openness to the other, and her story; and to psychological otherness within, forged in I/Thou qualities of dialogue; a kind of nomadic learning from experience, traversing borders, and sensitive to the good that may come from this. While also being aware of how myopic we can be without diverse encounters. Adult education, at best, has celebrated the gifts of insights and knowledge when we truly encounter the other, literally and symbolically.

DOI: 10.4324/9781003124412-5

Without such spaces, trauma's grip can stifle our humanity, and the quality of individual and relational experience. The capacity to engage with others, and otherness, in good and generous ways is constrained. Learning the ways of openness, dialogue, conviviality, and cosmopolitan self/other recognition—as opposed to relational and symbolic closure—is essential for everyone's well-being. The essence of good enough adult education is the nurturing of dialogue, sharing, caring, reciprocity, learning from each other, and the creative management of difference and disagreement; quite different, in fact, from instructing the other into firmly unquestioned, supposedly superior Western ways. Migration, in these terms, poses profound educational and democratic questions for 'hosts' as well as migrants; 'us' and 'them'; questions of the material, spatial, relational, emotional, embodied, cognitive, and maybe spiritual preconditions for learning from each other (Formenti & Luraschi, 2020). Forms of learning where I truly 'meets' Thou, in Martin Buber's (1922/1937) compelling words. The process is more than a kind of Habermasian cognitive journey into communicative competence, via rational debate. Rather, it encompasses the whole body, our senses, hearts, minds, imagination, empathy, as well as intellect (Honneth, 2007, p. 110–112).

However, hostility toward migrants, and others, in the contemporary world is often virulent, while migration frequently takes place in fractious, polarized societies, fanned by populist politicians playing on the anxieties of precarity and fragility. Social media can make delicate situations worse, acting as echo chambers in which people hear only those like themselves: 'us' against the 'dangerous', 'greedy', 'other', and 'out of control' migration. Moreover, the noise of social media can serve to highlight profound weaknesses in contemporary civil society. Historically, civil society offered in-between public space, free from the market or state, where people met, dialogued, debated, told stories, and experienced conviviality, sometimes across profound differences. There were many such in-between spaces in cultural organizations, fraternal societies, trade unions, cooperative movements, churches, and adult education, constituting a kind of participatory, inclusive cultural democratic experiment. It is still possible to observe something similar now, including virtually, but in general the space is much diminished. I focus in this chapter on illuminating, interdisciplinarily, what can be involved in creating democratic, cosmopolitan learning, drawing on historical and contemporary case studies where migrants and 'hosts' meet and learn together.

The reflections are set, as indicated, in a climate of increasing hostility and intolerance toward those crossing walls, oceans, barbed wire, or racism. A kind of collective, as well as individual narcissism, is holding sway among many toward what can seem like a threatening superdiversity: too much as well as too many. One way of dealing with this is to assume tribal superiority over others, especially migrants who threaten 'our' way of life. Primitive psychological fears are engaged: of being overwhelmed, things out of control, impossible levels of change etc., in a manic, confusing, conceptually illusive world—especially among those with relatively little stake or resources in the dystopia. People feeling marginalized and worried that what little they have—homes and jobs—will be taken away. From the interdisciplinary psychosocial perspective informing the chapter, the self and culture of our group, tribe, or nation becomes idealized in a kind of collective defense; while the racialized other, or otherness in general, is denigrated. This derives from fantasies about the other, far removed from actual people, their experiences and stories. Real migrants, in their wholeness, diversity, and complex narratives, rarely enter the frame. Once, adult education, as observed below, was good at bringing different people together to share stories, learning to listen, think, and imagine something better, collectively, in a creative fusion of difference.

Adult education was, is, and could be more like this again, in the face of xenophobia, racism, and diverse fundamentalisms. Even in the darkness of market, individualistic fundamentalism, and precarity, where dependence is considered spineless, and we must stand up for ourselves and not rely on others (Verhaeghe, 2014; West, 2016). Building walls, protecting 'us' from 'them,' and rejecting 'their needs,' is in the ascendant. 'We' must protect ourselves even from little children, as parents are forcibly separated from them at the border. Unsurprisingly, migrants who have crossed oceans and barbed wire can retreat unto themselves, into whatever safety they can find. They may be forced into 'detention centers,' where life is penal and about survival. Where it is difficult to escape the noise of the populist drumbeat from demonstrators banging at the door of reception centers as in parts of Kent, in England, where I live (Alex, 2020). Multiculturalism and the celebration of encounters with others, and new social and cultural possibility, are to be annihilated.

So, we should urgently think of how to create good enough, inclusive spaces for dialogue, reciprocal and cosmopolitan learning: transitional space, in the language of psychoanalyst Donald Winnicott (1971). Space where we learn to play, take risks, share experience, tell stories, laugh, and even break bread together; nourishing body, mind, and spirit. Space for rest, caring, conviviality. Space for taking stock, auto/biographically, of events and to find, in the company of others, mutual resources in the struggle for something better. These spaces, I suggest, represent a border country between people, and also between educational, therapeutic, caring, and potentially thoughtful, democratic processes (Formenti & West, 2018). Especially when enriched, in Buber's words, by I/Thou reciprocity and generosity, rather than I/It objectification (Buber, 1922/1937; West, 2017b). Border country can be a rich, diverse, and challenging space with room to walk, play, experiment, think, and imagine in a spirit of freedom. Or, of course, it can be riddled with barbed wire to keep others and otherness out.

Many of the dynamics of the transitional space or border country are, I believe, unconscious, and adult educators need greater awareness of them. Like transference processes, for instance, where we, teachers or facilitators, can represent, despite our efforts, untrustworthy and abusive authority figures forged in the biographies of migrants, or for that matter their 'hosts.' Or in the counter-transference, where we, as facilitators, are troubled and feel out of our depth, as we unconsciously internalize some of the messiness, confusion, pain, and anxiety of those we encounter. Alongside these psychosocial dynamics may also be neurobiological and physiological processes, as referenced below. Feeling safe is a deeply embodied, largely unconscious process between people. Our anxiety, fear, but also our receptivity, are communicated through bodily states, in visceral interaction. People know this without conscious thought. To create cultures where everyone can express thoughts, feelings, histories, and desire, in humane, relatively open, and respectful ways asks a lot of everyone. Sharing life stories can be a good if challenging place to begin.

Of course, not all migrants and migrations are identical, and not everyone responds identically to trauma. Migration can nurture resilience and the capacity to cope surprisingly well in certain lives. Nor must the other be reduced to a deficient, needy, and dependent subject. On the other hand, migration is frequently traumatic, as chronicled in my own auto/biographical narrative research (West, 2014). As educators, diverse professionals, and volunteers, we have to learn to imagine the world through migrants' eyes, as well as those of the people living in 'host' communities. 'They' too may feel unrecognized, disrespected, unloved, and unheard (West, 2016). To create good enough dialogical and educative space, in such border country, poses many questions. For one thing, we must reimagine our pedagogy and interrogate our self, cultural understanding, and life narratives in an interdisciplinary, hermeneutic spirit; and by revisiting the best of adult education, then and now.

Context: Migration in a Traumatized World?

Contemporary mass migration is located in a world of pandemic, ecological fragility and despoliation, 'natural' disaster, war, political upheaval, economic and cultural instability, as well as precarity and polarization; and maybe deep anxiety about the future. Context matters, as does scale. The World Migration Report (2020) estimates that there are currently 270 million people compelled to leave their countries of origin to move to new societies. Nearly 15 million new internal displacements were recorded in 120 countries between January and June 2020. Conflicts and violence in Syria, the Democratic Republic of Congo, and Burkina Faso, alongside cyclones, floods, bushfires, and locust infestations serve to paint a grim if complex picture (IDMC, 2020).

We seem, in response, to be witnessing a decline in compassion, at least in the richer countries of the 'North,' although the German 'welcome culture' has offered, for a while at least, a better alternative. But hate can feel stronger than love. The European Union has struggled to agree on refugee/migrant quotas for member countries and states like Hungary, Poland, and the old East of Germany, bear especial but not exclusive witness to the rise of right wing, nativist, and even fascist parties. In the United Kingdom, Brexit represents a kind of cultural retreat into the Anglosphere—under the mantra of taking back control. Not least of borders, which semiotically embody collective anxiety and retreat. There have even been suggestions from United Kingdom government ministers to ship migrants to holding centers on Ascension Island in the South Atlantic. Or to build plastic barriers in the English Channel to keep 'them' at bay. Migration, like Covid 19, is illuminating aspects of a confused and brutalized world. On the 28th of October 2020, as I write this chapter, a fifteen-month-old baby, two children aged 5 and 9, and their mother and father, 'Kurdish/Iranians,' died in the English Channel, on a flimsy overcrowded boat. These are deadly matters.

Of course, in addressing such issues, we must not forget the good that many do: the volunteers in countless settings, like 'the Jungle' of Calais, and in diverse adult education and caring initiatives. But the darkness is real, as is a ubiquitous precarity in Zygmunt Bauman's (2000) framing. Many feel unsafe and that life is perpetually insecure, despite our efforts (maybe there are exceptions for the richest 1%, who control so much of the world's resources, and retreat to private islands). For Bauman, in earlier, pre-modern times, we acted more like gamekeepers within a social and religious ethic of everything being best when not interfered with. The world, and nature, were divinely ordained, and our role was to cherish it, so we would be cherished in turn. In modernity, we became more like gardeners taking control of the world, molding it into our own image and desire. We even sought to rid the garden of weeds, that turned out, in Bauman's view, to be people and cultures not fitting in to the finely manicured artifice: like Jews or indigenous peoples in the Americas. Now, in late, liquid modernity, we are all hunters: competitive, fiercely holding on to what we have, in a Hobbesian war of each against all. We seek satisfaction in materialism, in conspicuous consumption, but it rarely satisfies, neither does the blissful 'fix' of a new job, partner, or even a degree. The past is often forgotten while the future can seem hope-less. Progressive narratives are marginalized, while the consumerist cult of desiring more from a diminishing eco-system, threatens the future of the planet and diverse species, including ourselves (McCarraher, 2019).

Education, including adult education, can be diminished too. It is often an instrumentalized space where we primarily learn skills for the market, to fit in, maybe to hunt more effectively, rather than pursue liberal goals (Fraser, 2018). Finding a job, any job, is the imperative, most of all in marginalized communities, even though jobs are scarce and casualized. Education, so one dominant mantra has it, must serve capitalism's seductions rather than social, democratic, and ecological ends. And maybe we turn, in our mental distress, to various addictions, whether drugs or losing ourselves in social media; or to hating others. Perhaps we seek a gang of our own, racist, neo-Nazi, or Islamist, in the war of 'us' against 'them'; a gang in which we seek respect and recognition, however perverse. Migrants then, who come to live in 'our' street, and threaten 'our' jobs and communities, are to be kept at bay, harassed, driven away (West, 2016). The problem for creating inclusive, dialogical space for learning in the neglected housing estates or rust-belt communities, is the strength of these feelings and of shared existential trauma. This can be the territory of closure, anti-learning, racism, and hate, under the banner of some fundamentalist, absolute truth, whether of white supremacy or the aggressive (and of course threatened) masculinity of the Proud Boys.

Trauma Reconsidered

Trauma affects both migrants and the communities they enter. It can be understood in different ways: at intimate, intrasubjective, and intersubjective psychological levels, as well as socio-culturally and politically. Abuse and violence against children, or vulnerable adults, as one example, play out at all these levels, while the abused can become the abusers in turn. Psychoanalytically, Freud conceived of every one of us as a conflicted individual, torn, in effect, by the adaptive need for civility and to fit in, but underneath driven by competitive, even destructive urges. His view on the origins of trauma changed, with implications for how the problem is framed. The focus initially was on the reality of actual sexual abuse and its traumatic consequences, but Freud shifted to more of a fantasized or imagined experience, emanating from the inner world. The shift for some was controversial, a retreat from reality, and a digression from engaging with actual experience (Gay, 1988). I prefer to think of trauma as rooted in historical or contemporary events that play out in our encounters with others and in our fantasies. Moreover, trauma is transmitted intergenerationally, as Rose (2010) suggests, in her work on the families of Holocaust survivors. There is silence, and silencing in many families: the sense of things being too difficult, awful, or dangerous to talk about, which is communicated intergenerationally, traumatizing the young, in turn. Silence, and the feeling of voids and untruths in a family story, creates a lacuna of emotional dread and avoidance, which can lead some to seek truth of an absolute kind, elsewhere (Alexa, 2020).

We are all of course, as psychoanalysts like Klein (1988a & b) suggest, born into the deepest vulnerability through our absolute dependency on others for survival, which can evoke anxieties over a life whenever we feel threatened or insecure, in childhood or as adults. Primitive anxieties surge through our bodies when threatened by 'them,' maybe, the migrants of a different skin pigmentation, or conversely when hateful 'hosts' scream abuse. We depend for survival on being fed— which operates at a physiological, unconscious, as well as symbolic level. When we are fed and content, and have, in the language of psychoanalytic object relations, good enough, reliable experience of the breast, we are nourished in our whole being. The world is then experienced as a relatively satisfying place, where needs are met and we can embrace new experience, and learn, openly. When we are poor, despised, desperate, and hungry, the world can be experienced in very different and fearful ways.

These are not necessarily conscious processes, but they stay with us, long afterward, in what Klein called 'memory in feeling.' Unsatisfactory feeding may give birth to unresolved frustration and bad undigested memory in feeling. A 'm(other),' in good enough environments, feeds us and contains anxiety, soothing away some of the bad. But there is always a mix of fulfilment and frustration. Sometimes, to protect ourselves, the bad feelings are split off and projected externally onto actual or fantasized others. This in turn evokes what Klein called paranoid/schizoid modes of functioning—to which we are all susceptible. The good is protected at all costs from the bad, maybe us from 'them,' in forms of splitting at a socio-cultural as well as an intimate level. Kleinian ideas have been applied in marginalized communities, in the stories people tell (Hollway & Jefferson, 2000/2020). Bad feelings, and what we least like in ourselves, get projected onto people of color or migrants; they become the no-gooders, spongers, indolent, over-sexualized, and even violent. Splitting is a desperate defense of 'self' and 'culture.' It exacerbates paranoia when the threat is projected out there. The Proud Boys, racists, or Islamists draw on these profoundly intimate and collective anxieties.

I have chronicled how, in post-industrial distressed communities, processes of rapid, bewildering de-industrialization and the loss of working class self-help traditions can traumatize whole communities. Anxiety combines with the loss of hope toward the future. People, the most vulnerable, like migrants themselves, are often caricatured in the mass media, and among elites, as feckless benefit cheats and the undeserving poor. As people who've had their chance, in the individualistic kingdom of capitalist meritocracy. They should know their place as a warning to skivers everywhere about what happens if you fail (West, 2016). They, the undeserving poor, are subject to, in Axel Honneth's (2007) language, profound disrespect from the powerful (who, in processes of splitting themselves, can over-idealize self and achievements while denigrating others as failures). This is a world in which a one-time Republican Governor of California, Arnold Schwarzenegger, emoted that he despised failures (West, 2016). Or where Donald Trump pronounces that he hates losers and shirkers of any kind, reaching back, perhaps to the traumas of his own family of origin, where vulnerability and illness were despised by his father (Trump, 2020). Or as in a recent biography of British Prime Minister Boris Johnson, an overblown, controlling personality is partly to be explained by reference to a bullying, violent, frequently absent father (Bower, 2020).

The welfare states that emerged in countries like the United Kingdom in the post-Second World War settlement, are now much weakened in this individualistic, social Darwinist world. The problem, under the banner of neo-liberal austerity economics, became the State and public expenditure, which, so the zealots of the Chicago School claimed, diminished personal initiative and self-reliance; and even threatened freedom (West, 2016; McCarraher, 2019). Migrants and mass migration were prime targets: 'their flight' from 'failed states,' and even failure itself, was a personal responsibility. I have chronicled stories of those deeply affected, migrants and 'hosts'; 'them' and 'us.' We are, in this sense, in it together.

Stories of people like Carol, for instance, who lives in a post-industrial, distressed community. Her husband died soon after being made redundant, as the last mine closed and the Thatcherite political economy unfolded. Carol sank into deep depression, and continued to struggle with the seeming hopelessness of self, children, and grandchildren, when jobs disappeared, her housing estate decayed, and life felt more dangerous. The older adult children were told to move elsewhere by employment agencies: in effect to migrate. Racist parties came near, however, in contrast to a diminished, denigrated local government, in the era of austerity. They listened to the stories of people like Carol. They sorted out 'the druggies' colonizing the estate, mended broken gates and fractured roofs that the local municipality had failed to. The racists won representation on the local municipal council. Carol felt listened to and understood; recognized, cared for even. And then, they pointed the finger at the newly arrived asylum seekers and how they, like the blacks and Asians, were the 'real problem.' Similar processes are documented among young South Asian people attracted to Islamic fundamentalism; and in the evidence gathered by documentary film makers like Deeyah Khan (Khan, 2020; West, 2016).

Interestingly, Deeyah Khan was able, after persistence, to interview particular leaders of an American neo-Nazi group. One leader, over many interviews, shared his story of trauma and abuse in childhood, and said he felt listened to and understood by Deeyah (who had suffered her own trauma, as a woman of Pakistani origin). He eventually quit the party. There are patterns here requiring understanding of transgenerational trauma; yet paradoxically we get glimpses of what caring, inclusive dialogue looks like as a basis for a revitalized adult education. One built on an epistemology of life stories, rather than premature abstraction, and listening, equality, mutual respect, empathic attunement, care, literally and metaphorically. Madelaine Bunting (2020) talks of care having to do with attentiveness; giving time and focus; it is not always about action, and can be wordless. It involves an endless curiosity toward people and their life stories. Maybe, care includes breaking 'bread' together, where 'we' meet 'them,' and I/Thou qualities find space. Carol found some of this in adult education, in a sewing class, as well as in listening to youngsters reading to her as a volunteer, at a local school; and eventually in community activism. She listened to the young reading and felt recognized herself, and more able to recognize others. We can be fed, nurtured, and animated in surprising ways (West, 2016).

There is a different but related story of trauma in the life of someone I called Mathew (West, 2014; 2017b). He fled a warzone in Africa, where some of his family were murdered. He crossed oceans only to reach a hostile environment in London, designed to keep people like him away. Mathew struggled, even though he was relatively well-educated and spoke four languages. He felt harassed by the authorities and was forced to register at a detention center on the edge of town, weekly, rather than every 14 days. He saw vans drive by with posters on the side telling, in effect, people like him to go home. (The vans, paid for by the British Home Office, were part of cultivating hostile environments.)

Matthew applied to a university, where he hoped to earn a degree. He failed in what labeled itself as an elite institution and dropped out. He could never fathom the Personal Tutor system, and, anyway, 'the tutor was never there.' He eventually enrolled at a local Further Education College on an Access to Higher Education course and began to enjoy the experience. But he was forced to report to a center more frequently and missed various sessions at college. Fortunately, two of his tutors noticed his absence, made contact, and listened to his story, care-fully. 'They were like parents really,' he said, and a campaign was launched, with a lawyer, to get him citizenship. They listened, Matthew said, to his life story. It was no easy process, and he easily slipped into self-blame. He also felt recognized by me and a colleague in research, when interviewing him, auto/biographically, over three years. In our last interview he was completing his degree in public health at a local, multicultural university. He eventually took on various advocacy roles for Black, Asian, and Minority Ethnic (BAME) and migrant students. He campaigned on mental health issues in predominantly BAME communities. He was good at this, not least because of the degree, but also his competence with languages, his cosmopolitan cultural insights, and his sympathy for those who suffered. He possessed a cultural eclecticism to understand how and why some people in particular cultures thought mental illness was a spiritual, rather than a purely 'mental' problem. He felt recognized, cared for, and was able to recognize and care for others in turn (West, 2014; 2017b). We have to imagine, as adult educators, how we can best bring people like Carol and Mathew together, in respectful and dialogical ways.

Re-imagining Care-full, Transitional, Eclectic Spaces of Self/Other Recognition

Exploring the border country between people has characterized the best of adult education. Donald Winnicott (1971) helps us think about this, in early and subsequent life; in the creative and imaginative play of a therapeutic and educational kind, including with anxious migrants. Winnicott suggests that psychologists often dwell purely on a person's inner life, separate from context and others. Those interested in the socio-cultural, on the other hand, can neglect internal life. He asks us to think of what happens when we are listening to a soothing piece of music, or are absorbed in an idea. Or when we are captivated in a sewing class, or listening to a child reading. Or when we tell our traumatic story to people who really listen and care. Or when we observe children on the floor, joyfully and creatively playing with toys, making whole imaginary worlds, under the loving gaze of a parent. Or what happens when a group of young people are absorbed by a rapper. This is not simply to do with inner and outer worlds, but with the creation of a particular quality of space between people. One neither simply inner nor outer, but in-between, as well as consisting of both me and not-me, at the same time. Winnicott was asking us to reflect on an adult or child's enjoyment of living, of beauty, most of all of play; maybe, the playfulness of walking and being absorbed in conversation and reciprocity. These spaces lie between individuals and their environment, between self, other, and symbolic objects, and can be vibrant with life.

They may take us back imaginatively to the creative gesture of the baby, reaching for the mother's mouth, and feeling its own teeth, and looking into her eyes and seeing her creatively. In these intermediate, transitional spaces of self-negotiation, safety is fundamental alongside the encouragement to let go, take risks, and play fulsomely. Maybe to experience care and soothing when things go wrong, and encouragement, after sufficient time, to try again. I have written of processes like these in adult education, when a student is wrestling with a new idea or a piece of literature, and struggles to articulate an insight, in relation to an 'object' of interest, like a character in a novel. She, the student, encountered a tutor who came alongside, listened, cared, was attentive, and enabled her to take risks. We are talking here of whole-body experience, in which the fear of being exposed and vulnerable or found stupid and wanting surfaces but is soothed; and we may learn to play, agentically. Such transitional space is neurological, physiological, embodied, psychological, socio-cultural, heartfelt, as well as cognitive at one and the same time. It is of fundamental importance when working with migrants and those, like Carol, whom they meet (Formenti & West, 2018).

I have referred to the concept of recognition, as Axel Honneth, the critical theorist, frames it (Honneth, 2007). He draws explicitly on Winnicott's teaching. Honneth uses the word love, in a Winnicottian sense, as foundational to human flourishing (Honneth, 2009). He calls this self-confidence (I think we need a word more like selfhood). Mathew, the migrant, found love—the giving of self to the other—in his encounters with the two tutors. Honneth adds to this the concept of self-respect, in which someone feels accepted as a member of a desired group, as Mathew did in the university. And then there is what Honneth terms self-esteem, in which as in Mathew's story, we can offer things back to the community; by listening to migrants and their stories, and in advocacy on their behalf. From such loving, caring foundations, new social solidarities grow. Strengthening social solidarities provides a profound rationale for adult education, above and beyond the meritocratic rhetoric of social mobility (West, 2016).

There is another helpful theoretical perspective to draw on: recent 'neurobiological' research emphasizes the importance of bodily and neurological communication between people in building safety and trust. Stephen Porges (2017) writes of how, when we are confronted with 'challenges,' our bodies act like polygraphs or lie detectors. We need to listen to our own body's responses while being aware of the bodily responses of others. He uses 'polyvagal theory' to make the point that 'we,' as mammals, have relatively highly developed neurobiological systems, because, unlike our ancient extinct reptilian ancestors, we require care and succor to survive. We are dependent on others for relatively long periods, and to greater or lesser extents, over the lifespan. The developed mammalian nervous system responds to signals that safety is available, or when we are threatened; safety matters evolutionarily as well as being essential for sleep, feeding, digestion, and play. Feeling safe, in other words, is a reciprocal and essential neurobiological process enabling other things, like learning, to happen. "For the social interaction to be mutually supportive...the dyad's social engagement need to communicate mutual safety and trust" (p. 50). For mammals, like us, the bidirectional system connecting bodily states with facial expressions and vocalization provides a portal for well-being, feelings of acceptance, and I/Thou qualities of interaction.

The Past and Future Role of 'Liberal' Adult Education

Historically, we can identify the power of transitional spaces of self/other recognition, of safety, and even love in the best of adult education. We should remember that adult education has been a site of ideological conflict in encounters between people. Dialogue can break down, bringing the danger that groups fracture along ideological or other lines. Adult education with migrants embodies the same dangers, maybe in acute form: it can be a caring but also challenging space for everyone. Especially when it seeks to achieve more than inducting people into some pre-established, uncontested cultural order. Rather seeking to be a space for negotiating difference, for divergent stories and perspectives on how we can learn to live together. On the whole, workers' liberal adult education classes—emerging in the United Kingdom at the beginning of the last century—did this well: they represented safe, facilitating environments in which adult students, with limited formal education, learned in their own localities to play in the symbolic order called higher education. If classes could be sites of turbulence—around ideology, class, or gender—the groups managed more or less to keep on keeping on and to learn from otherness in the room (Rose, 2010; Goldman, 2013; West, 2017a).

If mistakes were made, these were accepted, and people were encouraged to try again by empathic teachers—teachers like Richard Henry Tawney, steeped, as he was, in a Christian ethos where the spirit of the divine, as he saw it, existed in everyone. Where the classes represented microcosms of a diverse Kingdom, manifest on earth. He implicitly embodied I/Thou qualities of exchange. The point of adult education was to create space in which our stories and effort were care-fully encouraged; for love, as Mathew found. But there was frequent turmoil between 'them' and 'us,' as chronicled in students' memoires, diaries, and memorabilia (Rose, 2010). Students might react negatively toward a different other, a migrant, for instance. Nancy Dobrin was born in 1914, came to love literature but initially entered adult education classes, in her own words, in search of a man. There was a German Jew in the class, a migrant from Nazi Germany, and she wondered what on earth he was doing there. He should go back to where he came from, thought Nancy. But as she learned to love diverse literature—Tolstoy, Lawrence, and Joyce—she learned openness to other people too. Later, in fact, she married a German Jewish refugee, who she met in one of the classes (Dobrin, 1980; Rose, 2010; West, 2016).

Such spaces were not easy, and ideological conflict could claim space. One of the early workers' tutorial classes was dominated by members of a particular Marxist group—the Social Democratic Federation—members of which could take a rather economistic, reductive view of Marxism; a rigid stance based on economic determinism. They could clash with other socialists in the group. These were individuals who would cite *Das Kapital* with religious fervor. Others, including Tawney, were open to diverse perspectives. Once in one class, he was accused by a zealous student of hopping around like a bird, from metaphorical twig to twig. Bad temper pervaded the room. But Tawney made sure everyone took tea and food together afterward in a student's home, and they sang songs, quoted poetry, (in this case Walt Whitman was a favorite) and told many and diverse stories. Conviviality was restored and the class kept keeping on in a renewed spirit. There was opposition to the class from the Secretary of the local branch of the Social Democratic

Federation, and he instructed his members to leave. They stayed, engaging liberally with varied ideas and the diversity of the group. This included female elementary school teachers, and gender, no doubt, and its otherness, was a source of learning too (West, 2016). If there were no migrants here, per se, the students were educational migrants from working class backgrounds, in search of emancipatory experience. They collectively generated a learning, cosmopolitanism culture.

A Present Role: Telling Life Stories, on One's Own Terms; Sharing an Apple

There are many good and satisfying accounts of similar processes in contemporary adult education among migrants and their 'hosts.' Processes that include the breaking of bread, walking and telling life stories, chronicled in sensobiographic, ethnographic research. Formenti and Luraschi, (2020; and this volume) write of local people and migrants meeting in Lecco, on the banks of Lake Como, in Northern Italy, walking and eating together; learning in conviviality and understanding how otherness can inspire and succor. The wider context is of dramatic changes in the public discourse and reception systems for refugees. A diffused model was in place, in which education, tutoring, and local authority interventions were delivered where people were living. The provision was widespread across urban and rural areas. But a new, more bureaucratic regime was established. Educators and others were instructed to behave like controllers and administrators in a quasi-penal spirit, while the migrants were concentrated in specific centers (Formenti & Luraschi, 2020). In fact, rather like the hostile environment in the United Kingdom.

Despite tensions, some projects designed for migrants and 'hosts' to learn together, dialogically, flourished. In one case, the hosts included young men and women from diverse backgrounds. The aim was partly to help migrants find a job and to learn to speak the language, but also to search for harmonious co-existence, where migrants and hosts learned from each other. A transitional space, in fact, for play and building some social solidarity. Luraschi (2020) tells a moving story of changes, even transformational ones, in which migrants were repositioned from being 'deficits,' into experts and guides. Hosts and migrants ate different dishes together, from different cultures, which they then talked about: preparation, ingredients, and taste; a kind of sensory education in a 'slow' celebration of food. A process of reappropriating all the senses as a basis for mutual understanding. Hosts and migrants would walk to 'places of the heart,' in slow, barely perceptible rhythms. Walking in forests, or up mountains, or in urban landscapes to be seen anew by young 'hosts.' "Well, I never saw that before," they might say, including places of danger as well as respite. Two participants, Asad and Mateo, rested after climbing a mountain. It was Asad, the migrant from Pakistan, who took two apples from his pocket and washed them in a fountain, before offering one to Mateo. Mateo was astonished. Asad had been living in Lecco and was a refugee for religious reasons. His Italian was not good but here was a significant moment of communication between them. Asad felt at ease, it was recalled, and Mateo responded warmly to what might be seen as a trivial gesture, but one in fact pregnant with meaning. The migrant was no longer the needy one, but had resources and gifts to offer. Small, beautiful gestures, subtle in meaning.

Danny Wildersmeersch (2017), in his work, provides an example of dissensus entering a space, and how facilitators like him needed, reflexively, to think about what they were doing. The idea was for migrants to tell stories of arrival, and of their new home in Flanders, Belgium, in small groups. And to learn about local culture. On a particular night, the pedagogy was not working well. People were in small groups of five to six to learn Flemish but the spirit level was low. One of the asylum seekers interrupted the process. He wanted to tell a story of where he had come from, which included profound trauma. The story was of a Palestinian refugee camp near Beirut. Two suicide bombers killed 37 people and countless others were injured. But one man, the narrator continued, a father of three, threw himself at the second terrorist, avoiding more death and injury. The incident was barely reported, he said, in the Western press. The group took it upon themselves to research the incident. They discovered that the camp was tyrannically ruled by mafioso gangs. A process like this is quite different from a tutor acting as the master of the class with an agenda in which students get taught how to adapt. There can be colonialist assumptions of superiority in this while migrant voices are marginalized.

The facilitators learned how to manage difficult dialogue, and to accept in practice what they knew in theory: that everyone had something to teach as well as learn. But the process was strewn with difficulty. The boundary between education and therapy loosened in the story, as a deeply distressing trauma was shared. Creating more inclusive, narrative transitional space in which life stories are told in their pain as well as resilience, can challenge everyone's capacity to cope. But being able to tell such stories can be the beginning of healing.

Migrants bring diverse cultures and experiences into educational and cultural settings. Facilitators can easily assume that the migrant from the 'East' has much to learn about gender equality, for instance, or other 'Western' values. But multiculturalism is about respecting diversity as one step in negotiating how we must learn how to live together, and on what terms. Misogyny and gender exploitation are rampant in Western culture too, as is, a migrant might point out, materialism and irreligiosity that risks destroying the planet. Forms of exploitative usury in Western capitalism within broken communities could be another topic. The point is to learn how best to explore such issues together, in a generous, egalitarian, cosmopolitan spirit. Knowing the other's life history is a good place to start. Projects like these represent, in fact, in microcosm, what is required across whole fractious societies: transitional spaces, neither 'ours' nor 'theirs,' where playful risks are taken, in narrative ways, and the whole becomes bigger than the sum of the parts. We might call this a microcosm of the Kingdom on earth; or a good transitional space; or even a microcosm of good participative democracy traversing borders that often divide.

Conviviality, sharing food, listening, recognizing diverse others, and learning a shared hybridity, vulnerability, resilience, and community represent the best of adult education. Where Carol might share a story with Mathew about trauma, and Mathew in turn shares his; and both come to recognize the importance of an inclusive cultural imagination and dialogue. A place where Asad talks of his religious suffering while Mateo begins to perceive the world through a more cosmopolitan lens. The good that emanates can be a kind of resacralization, no less, of educational space. Wydra (2015) has written of how the sacred performs a hinge function between before and after, of political and other forms of brokenness. The sacred is found in communal practices that transcend, for a while at least, the fractures of experience and dissolution of certainty. Henry Miller, the American writer and migrant from Catholicism, reminds of everyday aspects of the sacred. He once complained of the profanity and alienation inherent in mass-produced bread in supermarkets. Such bread distanced people from awareness of everyday miracles in the making and breaking of bread that can, in turn, evoke thanksgiving for the bounty of the earth. Capitalism promised abundance though science and technology, but we ended up with processed food with most of the goodness lost. 'Life begins with bread,' Miller wrote, 'and with a prayer of thanks' (McCarraher, 2019, p. 643). Sharing apples, taking tea, slowing down, reciting poetry, teaching each other—hosts and migrants—the joy of different cuisines; walking, listening, caring for one another, opening space for the traumatized; avoiding judgementalism, the hard-heartedness of rigid texts, and giving thanks. Great solace may be found in glimpses of bodily, spiritual, mental, and collective healing. There can be thankfulness in new forms of social solidarity and the experience of emotional democracy. Cognition alone is insufficient for the task of cosmopolitan learning (Honneth, 2007).

Writing of love, and the importance of a cosmopolitan spirit, reminds us that these processes are often so much more poetic than rational. We need a poetry of cosmopolitan, dialogical learning and education, maybe inspired by the radical writing of people like William Blake and the Romantics (Thompson, 1993). A poetry in which 'selfish loves' (narcissism) diminish, and brotherhood and sisterhood (democratic, inclusive conviviality) increase. Reason alone, to repeat, is insufficient, especially if overly abstract, totalizing, and divorced from emotional empathy. Pontius Pilate exercised reason, as supposedly did the Committee of Public Safety initiating The Terror during the French Revolution. Adult education, at its most satisfying, is and has been quite different: where I 'meets' Thou in a poetic, celebratory, genuine, and sometimes transformative dialogue. In the perspective of the labor historian and adult educator E.P. Thompson, we may find here the great 'affirmatives' of Blake's glorious *Songs of Innocence and Experience*: of 'Mercy, Pity, Truth and Love' (p. 221). We need a more poetic, reflexive, embodied, hermeneutic epistemology to inspire us in our struggles for new, inclusive educational and cultural terrain. In doing so, we should never underestimate how small encounters between people may be beautiful, powerful, sacred, and ubiquitously relevant at one and the same time.

References

Alex, J. (2020). Asylum seekers protest in Napier Barracks in Folkestone. https://www.ken tonline.co.uk/folkestone/news/asylum-seekers-stage-protest-over-conditions-239831/.

Alexa, S. (2020). *Terrorism-affected Biographies Within Us. 'Terrorist Learning' as Pilgrimage Towards Death.* Ph.D. Thesis. Canterbury Christ Church University. https://repository.ca nterbury.ac.uk/item/8qyyw/terrorism-affected-biographies-within-us-terrorist-learning-a s-pilgrimage-towards-death.

Bauman, Z. (2000). *Liquid Modernity.* Polity Press.

Bower, T. (2020). *Boris Johnson: The Gambler.* W.H. Allen.

Buber, M. (1922/1937). *I and Thou.* Transl. by R. G. Smith, T. & T. Clark.

Bunting, M. (2020). *Labours of Love: The Crisis of Care.* Granta.

Dobrin, N. (1980) *Happiness.* The Sacombe Press.

Formenti, L., & West, L. (2018) *Transforming Perspectives in Lifelong Learning and Adult Education: A Dialogue.* Palgrave Macmillan.

Formenti, L., & Luraschi, S. (2020). Migration, culture contact and the complexity of coexistence: A systemic imagination. *European Journal for Research on the Education and Learning of Adults,* 11(3), 349–365.

Fraser, W. (2018). *Seeking Wisdom in Adult Teaching and Learning.* Palgrave Macmillan.

Gay, P. (1988). *Freud: A Life for Our Times.* Dent.

Goldman, L. (2013). *The Life of R. H. Tawney: Socialism and History.* Bloomsbury Academic.

Hollway, W., & Jefferson, T. (2000/2020). *Doing Qualitative Research Differently.* Sage.

Honneth, A. (2007). *Disrespect: The Normative Foundations of Critical Theory.* Polity Press.

Honneth, A. (2009). *Pathologies of Reason.* Columbia University Press.

IDMC. (2020). Internal displacements reach 15 million with still worst to come. *The Guardian.* https://www.theguardian.com/global-development/2020/sep/23/internal-displacements-reach-15m-in-2020-with-worst-still-to-come-report.

Khan, D. (2020). *Befriending the other: Seeing beyond Extremists.* Collective Trauma Summit, 2020. https://collectivetraumasummit.com/.

Klein, M. (1998a). *Love, Guilt and Other Works, 1921–1945.* Virago.

Klein, M. (1998b). *Envy and Gratitude and Other Works, 1946–1963.* Virago.

Luraschi, S. (2020). At dinner with "us": Exploring the conviviality space with newcomers and host communities. https://www.canterbury.ac.uk/education/conferences-events/docs/2020/esrea-abstracts/Luraschi-Silvia-At-dinner-with-us-exploring-the-conviviality-space-with-newcomers-and-host-communities.pdf.

McCarraher, E. (2019). *The Enchantments of Mammon: How Capitalism Became the Religion of Modernity.* Harvard.

Porges, S. (2017). The Neurology of Feeling Safe. In S. Porges, *The Pocket Guide to the Polyvagal Theory: The Transformative Power of Feeling Safe.* (pp. 33–54). WW Norton.

Rose, J. (2010). *The Intellectual Life of the British Working Classes* (2nd ed.). Yale University Press.

Shafak, E. (2020). *How To Stay Sane in an Age of Division.* Wellcome Collection.

Thompson, E. P. (1993). *Witness Against the Beast: William Blake and the Moral Law.* Cambridge University Press.

Trump, M. (2020). *Too Much and Never Enough: How My Family Created the World's Most Dangerous Man.* Simon and Schuster.

Verhaeghe, P. (2014). *What About Me? The Struggle for Identity in a Market-based Society.* Scribe.

West, L. (2014). Transformative learning and the form that transforms. Toward a psychosocial theory of recognition using auto/biographical narrative research. *Journal of Transformative Education,* 12(4), 164–179.

West, L. (2016). *Distress in the City. Racism, Fundamentalism and a Democratic Education.* Trentham Books, UCL Institute of Education Press.

West, L. (2017a). Resisting the enormous condescension of posterity: Richard Henry Tawney, Raymond Williams and the long struggle for a democratic education. *International Journal of Lifelong Education*, 36(1–2), 129–144.

West, L. (2017b). Love actually: Transformative learning meets Bildung, and the psychosocial concept of recognition. In A. Laros, T. Fuhr, & E. W. Taylor (Eds.) *Transformative Learning Meets Bildung: An International Exchange.* Sense.

Wildemeersch, D. (2017). Opening spaces for newcomers as democratic practice. *International Journal of Lifelong Education*, 36(1–2), 112–127.

Winnicott, D. (1971). *Playing and Reality*, Routledge.

Wydra, H. (2015). Spells of the sacred in a global age. *Journal of International Political Theory*, 11(1), 95–110.

PART II

Learning During Life Transitions

5

EXPLORING ADULT MIGRANTS' LEARNING NEEDS USING AN EMPOWERMENT-CRITICAL APPROACH

A Biographical Research

Georgia Barkoglou and Maria N. Gravani

Exploring adult migrants' needs is a core subject in migration studies. One focal area of the research focuses on migrants' health care needs (e.g., Chiarenza et al., 2019; Mohamed & Thomas, 2017; Van Loenen et al., 2018), while other research refers to migrants' needs in relation to their skills and capacities, education, and psychological support. A few recent research studies focus on refugees' and asylum seekers' needs, such as: a study by Rivera et al. (2016) that examines refugees' need for capacity-building activities to achieve integration in the host society; research by Trimboli and Taylor (2016) which investigates the relation between occupation, health, and well-being with regards to refugees' and asylum seekers' specific needs; an exploration by Dorman (2014) that examines the educational needs of Syrian refugees in Turkey and stresses the need for psychological support, apart from the language learning need. More recently, Lindsay and Seredynska-Abou-Eid (2019) underline the importance of language learning for both migrants' and refugees' adjustment and integration in the host country, as the lack of language proficiency prevents them from engaging with services, such as health care or education, and leads them to social isolation, negatively affecting their health, employment, and residential location. Oduntan and Ruthven (2019) present an information needs matrix for refugees and host communities to support integration, while other recent research deals with migrants' need to use modern technology (Demmans Epp, 2017; Lindström & Sofkova Hashemi, 2019).

Whereas the aforementioned and other relevant studies emphasize the diversity of migrants' needs, they frame these as being static and fixed across migratory experience, as a 'gap' to be filled, which prevents the integration of adult migrants in the host country. Nonetheless, migration is not a static phenomenon. Instead, it is regarded to be a dynamic, learning, and transformative process (Mirza & Mamed, 2019; Morrice, 2014; Webb, 2015). Accordingly, the study presented in this chapter builds on the assumption that migrants' learning needs are under formation

DOI: 10.4324/9781003124412-7

and reformation, depending on their diverse migratory experiences and the transformations of their identities in the new social space. Thus, it attempts to complement research on adult migrants' learning needs by seeking to gain a close and comprehensive account of the processes under which these needs are formed and transformed throughout the migratory experience.

In doing so, the study harnesses the biographical approach, drawing from the narratives of the life stories of four adult migrant learners who have been attending the Greek language learning program at Odysseus solidarity school in Thessaloniki, Greece. This approach places at the core of the investigation the individual, ordinary life, the social practices, and the meaning that these practices have for the individuals themselves (Tsiolis, 2006). By doing so, it also challenges the dominant, homogenizing understanding of migration (Cederberg, 2014). The life stories provide research participants with the space to construct personal meaning of their own learning needs and their struggles to meet these, their aspirations and hopes for the future.

As the exploration of learning needs has direct implications on pedagogical interventions (Diep et al., 2019; Pearce, 1995), another implicit aim of the presented research is to identify the kind of educational interventions needed for the support of adult migrant learners. In relation to this, Manninen et al. (2019) recognize two basic directions in adult education: the 'not change oriented' (Manninen et al., 2019), which contributes to the maintenance of the social order by helping learners to adapt to their social environment; and the 'change oriented,' which aims at improving the system and, in some cases, provoking structural transformation. In this context, learners reform and transform themselves, while actively engaging in the new social space.

In what follows, the approach of critical-empowerment theory on learning needs, adopted in the research, and the methodological considerations, including the context, participants, data collection, and analysis process, are critically presented. Then research findings are reported under two main axes: migrants' learning needs upon arriving in the host country, and their current needs and future aspirations, both as viewed presently. Finally, conclusions are drawn, followed by a discussion and implications of the research.

An Empowerment-Critical Approach to Learning Needs

Most definitions of learning needs describe them as a gap or difference between an existing and desired situation. Consequently, identifying needs is a process of describing 'gaps' that a target group has. However, viewing learning needs from this perspective implies a deficiency between the two situations; therefore the starting point of an educational program is the 'weakness' of adult learners (Sava, 2012, p. 30). This is especially evident in the case of adult migrants, as relevant research usually describes migration as a "biographical crisis" (Boldt, 2012, p. 93) and highlights the disruption "of inherited frames of meaning and the accumulated biographical repertoire of knowledge and understanding" (Morrice, 2014, p. 152). In contrast, the empowering impact that migration may have is acknowledged very little.

Pearce (1995) discusses two perspectives in identifying needs: the *functional* perspective that focuses on what people need to know to improve their way of doing something; and the *empowerment* frame that aims at the empowerment of individuals, communities, and even societies. In this, the discrepancies or gaps between the two situations are not seen as weakness or lack of something, but as the basis for asset building, self-improvement, and a stimulation of higher goals. Besides, Brookfield, Knowles and Tyler emphasize that the identification of learning needs is a learning process itself, as it reinforces learners' responsibility and capacity of pinpointing realistically what they need to learn (Gravani, 2007).

The aforesaid approaches express two different ways of understanding and assessing needs. The former, harnessed primarily in quantitative studies, assumes that needs can be identified objectively in relation to the needs of a society or a company; whereas the latter, mostly followed in qualitative research, assumes that needs, including interests, wants, and desires (Pearce, 1995) can be subjective, as learners express them from their own point of view (Sava, 2012, p. 33). Ayers (2011), without denying the existence of 'natural—objective needs,' believes that needs may also be socially constructed and consequently subject to social inequities, as in modern, capitalist societies people only rarely have direct access to their natural needs (e.g., food and health care). From the perspective of Marxist theory, Ayers (2011) argues that workers "sell their labor power to gain the money form, which is then exchanged for the objects of need" (p. 352). Thus, natural needs are usually mediated by social structures, and therefore, people need "the capacity to navigate social structures" (p. 352). Discourse is one of these social mediators; needs are mediated through discourse, but discourse on needs is imperfect and a partial representation of natural needs. Needs themselves may be natural and objective, but not discourse about needs, since, for example, current knowledge about a specific need may go under correction, transformation, or even evolution (Ayers, 2011).

Given their critical orientation when referring to adults' learning needs, Ayers et al. (2008) consider a broad array of needs, such as material, emotional, spiritual, and relational needs. These needs may be felt or expressed, but sometimes they cannot be reduced to people's knowledge of them and they must be seen "as a process or an event, whereby causal mechanisms interact, counteract, or remain latent" (Ayers, 2011, p. 354). This process includes a complex interaction between natural needs and social structures, which lead to what Ayers (2011) calls 'emergent needs.' Building up on these notions, an empowerment-critical approach to learning needs has been adopted in the chapter to avoid a mere description of migrants' learning needs without reflecting critically on their emergent needs.

Methodological considerations

Context and Participants

Through the lens of the empowerment-critical approach, this study attempts to deeply understand how migrant learners perceive their learning needs over time and in what ways these evolve, change, and/or are being transformed in the new social context; the purpose being to identify the kind of educational interventions that might be useful to adult migrant learners.

A purposeful sample of four adult migrant learners, two men and two women, who had been attending Greek language courses at Odysseus School, was selected. Odysseus is a solidarity school for migrants, refugees and repatriated, which has been operated by volunteers since 1997. It has been attended by more than 8,000 adult learners from various ethnic, cultural, and linguistic backgrounds. In the chapter, the term 'migrant' is used interchangeably with 'immigrants,' 'refugees,' 'asylum seekers' and 'repatriated,' as it is beyond its scope to distinguish the different terms. Participants were selected on the basis of two criteria: first, they could speak Greek in a satisfactory level, hence communication with them was feasible; second, they have been living as migrants in Greece for more than twenty years, so their learning needs could be explored over time. Their names have been disclosed, and pseudonyms are used to ensure anonymity and confidentiality. Their profile is presented below, Table 5.1, following their life experiences.

Data Collection and Analysis

Data were gathered through open biographical interviews. Participants were invited to talk about their lives since they remembered themselves, aiming at enabling them to select the life experiences they regarded worth sharing. Throughout the interview only some clarification questions were made, and prompts were given to the interviewees to continue their stories, the purpose being to avoid participants' accommodating the perspective of the researcher (Ayers et al., 2008). A consent form was signed by participants before the interview.

For the analysis of the data, thematic and discourse analysis strategies have been applied. More specifically, the theoretically flexible six-phase thematic analysis was adopted (Braun & Clarke, 2006), which includes: transcription and familiarizing with the verbal data; generation of initial codes; search, review and definition of themes, and production of the report. The thematic analysis followed an inductive process of coding the data without trying to fit it into any pre-existing coding frame. It also went beyond the surface by examining latent ideas and conceptualizations (Braun & Clarke, 2006), with nuances from the Discourse Analysis which provide a critical perspective on data (Phillips & Jorgensen, 2009), and "moves away from the realm of what is being said into the realm of how things are being said" (Molina et al., 2020, p. 480). This kind of analysis sometimes is called 'thematic discourse analysis' (Braun & Clarke, 2006; Molina et al., 2020; Taylor & Ussher, 2001).

Findings

From the thematic discourse analysis of the data, different categories of learning needs emerged, with the language learning need being eminent amongst them.

TABLE 5.1 Participant Profiles

	Experiences in home country	Experiences in Greece
Ahmed from Afghanistan	- He grew up in war; attended elementary school and started working in the age of six. - After experiencing problems with the Taliban, he migrated to Iran, Pakistan, Turkey and then Greece.	- He arrived 20 years ago. - After experiencing a wandering period, working in the fields in different places in Greece, he moved to Thessaloniki, working in industry. He learned some Greek, in a refugee camp.
Irene from Russia	- She studied History in Moscow and was teaching at a high school when the Soviet Union collapsed. - She married Boris, the next participant, and gave birth to her first daughter. - She migrated to Greece due to financial difficulties.	- She migrated to Greece 20 years ago and initially worked in industry. - She gave birth to her second daughter. - She has been working seasonally as a tourist guide for the last seven years.
Boris from Georgia	- Irene's husband—they met at University. - He has Greek origins from Pontus, born in Georgia from well-educated parents. - When the Soviet Union collapsed, he was persecuted from Georgia. - He migrated from Russia to Greece as he did not want his degrees to be devaluated.	- He arrived 21 years ago. - His first job was working in the fields and industry. - He has been working in tourism industry for the last 10 years in Crete.
Netty from Albania	- She was born in a poor family in an Albanian village and did not finish high school. - She was in a relationship with a man who abused her systematically. - She decided to migrate to Greece to avoid that man.	- She entered Greece 27 years ago by walking through the mountains. - She started working as a housekeeper. - Her boyfriend followed her and they had a child. She was then abandoned. - She attended and is currently supporting voluntarily a therapeutic group for abused women.

This seems to be interrelated to a number of other needs, for example: the need to learn and have access to accurate information, material, social needs, needs for personal development, recognition and self-fulfillment, relational needs. These needs appear to be shifting across time in relation to the dynamics of migrants' lives in the new socio-cultural place. They are described below chronologically under two broad headings: retrospection on migrants' learning needs upon arriving in the host country, and migrants' present needs and future aspirations.

Migrants' Learning Needs upon Arriving in the Host Country

In this section, participants' learning needs during their first period in Greece, as viewed retrospectively from a present perspective, are discussed under two broad categories: the language learning need and the need to have access to accurate information. These learning needs emerge through participants' discourse as the necessary mediators in order to meet their natural needs and ensure their survival in the new social space.

Language Learning Need

All the participants, when describing their first years in Greece, stressed the need to learn the Greek Language and linked this to their professional reintegration. Greek is not widely spoken, and those who move to the country without having planned it, almost never speak the language when they arrive. Boris, a Russian with Greek family origins, commented that his grandmother was speaking Greek, but he did not: "I'd never thought I'd need it." Netty said: "The first two-three months I had to learn some Greek, at least the basic, to get a job." She did so by listening to Greek songs and watching television. Ahmed also stated that he had his first Greek lessons in a refugee camp in Thessaloniki. He commented: "It lasted four months, around 80 hours, something like that. It was better than nothing...After that, I found a job at a factory in Panorama...and a bit later I found the job I've been doing for the last 13 years." Irene noticed: "We came to Greece with two suitcases...and a child of two years old. It was very difficult, because we didn't know Greek, or English."

Language learning was related to their survival in the new social context and, therefore, it was very important at a primary stage. Since most of the basic human needs are mediated by social structures (Ayers, 2011), language learning is essential for migrants in order to find a job, which means access to material goods, such as food and clothing, but also to health care (Lindsay & Seredynska-Abou-Eid, 2019).

Three out of four participants associated the language learning need with the need for self-fulfillment, self-actualization, personal and professional recognition.

Ahmed, who migrated to Greece in the age of twenty, was alone in the host country, with no money and legal documents: "Before coming to Thessaloniki I was in different places in Greece...I couldn't understand where to go, in which city. And I didn't know the language! This was the biggest problem I had. I couldn't decide what to do, where to go." Due to language deficiency, Ahmed could not make decisions about his life. He was deprived of the right to act as a free man for himself.

For Irene and Boris, a couple from Russia, the lack of knowledge of Greek language meant the devaluation of their university degrees. Boris could not work as a historian in Greece when he first arrived. Instead, he was working in the fields, collecting strawberries. He commented: "It didn't matter, ok, uh...it did matter, but what could you do? You couldn't do anything. At least, you could earn some money." Irene added: "Most people were in the same situation. If somebody else was in a better situation, perhaps we would feel worse. But we were all in the same.... There were University Professors who, when they came here, were washing dishes in tavernas."

Both participants had to re-define themselves in the host country, shift aspects of their former identities, and accept their current opportunities for low level employment. However, their discourse reveals that this was not pleasant for them. Hence, the need to learn Greek emerged as a need to raise their self-respect and esteem in the new social context.

Need to Learn Accurate Information

The need to know how to access accurate information in the new social space emerged in a latent way in various parts of Irene's discourse. Upon her arrival in Greece, she used networks of Russian migrant women, who arrived in the country before her, to collect information on surviving in the host country. This is a common practice among migrants to socialize, access employment opportunities, and get emotional support (Ryan et al., 2008) from other migrants of the same ethnic or national group. In the "new capitalistic society" as she claimed, Irene felt responsible for finding access to information. However, it was only after being in Greece for many years that she learned that, if both her and her husband were certified as proficient in the Greek language, they could work in jobs related to their studies, ensuring higher income and social status: "We didn't know. Nobody told us that if you learn the language, you can recognize your degree. Many years later I found out that I can work as a Historian...it was too late already."

Ahmed also mentioned that during his first years in Greece he did not know where to go and what job opportunities were available to him. In fact, migrants usually ignore the social structures and norms that lead to specific professions and social positions, because these structures and norms are totally different in their countries (Kloubert & Hoggan, 2021). Thus, what they really need is not random information, but information on how to access accurate information in the host country. Perhaps, the other research participants did not express such a need because sometimes migrants "do not know what they don't know" (Hoggan & Hoggan-Kloubert, Chapter 9, this volume), in the new social context.

Migrants' Current Learning Needs and Future Aspirations

In this section, participants' current needs are described under the headings: language learning need and the need for self-development. As in the previous section, the need for language learning is connected to other needs, such as professional growth and relational needs. Apart from language learning, all of the participants expressed their intrinsic need for personal development.

Language Learning Need in the Context of Future Development

At the time of the interview, Ahmed, although being fluent in Greek, returned back to Odysseus School, which he had left two years ago, to improve his writing and reading and to learn English, because he aspired to become a translator. After having lost his job, he started helping Doctors Without Borders voluntarily:

> There...I translate from Dari, which is my mother language, and Farsi, an Iranian language I've leant when I had lived in Iran, in Greek. I also translate Odoo in Greek, which I've learnt since I had lived in Pakistan. I decided to improve my Greek. That's why I've been back to school...I'll try to work as a translator.

Ahmed was determined to invest in language learning and work as a translator. According to Norton (2001), an investment in the target language is in fact an investment in the learner's own identity. This resonates with Ahmed's case, who needed to learn to speak Greek correctly to find a better job, through which he could improve his social status.

Irene, decided to join the Greek language course in Odysseus School, since proficiency in Greek is a requirement to enter the Tourist Guide School and become a Certified Guide. She was also thinking of attending, additionally, the Greek Language School of the Aristotelian University of Thessaloniki to further support her language learning. Irene has been working as a tourist guide, underpaid since she had no license. She commented:

> In Crete, colleagues say: 'Irina, you're a good guide; you have to become certified... An unlicensed guide earns 50–60 euros per day, while Certified Guides earn 150–200. You see?...I've got nothing, but I tell you, I deserve more as a professional...I'm getting exhausted for this money."

Irene, after working hard for years, experienced a change in her learning needs. She was not satisfied having a job for survival; on the contrary, she was looking for professional recognition that would bring her a better salary and social position in the host country.

In all four participants' discourses, another need emerged in the course of attending the language learning courses: the need to be connected to their home country, through migrants of the same nationality, to interact with others and build up friendships. Irene stated:

> ...we [the Russian learners] were talking about Dostoyevsky and other Russian writers, who have a particular Russian style of writing... It's not only the Greek language we talk about in the course, but many other things. I'm also learning from newcomers about recent developments in my home country".

Boris shared the same discourse as his wife. Ahmed identified interactions in the new social space as being necessary, and viewed language learning as a means to achieve these. He argued:

> ...it's another thing learning a language like this [i.e., from everyday practice], and another thing to go to school and learn how to speak to others. When you don't speak well, you cannot really communicate; others don't understand you. That's why school is needed, and I decided to come, because I wanted to improve the way I speak. I need to...Everybody wants to go to school to learn how to speak and behave.

Ahmed realized that language is a culture carrier, which enables seamless communication and contact. In contrast to the others, he expressed the need to socialize more with Greeks rather than other migrants. Harnessing the logic of equivalence, according to which members of a group tend to overshadow their differences (Laclau & Mouffe, 1985; Phillips & Jorgensen, 2009), Ahmed identified having more in common with Greeks than with other migrants, with whom he said that he had developed no relationships: "...with my classmates, no, uh, we aren't many. Ok, sometimes we may talk... I don't have many friends, but most of my friends are Greeks."

According to Laclau and Mouffe (1985), the logic of equivalence plays a crucial role in the formation of group identity, since it overshadows differences and creates a myth that attempts to construct a society as a totality with a positive identity. When a myth succeeds in doing so, and thereby creates a hegemony of one particular vision of social order, it can be said to have reached the level of social imaginary. Norton (2001) argues that language learners often aspire to enter to an imagined community. Thus, for many language learners, the community is one of the imagination, "a desired community that offers possibilities for an enhanced range of identity options in the future" (Norton & Toohey, 2011, p. 415). Probably the fact that Ahmed felt he had been wandering for years, created for him the need to integrate into Greek society, being that he has lived in Greece for more years than previously in his home country.

Need for Self-Development

All four participants expressed the need for self-development. Boris, before joining Odysseus School, believed that he knew Greek. However, he had decided to join the school when his wife, Irene, did so, just because he had nothing better to do. He commented:

> I thought I knew Greek, but once I've started learning I realized how little I knew... The more you learn, the more you realize you don't know. Now, I understand that there're many things I don't know... I need these language lessons for me. I don't think I'll have the time to go on for further studies, but I'll express myself better, so that others can understand me.

Boris' self-reflection shows development, self-awareness, and a change in the way he sees learning, and himself as learner and social human being, who needs to communicate with clarity.

Irene supported in her discourse that it was time to do something for her own development:

> ...it's very important to learn. And I like it. I like that I'm having lessons. Previously, I had no time at all. Work, home, home, work... And my children were too young. But, now, I think, it's finally time for me. My children grew up and it is time to do something for myself.

Similarly, Ahmed, who had little time to attend language courses previously, joined the school for the reasons he explained:

> I always wanted to correct the way I speak and write. But I had always been working and I had no time. That's why I decided now to improve what I know... I had to do it for me. Even if you are an adult, it's important to learn always. What counts is the effort.

At the time of the interview, Ahmed seemed to recognize the importance of life-long learning and constant self-development.

Netty had never gotten involved in any structured educational program before attending Odysseus School. However, she had received some informal learning in the context of a therapeutic group for abused women, which she attended as an abused woman herself. At the time of the interview, she was volunteering in this group as a supporter of other women and also as an activist, supporting women's rights and newcomer Albanian women's integration in Greece. Through them she had been informed about Odysseus School, which she decided to attend, as she needed to improve her speaking and writing. She enjoyed the educational process:

> I liked it very much! Let me tell you something: up to now my life was work and home; sometimes going around with my friends...this thing [the course] gives me life. Even if I'm tired, I go and write. I'm attracted by the course, and I'm counting days to go to classes, because I regard it as being very good...I've started writing in Greek. I go home at night and I do my homework. Why losing time on Facebook and Instagram?

Netty was enthusiastic with her development. In her biographical discourse, the educational program was articulated with signifiers such as: writing skills, thinking, and knowledge. Throughout her narrative, she seemed to realize that her educational experience at Odysseus School was a transformative experience, mostly regarding her learning identity. This resonates with the empowerment view that "needs assessment...is a learning and needs-meeting tool of its own" (Pearce, 1995, p. 407). In this spirit, at the end of the interview, she added: "You know what?

Even if I don't get the citizenship, I don't mind at all. I'm happy for what I've learnt!"

Discussion and Implications

Building on the critical-empowerment perspective, this study has attempted to critically explore adult migrants' learning needs from their subjective point of view, considering that needs are socially constructed, constantly changing (Ayers, 2011; Pearce, 1995), and usually, the necessary mediators of meeting natural, objective human needs (Ayers, 2011). In this framework, it was sought to detect the processes under which these needs are formed and transformed throughout the migratory experience.

Though it is small-scale research, its findings are indicative of the great heterogeneity amongst migrants and the complexity of the way in which their learning needs, aspirations, and hopes get formed and transformed across living in the host country. Every story articulated is unique. Nonetheless, a common pattern is repeated: participants' initial need to learn the language of the host country to get a job for survival gradually changes into the need to become proficient users of the language of the host society, to accomplish professional recognition with high salaries, improvement of their social status, new relationships and social interactions, social integration, self-development, and self-realization.

Additionally, the need to know how to access information in the new social space emerges only latently in Irene's and Ahmet's discourse. This might indicate that migrants ignore what they need to know in the new social context because of the great cultural differences and gaps between the country of origin and the host country.

All the above needs evolve gradually across migratory experience, having different dynamics in each case, as they change and shift in relation to individual migrants' experiences in the new social context. This has implications for the education of adult migrants, as the mainstream adult education which aims at helping individuals to adapt in a given society and equip them with necessary survival skills (Manninen et al., 2019) proves to be insufficient. It is based on the analysis of "objective" learning needs, mostly defined by "the rulers" (Manninen et al., 2019, p. 13) or on the current needs of migrants, ignoring the fact that their needs evolve and transform, and sometimes, oppressed individuals are not aware of their own needs (Manninen et al., 2019).

In the light of the above, this chapter argues for a liberating, emancipatory, change-oriented education of adult migrants, which enhances critical awareness, self-efficacy, personal development, and active engagement with the new social space (Manninen et al., 2019). In the same direction, Borg (2021) endorses Emancipatory Learner-Centered Education (ELCE) community-based adult education projects, which aim at addressing the immediate needs of migrants (and other adults) while engaging in consciousness-raising, confidence-building, networking, and transformative action. ELCE initiatives are rooted in participatory democracy, rather than abstract rhetoric, and revolve around the pedagogy of authentic dialogue (Borg, 2021).

To this end, more research should be conducted, focusing on different critical aspects regarding migrants' learning needs. For instance, research on both migrant learners' and their educators' perceptions of the learning needs of migrants would be valuable, since change-oriented adult education involves both migrants and their educators in the host societies. It could also be explored how power relations in the host country enter migrants' discourse on their learning needs. Given the challenge that adult education faces in the modern era of transnational migration, more critical research on the topic is needed.

References

Ayers, D. (2011). A critical realist orientation to learner needs. *Adult Education Quarterly*, 61 (4), 341–357.

Ayers, D., Miller-Dyce, C., & Carlone, D. (2008). Security, dignity, caring relationships, and meaningful work. Needs motivating participation in a job-training program. *Community College Review*, 35(4), 257–276.

Boldt, T. (2012). Migration biography and ethnic identity: On the discontinuity of biographical experience and how turning points affect the ethnicisation of identity. In C. Négroni, F. Kupferberg, & K. B. Hackstaff (Eds.), *Biography and Turning Points in Europe and America* (pp. 93–124). Policy Press.

Borg, C. (2021). Reading the migrants' world through emancipatory learner centred education: Parting reflections on the micro pedagogical contexts. In M. N. Gravani & B. Slade (Eds.), *Learner-centred Education for Adult Migrants in Europe: A Critical Comparative Analysis* (pp. 168–181). Brill/Sense.

Braun, V., & Clarke, V. (2006). Using thematic analysis in psychology. *Qualitative Research in Psychology*, 3(2), 77–101.

Cederberg, M. (2014). Public discourses and migrant stories of integration and inequality: Language and power in biographical narratives. *Sociology*, 48(1), 133–149.

Chiarenza, A., Dauvrin, M., Chiesa, V., Baatout, S., & Verrept, H. (2019). Supporting access to healthcare for refugees and migrants in European countries under particular migratory pressure. *BMC Health Services Research*, 19, 513.

Diep, A. N., Zhu, Ch., Cocquyt, C., De Greef, M., Vo, M. H., & Vanwing, T. (2019). Adult learners' needs in online and blended learning. *Australian Journal of Adult Learning*, 59(2), 223–253.

Demmans Epp, C. (2017). Migrants and mobile technology use: Gaps in the support provided by current tools. *Journal of Interactive Media in Education*, 1(2), 1–13.

Dorman, S. (2014). *Educational Needs Assessment for Urban Syrian Refugees in Turkey*. YUVA Association Press.

Gravani, M. N. (2007). Unveiling professional learning: Shifting from the delivery of courses to an understanding of the processes. *Teaching and Teacher Education*, 23(5), 688–704.

Kloubert, T., & Hoggan, C. (2021). Migrants and the labor market: The role and tasks of adult education. *Adult Learning*, 32(1), 29–39.

Laclau, E., & Mouffe, C. (1985). *Hegemony and Socialist Strategy: Towards a Radical Democratic Politics*. Verso.

Lindsay, C., & Seredyńska-Abou-Eid, R. (2019). Addressing the need for language support for the migrant and refugee community in the East Midlands, UK. *Andragoška spoznanja/ Studies in Adult Education and Learning*, 25 (3), 61–73.

Lindström, N., & Sofkova Hashemi, S., (2019). Mobile technology for social inclusion of migrants in the age of globalization: A case study of newly arrived healthcare professionals in Sweden. *The International Journal of Technology, Knowledge, and Society*, 15(2), 1–18.

Manninen, J., Jetsu, A., & Sgier, I. (2019). *Change-oriented adult education in the fields of democracy and digitalization. FutureLabAE project intellectual output* 01. EAEA. https://eaea. org/wp-content/uploads/2020/02/FutureLabAE_updatedversion2.pdf.

Mirza N. M., & Mamed M. D. S. (2019). Self-narration and agency as interactive achievements: A sociocultural and interactionist analysis of migrant women' stories in a language learning setting. *Learning, Culture and Social Interaction*, 21, 34–47.

Mohamed, S., & Thomas, M. (2017). The mental health and psychological well-being of refugee children and young people: An exploration of risk, resilience and protective factors. *Educational Psychology in Practice*, 33(3), 249–263.

Molina, P. A., Palinkas, L. A., Monro, W., & Mennen, F. E. (2020). Mothers' perceptions of help-seeking for depression in head start: A thematic discourse analysis by language group. *Community Mental Health Journal*, 56, 478–488.

Morrice, L. (2014). The learning migration nexus: Towards a conceptual understanding. *European Journal for Research on the Education and Learning of Adults*, 5(2), 149–159.

Norton, B. (2001). Non-participation, imagined communities and the language learning classroom. In M. Breen (Ed.), *Learner Contributions to Language Learning: New Directions in Research* (pp. 159–171). Pearson Education Limited.

Norton, B., & Toohey, K. (2011). State of the Art article: Identity, language, learning and social change. *Language Teaching*, 44(4), 412–446.

Oduntan, O., & Ruthven, I. (2019). The information needs matrix: A navigational guide for refugee integration. *Information Processing & Management*, 56(3), 791–808.

Pearce, S. (1995). Needs assessment: Constructing tacit knowledge from practice. *International Journal of Lifelong Education*, 14(5), 405–419.

Phillips, L., & Jorgensen, M. W. (2009). *Discourse Analysis as Theory and Method*. Papazizi (in Greek).

Rivera, H., Lynch, J., Li, J.-T., & Obamehinti, F. (2016). Infusing sociocultural perspectives into capacity building activities to meet the needs of refugees and asylum seekers. *Canadian Psychology/Psychologie Canadienne*, 57 (4), 320–329.

Ryan, L., Sales, R., Tilki, M., & Siara, B. (2008). Social networks, social support and social capital: The experiences of recent Polish migrants in London. *Sociology*, 42(4), 672–690.

Sava, S. (2012). *Needs Analysis and Program Planning in Adult Education*. Budrich.

Taylor, G. W., & Ussher, J. M. (2001). Making sense of S & M: A discourse analytic account. *Sexualities*, 4(3), 293–314.

Trimboli, C., & Taylor, J. (2016). Addressing the occupational needs of refugees and asylum seekers. *Australian Occupational Therapy*, 63, 434–437.

Tsiolis, G. (2006). *Life Stories and Biographical Narratives: The Biographical Approach to Sociological Qualitative Research*. Critiki (In Greek).

Van Loenen, T., Van den Muijsenbergh, M., Hofmeester, M., Dowrick, C., Van Ginneken, N., Mechili, E. A., & Lionis, C. (2018). Primary care for refugees and newly arrived migrants in Europe: A qualitative study on health needs, barriers and wishes. *European Journal of Public Health*, 28(1), 82–87.

Webb, S. (2015). Learning to be through migration: Transformation learning and the role of learning communities. *International Journal of Continuing Education and Lifelong Learning*, 8 (1), 62–84.

6

THE CONSTANT NEGOTIATION OF BELONGING

Experiences of Aging Polish Migrants in Sweden

Małgorzata Malec Rawiński

The Context of Migration and Research Background

For at least the last half century in Europe, we have observed that both 'population aging' and 'migration' have been dominant processes in socio-demographic changes, as both issues have been studied intensively. However, older adult migrants do not seem to represent an *interesting* group to research in modern Western society (Malec Rawiński, 2017). This group is marked by a double stigma: migration and aging. Migration—including for some the process of becoming a refugee—involves complex and multi-contextual processes that affect every social dimension of human existence (Castels & Miller, 2009). Migration is a challenge, which causes many struggles that either lead to personal development or attachment to a place. Migration invariably leads to a confrontation with the boundaries of our heritage (Chambers, 1994), to seeking out roots, the migrant's place in the world, and a discovery of the migrant's limits.

I would like to focus attention onto a particular group of older adults who migrated many years ago mostly due to political reasons. Scattered throughout the world, they exemplify diverse characteristics and have emigrated—some from the most deprived and socially excluded, and some from the most affluent and accomplished countries. All of them, though, are aging while living in a place in-between two cultures and two countries. In my study, I am particularly interested in Poles who have migrated to Sweden. The current Polish migrant group in Sweden is one of the largest in the Nordic countries—according to Eurostat there is a total of over 90,000 people in Sweden who have Polish ancestry. However, Finns still constitute the largest ethnic group (about 39% of the total), which is probably why much of the literature on elderly immigrants has focused on elderly Finns (Torres, 2006). Immigration from Poland is substantial in all of the Nordic

DOI: 10.4324/9781003124412-8

countries. While immigrants in Norway are dominated by relatively newly arrived Polish people, there are already a great number of Polish former political refugees in Sweden and Denmark who have been living in the country for a long time, and who are often well established in the community (Pettersen & Lars, 2013). While analyzing their integration and participation in the host society, the differences in length of stay and reasons for migration to Sweden are meaningful. The heterogeneity of the migrant population of older Polish people leads to diversity in many aspects: values, needs, problems, lifestyles, and learning. There are as many reasons for migration as there are migrants and, of course, there are positive and negative sides to any migration. There are many 'faces' to each migrant's world, and the 'world' of Polish migrants in Sweden is similarly multi-faceted.

The process of migration may be viewed from many perspectives: sociological, economic, political, demographic, historical, psychological, and also from the subjective perspective. The biographical research approach is one powerful way to explore the subjective perspective of migration (Malec Rawiński, 2017). The subjective perspective is impacted by cultural aspects and social contacts in the host country. Living in a host country triggers the process of rethinking culture, language, tradition, the functioning of institutions, and history in the context of a 'new' place and time (Malec Rawiński, 2017). The concept of 'superdiversity'—described as the 'diversification of diversity' (Vertovec, 2007, 2019)—can be helpful in understanding the complexity of the contexts, including migrants' age and the various factors that shape migrants' life experiences and trajectories from a biographical perspective. Aging of migrants is associated with political, economic, cultural, and social changes in the country of origin of migrants and in the host country, which also play a role in the process of aging recognizable in a long life—biographical perspective. As Vertovec (2007) states, "the experiences, opportunities, constraints and trajectories facing migrants and the wider set of social and economic relations within the places where they reside are shaped by complex interplays" (p. 1049). Aging and migration experiences are parallel processes, and therefore they need to be considered in their interconnection.

Understanding Aging in the Light of a Biographical Approach

The world we live in is changing, and this fact affects the dynamics of aging as well. Aging is no longer preordained and scheduled, and there is no single pattern for it. Although aging is socially constructed, we age individually. Aging is a learning and transformation process related to subjective life experiences. As we age, we learn and transform the frame of references and meaning perspectives (Mezirow, 1991; see also Hoggan-Kloubert & Hoggan, Chapter 9, this volume). The process of aging is managed and negotiated by individuals in various ways, through several resources and strategies at various points in life, and with different consequences and effects (Hockey & James, 2003). In this sense, aging becomes more variable and multidimensional for both individuals and the society. Aging is a process of growing older, which is dynamic, interactive, and subject to the twists and turns of life. It involves changes and complications that are exemplified by complexity. In this sense, as Randall (2007) states, we become more unique and more distinctive with age. Understanding aging as a process means *becoming* older instead of *being* older. We can determine the objective age; nevertheless, each of us learns individually what aging is and then we feel or label ourselves 'old' across our life's course.

According to Giddens (1991), the post-traditional self has become an ongoing, embodied project. I argue that aging has also turned into an ongoing lifelong project. Aging is a significant resource through which individuals construct their biographical narratives, both in terms of the past, looking back from old age, and looking forward (Hockey & James, 2003). As Randall claims:

> One of the more exciting developments in gerontology at present lies in the use of narrative approaches and perspectives in exploring the complex—yet under-researched—'inside' of aging. With a focus on biographical more than, say, biological aging, the resulting subfield, known loosely as 'narrative gerontology,' is enriching our understanding of how we change subjectively over time; of how we change, that is, with regard to our sense of identity as a consequence of the continual weaving and reweaving within us of memory, emotion, and meaning.
>
> *(p. ix)*

Ruth and Kenyon (1996) also stress the importance of narrative within aging studies, which provides an excellent medium for investigating both the similarities and differences of human aging over the life course. They emphasize that narratives may reveal some of the complexities and contradictions that are embedded in the experience of aging and show the (re)construction process of different identities. Moreover, by employing the biographical approach to gerontology, we can also identify how cultures, subcultures, or family patterns are reflected in individual lives, and how people adapt, fight, or expand the possibilities and limitations of the historical period in which they live (Ruth & Kenyon, 1996). By exploring aging through narratives, we can explore the complexity of aging, which is located 'inside' aging. It means recognizing the life experiences which are embodied in the aging process, making each human life unique.

Humans build up the biographical plan of everyday actions, dealing with external structures and objective facts, life struggles (crises and successes), hobbies, emotions, habits, and values. This means that aging—as part of our lives—has its own dynamics with transitions, transgressions, and variable periods, which lead to a unique biographical aging. Each older adult has an individual ongoing biography which might be captured by telling life stories. Narrative interviews are designed to provide the interviewee a maximum of freedom in expressing his or her own life story from their individual life course perspective. Awareness of responsibility for our life can help us to deal with life crises, but on the other hand, it may lead to troubles, which might be difficult to overcome. Living longer and reflecting upon our life, we realize that while aging we become more aware of various expectations that we had difficulty meeting, and that we have been living differently than we planned due to particular unplanned events in life, but also the impact of a changing world.

The Research Design

As my main research field is aging, specifically old age and learning, I have focused my study on older migrants in Sweden and analyzed their life experiences from the biographical perspective. The research method of the project was based on in-depth narrative interviews with older adults: Polish senior migrants who live in Sweden. The life perspectives of recent migrants seems to be quite different from those of Polish migrants who came to Sweden 30–40 years ago. It was desirable to include diverse interviewees from a range of professional, educational, and gender backgrounds. The research was conducted in 2010 and 2011 as part of a post-doctoral fellowship[1]. I collected data from 17 older migrants (men and women) who came to Sweden many years ago. All were over 60 years of age and most had been in Sweden for at least 30 years. Living within both the Swedish and Polish cultures was the main criterion of participants' selection. To locate interviewees, I used the snowball technique, which allowed me to regard the first interviewee as an 'opener' who introduced me to the next subject. The main purpose of this chapter is to illustrate the life experiences of two older Polish migrants from the biographical perspective. Therefore, to accomplish this purpose, the following research questions are posed: What are the life experiences of older Polish migrants in Sweden? What kind of difficulties do the migrants face? What do they struggle with? What does one's place of living vs. place of belonging mean for older migrants?

Analysis of the data, in the whole project, was based on a grounded theory (GT) approach (Glaser, 1992, 1995). As GT requires, I did a careful and discrete sequence of analysis: open coding, selective coding, discovery, and naming categories (Glaser, 1992) for all narrative interviews. The analysis of life stories showed both some similarities and differences in accordance with the biographical patchwork of their life experiences. Themes that emerged from the analyses were coded.

In this chapter, I focus mainly on two chosen narratives. Additionally, it is worth mentioning that the research project became a longitudinal study. Some of the interviewed older migrants I meet quite often—I talk, observe, and establish close relations with them. Among them were Robert and Irena, whose narrations I have chosen to analyze and present here. The reason for choosing Irena's and Robert's narrations is grounded in differences and similarities identified during the analysis. However, the most important reason was that both were suffering from cancer and recently passed away. They presented different attitudes towards Sweden—Irena liked and Robert disliked Sweden. The common themes that emerged from the analyses are presented in the following section.

Place of Living vs. Place of Belonging: Challenges and Changes

In 2010, I met and became close to both Irena and Robert. Irena was 81 and Robert was 64 years old at that time. I used to visit them quite often at their homes, which allowed me to observe the changes and health problems they both coped with, especially at the end of their lives because both have passed away. Irena died in 2018 (liver cancer), but despite the pain she suffered and until the last days of her life, she was very conscious of the process of dying. One day before her death, she called me on the phone just to say 'good bye forever.' Robert died in 2019 (lung cancer)—although he remained at home getting very good care, he suffered a lot. His son and wife were with him to take care of his health.

Irena migrated to Sweden in 1981, thus she was 52 years old and already had many years of life experiences in Poland. "Becoming old as a migrant poses different challenges to those faced by people who migrate as elders" (Torres, 2006, p. 1344). In Irena's case, it seems that she converted her challenges into opportunities. She was not afraid to migrate to Sweden at an advanced age. "I look at everything positively. First, in a place where I am, I gather around garbage to be clean. And then (...) I take my life by the hand and go with it. Because you have to 'appease' this life so that it is not hostile." Thus, Irena's sense of life and place make life flow. She lived in Tensta, one of Stockholm's districts where many migrants live, mostly those from outside the EU and the Nordic Countries. The district is called a 'no-go zone' by some, and according to police reports from December 2015 it is the most severe category of urban areas with high crime rates. However, Irena loved this place and saw the diversity of cultures as an opportunity to become a better human being.

In 1977, Robert migrated to Sweden. At 31 years old, disenchanted with the political situation in Poland and reluctant to illegally migrate to Sweden, he and his wife (she is Jewish, and she was pressed to leave Poland) finally made the decision to emigrate to Stockholm. Robert was an artist, and he lived a very artistic life in Poland—he arrived with a car packed full of paints. He felt uncomfortable, as the challenge of a new place, language, and socially-distant Swedes overwhelmed him. Gradually, he started to teach painting courses and got a job at a bank, which made him feel much more rooted in Sweden.

Robert, being an artist (painter), had a deep desire for independence that did not change when he migrated. Robert chose not to buy a house in Sweden since he was afraid of being attached to the place. He "did not want to be linked with something—he wanted to have a rented flat, so he could say at any time: 'I'm leaving—I'm not there.'" Throughout the first 15–17 years of being in Sweden, Robert's family was terribly poor. He said, "We earned zero but then we bought the first house, which needed a lot of repairs, so we sold it." Afterward, thanks to Robert's work at the bank, they got an exceptionally good mortgage rate and bought a very nice new house. Although Robert had a house, he did not associate with Sweden. "I was even afraid when I landed in Sweden, I thought, what am I doing here?" His sense of belonging blurred because of the cheap flights to Poland that gave him independence in traveling to Poland at any time. However, the place of belonging was neither Poland nor Sweden, but rather Robert's studio. As he said, "an asylum where I feel 100 percent good is my studio where I know where everything is, I can paint, I can browse the internet." Thus, his place of living was Sweden, but his place of belonging was Poland or even Polish culture. Robert described himself as a happy man, and he said, "I regret only one thing: losing time when I was young and did not work more on art." He had many hobbies, like reading books, writing poetry, driving fast cars, and shooting, but his biggest passion was painting, which gave him an illusion of an unchanging life. He said, "My life is guided by my attitude towards art and in this sense, nothing has changed after migration." However, the analysis of Robert's life shows that the slow process of changes had started already in Poland when they made the decision to migrate. In many ways, the process of migrating reset his life: "If you are not tough, you will simply die because you start from zero, and from this zero, you have to start living again." When Robert was 16 years old, he started to be an artist. However, after migrating to Sweden, he had to change his priorities, as he said, "Sitting behind a desk is a prison (…) but sometimes, you have to do it. I did it despite myself, but I just stated that when the courses end, there will be nothing to eat; no discussion."

Irena was born and grew up in the east of Poland, close to the border with Belarus and Ukraine. The borderlands are a place where many cultures and ethnic groups used to live together; they share space. However, as Irena said, "there is always confusion on these borders" which was caused after World War II when Irena's family (without a father—he was in the army) was displaced to Siberia where they spent three years. In this way, Irena learned Russian and Ukrainian as a child, which helped her start studying Russian philology at the University of Warsaw. Irena was keen to learn throughout her life—as a child and as an older adult, "I always dreamed about learning. (…) I was most interested in school."

A few months prior to martial law being declared in Poland in 1981, Irena moved to Sweden to work as a babysitter and home help. Because of the political situation in Poland, the Swedish government granted her the right to stay in Sweden. She took some Swedish courses and soon got a job as an assistant for older people. She left the family that she worked for and got her own apartment—this gave her independence. Irena was already divorced in Poland, but she had a daughter, Ana, whom she managed to bring to Sweden. However, after a few years in Sweden, Ana became sick. She suffered from schizophrenia, which started an extremely tough period for Irena. "It was a time of suffering. They took her away from me because she started beating me, torturing me, all for that money for cigarettes. (…) They could do nothing more, so I had a terrible life." Nevertheless, Irena did not complain. On the contrary, she tried to see the bright sides of her life.

I learned a beautiful thing: maybe I came into the world to enjoy someone's success. For example, the success of somebody's children, that I was not successful with my child is difficult, but this is not such a scary story when you

live in Sweden. (...) I succeeded in Sweden, in Poland I would not be
wise for sure, especially because of the material part. (...) I worked only
seven years and just because of that I have a pension which is enough for
me. (...) I don't feel comfortable with it [getting a pension every month].

Irena's needs were not connected to money and wealth. She said, "I don't
care how rich people live if I have decent conditions, especially since I'm
retired and I have such a flat (...)." Even though she had very difficult time
with her daughter, when she had started suffering from schizophrenia, Irena
had a very happy life in Sweden. As she said, "I managed to land very softly,
that great misfortune happened to me, well (...)." She appreciated the place
where she lived saying, "the gentleness of Swedes, the colors, the architecture,
(...) that the poor man had a dignified life, and that just when I stood on my
own feet, I could know that there would be no harm to me here, that no one
would hurt me because I see that they are kind." Irena loved nature in Sweden
and related closely to the Swedes' attitudes toward nature. She said, "I took
everything from Swedish culture as such a blessing, and you know, with a kind
of (...) with gratefulness because everything is so different (...) everything was
different and everything in favor, everything as a positive for Sweden."

On the one hand, Irena said, "I do not like changes, I got used to myself as
I am, and I don't need to change. I feel good in my skin," but on the other
hand, she had been changing all the time because of her commitment to
learning. As she said, "I have a desire to learn. I have never worked in such
conditions with sick people as here. I went to school. I learned. I mastered the
language in such a way in which it is needed, and besides all that, I have
'learned people.'"

While she was aging in Sweden, she referred to the past, to her childhood,
family, and the place where she had grown up. Irena reflected upon her life,
experiences, and the world. She said, "I live, connecting my thoughts with
my family every day. This bond which is getting stronger, and placing me
here in Sweden, gives me the strength to live in this foreign country."

Since I met Irena and Robert, I had been in constant touch with them. I met
them quite often (separately) and observed how they cope with their diseases
(they both suffered from cancer). For several years, Irena knew about the cancer
and she accepted it, trying to live as much as possible without pain. She was an
atheist and was persistent about not wanting to have a funeral. She said, "I just
want to dedicate my body to students who research a body after death." Robert
learnt about his cancer several months before his death. He was reluctant toward
Sweden almost throughout the entire migration period.

As I go from Sweden to Poland, I know that I will make myself very
tired, because I have a lot of work always in Poland. Then I return to
Sweden I do not have the feeling that I am coming back, as someone
might say to the second homeland, in no case, I am coming back to my

studio. And now, the question is whether I have any country at all, I do not know? Most likely Poland, subconsciously yes, but not Poland as Poland, but people.

However, his attitude changed fundamentally when he became ill and began to receive treatment and care. He was grateful that he was aging in Sweden. The needs he faced changed him. His resistance to the place of living turned into a blessing.

The Process of Biographical Aging within Transformation in the Context of Migration

Although I present an analysis of only two cases of Polish older migrants, their stories showed that the life experiences of Polish older migrants in Sweden are diversified and illustrate a specific patchwork of aging processes. To understand such a variation and complexity of life experiences, I used the biographical perspective that helped to grasp the correlation between the past, present, and future life of migrants and their process of aging.

The analysis of these two chosen cases shows the process of transformation, the struggles, changes, challenges, and the constant negotiation between the place of living and place of belonging. The migrants learned not only about adopting and integrating with the new place and culture, but also the acceptance of differences which they face in comparison to those they are familiar with. The differences are recognized in everyday situations, at the workplace, in contact with others in the host country, and in the natural environment. The learning process includes all the life experiences, including those before the migration, as well as the collected experiences of being a migrant. The analysis of Irena's and Robert's lives show that migration is a parallel process with the process of aging—from a certain date and time. At the beginning of migration, the migrants are mainly involved in finding their way of living (in many cases surviving) in the new place, which is not free of struggles and disappointments, as presented in Robert's case. Nevertheless, some of the migrants, like Irena, take the struggles as challenges to overcome the difficulties, and as an impulse to recognize the new place and culture.

Living in between two cultures—Polish and Swedish—starts the process of constant negotiation, 'where do I belong?' Irena accepted Swedish culture and nature which anchored her in this place. She took care of that place of living, but her Polish heritage and culture were deeply embodied in her every day until the end of her life. Over the years, Irena reflected a lot upon her childhood and pre-migration life experiences. In Robert's life story, the process of negotiating between Poland and Sweden, had started already in Poland. He struggled with the hindrances of being a migrant from the first day of migration—even though he unconsciously turned the obstacles into challenges. Sweden was definitely the place of living, but Poland or Polish culture was a place of belonging for Robert. The changes of Robert's life were evidently recognized at the end of his life when he was ill. Robert's perspective of Sweden had changed, as he transformed his meaning perspective (Mezirow, 1991).

Thus, employing the biographical approach brought more understanding to aging, as a process where transformation can appear in various forms throughout it. It can be embedded as a constant learning process (Irena's case) or as a result of learning from critical life events, such as cancer (Robert's case). The concept of 'superdiversity' helped me in understanding the complexity of the place and contexts in which older migrants constantly negotiate between the place of living and place of belonging.

Whilst my chapter provides analyses of only two life stories, the case studies are illustrative of many other diverse life stories of older migrants from diverse countries who have experienced similar or different transformations in their lives. The results of the data analysis show that aging—from a biographical perspective—is a learning process throughout which people re/construct their lives with social, educational, and cultural contexts, while drawing from their experiences related to social practices and historical events. Aging is a learning and transformative process—with ups and downs—related to life experiences. As Alheit (2018, p. 14) claims, "the learning process takes place 'between' subjects and the worlds relevant to them—and these worlds change and are themselves historically variable." Aging is immersed in the biographies. It is complex and unpredictable, but an organized process with multi-layered social contexts of varying levels of relevance. The variety of life situations, life-settings, and structured historical-social-political events show that aging is socially constructed and contextualized. Thus, biographical aging is a complex process of learning to deal with various life experiences through one's entire life course. Migration, the new place of living, is in the constant process of negotiating with the place of belonging—negotiating between Poland and Sweden. Taking the migrants' position, it might open a new perspective to reflect upon who we are as migrants—where do we belong? To the place where we live or to the place where we grew up? Which culture is dominant, the Polish or Swedish one? While aging, life experiences intertwine with each other—work experiences, health problems, family problems, needs, social problems, language problems, stigmatization, and disappointments in the context of migration lead to transformation through learning to cope with them. However, while reflecting upon an entire life, we see all the life experiences as an intertwined mosaic. I understand the aging process as the construction of life trajectories and transformation as a lifelong process. This entanglement of various and unlikely life experiences makes the person's life unique, uncommon, and unpredictable. The place of migration opens new perspectives for aging that might be seen as a challenge and opportunity to develop (as in Irena's case), or as struggle and resistance (in Robert's case). Thus, it might be observed that transformation or transformative learning takes part constantly and sometimes incidentally.

This study suggests that there is still a lot of research required in the context of migration and learning in host countries, especially for diverse groups of older migrants. While this research focuses on two older migrants, it might be seen as a small contribution. However, I consider that the insights in this paper provide enough evidence to suggest a need to pay more regard to the process of aging (as a subjective process in an objective world), and transformation in the context of migration using a biographical perspective.

Note

1 Financed by the Swedish Institute.

References

Alheit, P. (2018). The concept of 'biographicity' as background theory of lifelong learning? *Dyskursy Młodych Andragogów*, 19, 9–22.
Castels, S., & Miller, M. J. (2009) *The Age of Migration: International Population Movements in the Modern World*. Palgrave Macmillan.
Chambers, I. (1994). *Migrancy, Culture, Identity*. Routledge.
Giddens, A. (1991). *Modernity and Self-identity*. Polity Press.
Glaser, B. G. (1992). *Basics of Grounded Theory Analysis*. Sociology Press.
Glaser, B. G. (1995). *Doing Grounded Theory: Issues and Discussions*. Sociology Press.
Hockey, J., & James, A. (2003). *Social Identities Across the Life Course*. Palgrave Macmillan.
Malec Rawiński, M. (2017). Ageing and learning experiences: The perspective of a Polish senior immigrant in Sweden. *Australian Journal of Adult Learning (AJAL)*, 57(3), 421–439.
Mezirow, J. (1991). *Transformative Dimensions of Adult Learning*. Jossey-Bass.
Pettersen, S. V., & Lars, Ø. (2013): *Skandinavisk komparativ statistikk om integrering. Innvandrere i Norge, Sverige og Danmark. Samfunnsspeilet 5/2013*. Statistisk sentralbyrå.
Randall, W. (2007). Narrative and chaos, acknowledging the novelty of lives in-time. *Interchange*, 38(4), 1–24.
Ruth, J.-E., & Kenyon, G. (1996). Biography in adult development and aging. In J. E. Birren, G. Kenyon, & J.-E. Ruth, (Eds.). *Aging and biography: Explorations in adult development*, pp. 1–20. http://ebookcentral.proquest.com.
Torres, S. (2006). Elderly immigrants in Sweden: 'Otherness' under construction. *Journal of Ethnic and Migration Studies*, 32(8), 1341–1358.
Vertovec, S. (2007). Super-diversity and its implications. *Ethnic and Racial Studies*, 30(6), 1024–1054. doi:10.1080/01419870701599465.
Vertovec, S. (2019). Talking around super-diversity. *Ethnic and Racial Studies*, 42(1), 125–139. doi:10.1080/01419870.2017.1406128.

7

SEEKING HOPE, SAFETY, AND NEW PERSPECTIVES

Learning and Adapting for Adult Migrants

Larissa Jõgi and Meril Ümarik

In recent decades, scholarly interest has increasingly focused on different dimensions of migration, including the cultural, societal, and social integration of migrants. Historically, scholars have often used the acculturation approach developed by Berry (1997, 2003) to explain the acculturation process along two dimensions: adjustment (to the receiving culture) and retention (of the original culture). More recent approaches tend to challenge such acculturative approaches, which see migration as unidirectional border-crossing leading potentially to assimilation and adaptation in the receiving cultural contexts and the loss of existing ties. Contemporary approaches focus rather on migration as a process by which the migrants sustain activities, ties, and relations across multiple national borders. Since the 1990s, scholars have explored the complex dynamics of migrant transnational mobility, the emergence of transnational spaces that transcend geographic, political, social, and cultural borders (Portes, 1999; Faist, 2000) and the agency of transnational migrants transforming the space (Pitkäinen, 2012) and their own personal and professional careers.

Emerging research has been interested in the adaptation of migrants and the transformative learning in that process (e.g., Qi, 2009; Brigham, 2011; Grzymala-Kazlowska & Phillimore, 2018; Morrice et al., 2017; Wise, 2005). Migration constitutes different life-shaking incidents or triggering events in the host country, prompting one to re-interpret previous life-views and personal beliefs. Transitions in adult life and transformations become a learning experience. For learning to occur, an experience needs to be discomforting or puzzling enough not to reject or ignore it, but also significant enough to attend and reflect upon it. It is then that learning takes place (Merriam, 2005, p. 7).

In this chapter, based on collected data from narrative research, we have made use of the transformative learning approach, drawing from Jack Mezirow's

DOI: 10.4324/9781003124412-9

transformative learning theory (1991) in order to provide an in-depth analysis of the adaptation stories of new migrants in Estonia. Narrative research is undertaken on the assumption that human beings give meaning to their lives and experience through telling and constructing stories (Bau, 2016, p. 375).

As migrants' experiences of adaptation tend to vary and are always unique, it is worth studying what factors contribute to more or less positive transformative experiences, and how this process can be supported by adult education institutions. In order to better understand how migrants adapt to life in Estonia, the following research questions are posed: (1) What kinds of learning experiences and possible transformations are involved in the adaptation process? (2) What are the roles of individual agency and contextual factors in this process? Therefore, our aim in this chapter is to understand the interplay of individual and social resources, and contextual factors shaping the adaptation of migrants as a transformative learning process.

Transformative Learning and the Adaptation Process in the Context of Migration

The findings from earlier research indicate that migrating to a new country is a complicated and diverse socio-cultural and psychological process with multiple challenges involved (Baumgartner, 2019; Erichsen, 2011; Nada & Araújo, 2018; Sharpe, 2016). Migration brings with it different social and personal life events, and disorienting dilemmas with potential for transformations and learning. In this chapter, the concept of transformative learning (Mezirow, 1991) has been applied as a useful lens for understanding migration as an adaptation process.

The essence of transformative learning, and adult learning in general, is the experience (Taylor & Cranton, 2013, p. 35). Formulating meanings, constructing new or revised interpretations of one's experience, and becoming aware of one's assumptions, are central to an adult learning process (Mezirow, 2000, p. 5). According to Mezirow, learning occurs by elaborating existing frames of reference, learning new frames of reference, or transforming points of view or habits of mind (Mezirow, 2000, p. 19).

Habits of mind are a set of assumptions that act as a filter for making sense of one's experience. A frame of reference is a meaning perspective. It provides the context for meaning making within which we choose how experience is to be constructed or appropriated (Mezirow, 2000, p. 16). Transformative learning is related to reflecting and interpreting experiences, which involves subjective reframing. Mezirow (1991) distinguished between ten different phases, which may be experienced iteratively in the transformative learning process: a disorienting dilemma, self-examination of assumptions, critical reflection on assumptions, recognition that dissatisfaction is shared by others, exploration of alternatives, plan for action, acquisition of new knowledge, experimentation with roles, competence building; and the final phase, which is the reintegration of new perspectives into one's life. Since then, it has been argued that in reality these phases may not be easily separable (Qi & Cesetti, 2019). Transformative learning, when it involves subjective reframing and self-reflection, is often an intensely threatening emotional experience in which the person has to become aware of the assumptions undergirding the ideas, and those supporting the emotional responses to the need to change (Mezirow, 2000, p. 6).

The transformative dimensions of learning refer to aspects of the learning process that hold the potential to change people in dramatic ways. When such dramatic change occurs, Mezirow calls it a perspective transformation, which can be epochal or cumulative (Mezirow, 2000, p. 19). Perspective transformation is most often explained as being triggered by a significant personal event (Taylor, 2000, p. 298), turning point (Elder, 1998), or disorienting dilemma (Mezirow, 1999). Transformative learning resulting from a triggering event or disorienting dilemma involves transformation in how the person views themselves in relation to the world, or a transformation in how the person responds to challenges or opportunities (Cappeliez et al., 2008).

Some events initiate reflection and others do not. The most provocative events are crises, which force change (Mezirow, 1991, p. 87) and provoke reflection (Mälkki, 2012; Mälkki & Green, 2014), or events that involve questioning existing social norms (Cranton, 2016, p. 78). Transformative learning means that an individual shifts from unreflective thinking to more reflective and critical ways of making sense of the world (Mezirow, 1999).

Migration brings with it disorienting dilemmas with the potential for the transformation of the migrant's identity, but can also trigger resistance to a transformation (Qi, 2009). Positive transformation of identity involves the formation of an intercultural identity, being more inclusive than the original, and a by-product of social contact with others. Based on research into Chinese migrants in Canada, Qi concluded that those migrants reporting the highest amount of integration into the host country's society and general satisfaction had more flexibility in re-evaluating their perceptions and learning from a new environment, without losing contact with their original culture (Qi, 2009, p. 344). Based on that, it can be argued that a strong identity is a prerequisite for transforming one's perspective, and the role of transnational ties are essential for re-constructing one's identity.

However, the aim of the change might not be limited to individual transformation. For critical educators following the Freire approach, the ultimate aim would be social transformation against poverty, oppression, and injustice (Lange, 2015). Having been inspired by Freire, Schugurensky (2002) distinguishes between three kinds of transformation: transformation of individual consciousness, that of individual behavior, and social transformation. Although these three kinds of transformation are related, the pathway through different kinds of transformation is a complicated process. Several studies have applied transformative learning theory to study the psychological and socio-cultural adaptation of migrants (e.g., Qi, 2009; Brigham, 2011; Grzymala-Kazlowska & Phillimore, 2018; Morrice et al., 2017; Wise, 2005).

Adaptation means using resources to manage different life and personal demands (Kuo, 2014). There are social and psychological resources for the adaptation—social resources related to personal and social competence in managing everyday life, and psychological resources related to well-being and mental health (Ward et al., 2001; Hobfoll, 2002). For instance, social support has been considered by scholars as a complex meta-construct of social resources (i.e., family resources, supportive communities, meaningful others) that include aspects of the supportive interactions, perceptions of the receipt of support, and aspects of the self and whether it is viewed as supported (Sarason et al., 1986, cited in Hobfoll, 2002, p. 309). The roles of the social support and wider social context, networks, and communities are essential in supporting adaptation as a transformation process.

Moreover, according to Qi and Cesetti (2019), there are at least two essential elements of personal resources—the individual's own acts and past experience. Therefore, some disorienting dilemmas might start the transformative learning process, when both internal (personal resources) and external conditions (social resources) are met. On the other hand, when individual agency is not persistent enough, the person lacks the necessary abilities, or the environmental influences are not supportive, the transformation process might be disrupted (Qi & Cesetti, 2019, p. 10).

Inspired by Giddens, we consider the social structure as always both enabling and constraining (1984/1991), although we do not underestimate the 'transformative capacity' of agents (Giddens, 1976) to make a difference in the social world. Personal agency is essential in transforming all kinds of practices (Giddens, 1984/ 1991), and agency is transformational (Eteläpelto et al., 2013), being both evidence and a means of change.

The narrative interview data from ten new migrants enable us to analyze how those processes of learning and adaptation might take place in diverse ways, resulting from an interplay of individual agency with personal resources and the social context.

Studying the Stories of Migrants: Methodological Approach

The empirical data were collected and constructed in an interactive process between two researchers and the interviewees. In this chapter, we base our arguments on the findings from a secondary analysis of two data sets of semi-structured interviews conducted in 2017/2018, and repeat interviews conducted in 2020. The aim of the repeat interviews was to give the participants the opportunity to speak and reflect on their lived experience in Estonia since 2018.

The purposeful sampling for the interviews in our study involved ten migrants living in Estonia with migration experience of less than five years, with diverse ethnic, family, and professional backgrounds. The interviewees migrated because of diverse motivations, including: economic reasons, for study, family, or an insecure situation in their homeland. All interviewees had had shorter or longer periods of contact with adult learning institutions, by participating in the national welcoming program[1] for migrants, Estonian language courses, or formal education (at university).

All interviews were conducted in English. The interview started with an open narrative question asking the respondents to describe their migration story, starting from the very beginning to present day. Next, a set of pre-designed thematic questions were asked, but providing flexibility for the interviewees to introduce topics they deemed relevant (Mason, 2002). The topics asked were about life before migration, motivations for migrating, life in Estonia, networks, and future plans. The questions were asked so as to encourage the participants to critically reflect and add more detailed reasoning. The interviews lasted between one and two hours.

The hybrid approach to thematic analysis (Braun & Clarke, 2006) has been applied in the secondary analysis of the interview transcripts. The analysis started with text-driven coding. The transcripts were read, and initial text-driven codes were generated. The codes were graded into themes and sub-themes, reorganized and named. The broader themes involved: *the motivation for migrating, supporting resources and barriers in adaptation, integration into adult education, labor market experiences, the role of networks, support and future perspectives.*

As a result of the thematic analysis, we present in the next section two narrative portraits about *Elias* and *Fatima* as two diverse empirical examples constructed and written by us, based on the interview data and following the structure of the migration story. The narrative portraits offer useful analytical tools for presenting the empirical data (Rodrigez-Dorans & Jacobs, 2020), and in our case, aim to exemplify how the interplay between individual agency and context can lead to diverse adaptation patterns.

In the later stages of the analysis, the conceptual approach of transformative learning theory was taken as a frame to make sense of the data and the categories formed, including identifying the disorienting dilemma as constructed in the migrants' stories and the strategies for making sense of the situation and oneself in a new light, and the role of agency and contextual factors, including supportive communities of co-workers, co-learners, and family members supporting the adaptation.

We would like to emphasize, as qualitative and narrative researchers, that meeting people and writing about their personal experiences is always ethically demanding. Research questions and several ethical decisions guided us in the writing process of the stories of Fatima and Elias. We chose to use these pseudonyms and omitted sensitive details related to their life and personal experience. In the case of Fatima, we have disclosed all details related to her family and personal relations. In the case of Elias, certain aspects and facts about his previous life experience are not presented. We decided to use narrative portrayals to present our findings, as we agree with scholars who believe that this strategy minimizes the risks of stereotyping and oversimplifying migrants and their experiences in the host countries (e.g., Golsteijn & Wright, 2013).

Findings: Learning and Adaptation, the Role of the Personal and Social Resources

The choice of Estonia as a host country was often made by migrants without knowing much about the Estonian context. Often the decision to migrate to Estonia was by chance, meaning that the motivation to migrate might have been different, for example, to leave the country of origin in order to escape war or discrimination (e.g., Syrians or Kurds in Turkey), or a weak economic situation, to find a secure job or build a business. Other cases were triggered by family reasons, primarily by female migrants following their husbands residing in Estonia.

Most of the migrants interviewed touched upon events or 'culture shock' encountered when arriving to Estonia. In many cases, the different local environment (cold weather), different cultural norms, and attitudes of the people, e.g., being more reserved in general, was considered unusual. Most of the migrants remembered encountering racism directed at them. For example, people with Arabic background often had difficulties renting an apartment or a place for a business in Estonia. "It was for me a shock really," recalls Ammun, an entrepreneur from Sharm el Sheik. He remembers that several landlords refused to rent him a place to start a restaurant business in Estonia.

These incidents were usually considered a shock at first by all, but different strategies were applied in response, making sense of these incidents and oneself in a new context. Ammun was ready to take a paid job as salesman, but soon realized that without knowing Estonian, nor having sufficient knowledge about the field, he could not manage. He started his Estonian lessons and took an offer by an Egyptian friend in Estonia to replace him in his restaurant, followed by another apprenticeship period in another restaurant. He values these opportunities as the experiences he needed, as now he has finally opened his own pizza restaurant. Being able to learn from the negative incidents and be flexible, he has managed to adapt to a new context.

Although our interviewees had different reasons for migrating and different life-plans (e.g., building up a business, continuing education), the importance of Estonian language skills soon became apparent, sometimes pushing the participants to rethink their original plans, for example, taking up a paid job (pursuing a different professional field or at a lower position than their actual professional background), starting intensive language learning, or strategically building up a network of locals to learn the language, local culture, and habits.

In addition to personal resources like individual agency, the ability to reflect and be flexible in re-thinking previous life-orientations, the role of social support and relationships with others have been significant in the migrants' journeys. The migrants had some significant others left at home; therefore, connections with the home country were maintained and considered meaningful. In adapting to the host country, the network created through work, educational institutions, migrant community, or family members residing in Estonia played an essential role, in both positive and negative ways.

For example, for Ammun, the community of Egyptians in Estonia helped him settle down into the local restaurant business. Layal (Syrian-Armenian woman) considers the circle of Estonian friends introduced by her husband as an important source for learning about the Estonian education system, healthcare, and finding tips for kindergarten places. On the other hand, Chang (Chinese teacher), who is married to a Russian-speaking husband, lives in a Russian-speaking area, and works at a Russian school, feels rather isolated from Estonian speakers and has limited opportunities to practice the language skills necessary for progressing in her professional career.

Moreover, international companies, where the working language is English, serve as important buffering environments for new migrants. As English is the lingua franca, there is no language barrier at the workplace. Nevertheless, migrants often experience a strong contrast between the working cultures of Estonia and their home countries; therefore, learning by doing, especially learning about the work culture and norms, is an everyday practice. Although the community of practice at work is international, some migrants, such as Bazan (Kurdish from Turkey), have pointed out that when not at work, they usually try to interact with Estonians in order to learn about local life: "I do not like to go out with Turkish friends. I want to meet new people and learn the new culture. I often ask people to recommend Estonian books." Similar to the work environment, educational institutions (whether long-term programs or language courses) serve as channels for building a social network and relations with other migrants and locals, as illustrated by the portraits of Elias and Fatima below.

The following two narrative portrayals of Elias and Fatima are presented as illustrative examples and discussed in order to exemplify two stories of adaptation that contrast in diverse ways.

Elias

Elias, born in Syria, is a young man in his 20s who moved to Estonia two years ago.

His motivation for migrating was related to education, but the migration decision was also triggered by war. Elias was born in Syria and used to live in Syria. Even before the war he always dreamed about studying abroad, but war prompted him even more to strive for this opportunity. He studied IT technology in Syria, had finished bachelor level studies and was continuing with MBA studies, but the university was not up to date in that field. He also worked for an NGO in peace resolution. He understood that studying might help him to get abroad, and therefore applied for a scholarship with an extremely high competition rate (6000 applicants for 14 scholarships). He won the scholarship and chose the Human-Computer Interaction master's program at one of the Estonian universities. He argued that the decision was made based on the program, without knowing much about the country.

Although he was lucky to receive the scholarship, the first couple of months were stressful, or rather 'eye-opening.' First, he realized that his educational background was weak in comparison to others who came from better universities. Second, as he only had the scholarship for 10 months, he needed to find a job immediately in order to be able to continue the two-year program. He remembers 'applying like crazy' and managed to get a job as a project manager at an international IT consultancy company that was part-time for him at first, but soon he continued with full-time study combined with full-time work. He recently graduated Cum Laude and finished one semester earlier than others.

He has a lot of local friends and a wide social network, created at the university and at work, who support his adaptation. He has noticed racism in Estonia but does not talk about specific incidents. Rather, he talked about how he, as a Syrian, often gets approached by people asking for help, and has gained many friends that way. In addition to full-time study and work, he is involved as a volunteer in an NGO, and for the last year and a half has been touring around Estonian highschools speaking about Syria. He argued that his aim is to give something back to the society and to contribute to decreasing the level of xenophobia in society, as the media often portrays Arabic people as extremists.

He is very positive about the future, arguing that "it is your choice if you want to do something with your life or not." He sees his future in Estonia: "I feel that this is my place, my country" However, as his girlfriend in Syria is planning her career in architecture, and no such high-quality training in that field exists in Estonia, Elias foresees that they might live temporarily in some other European country. He has some ideas for a start-up business, and in the long-term perspective hopes to get a residence permit in Estonia. When thinking about his journey, he emphasizes the role of his untraditional family in the context of Syria. They used to form a small family (4 people), not religious or ideological in any sense, but rather valuing freedom of thought. He said that while in school he already knew that he wanted to do something meaningful in his life. All of these elements have helped him to become successful. Nevertheless, Elias ends his story rather emotionally by saying, "Sometimes I am very angry that I was born where I was born. I did not get a visa to go to US as I am Syrian. There is one positive aspect that it gives you motivation."

While Elias's migration story seems rather smooth and planned, it is visible that there had been several trigger incidents (disorienting dilemmas in Mezirow's sense) before migration (e.g., war in Syria) and during the migration path (e.g., being less competent in the MBA studies compared to his peers, needing to find a job in order to continue his studies), that required him to mobilize his existing resources, broaden his social network, and find new perspectives in life. Becoming a project manager in an international IT company just a few months after migrating is a big transformation. He sees Estonia as 'his country, his home,' but on the other hand, he is highly global in his perspectives both professionally and concerning his family life.

His adaptation process has involved learning from difficult situations, receiving support from local networks created at school, work, and his family back home, and societal transformation, as he considered himself responsible for helping the host society become more tolerant and less xenophobic.

Fatima

Fatima is a Sri Lankan woman in her late 30s, who migrated to Estonia four and a half years ago with her husband and two children. She presents herself as an optimistic and positive person, mother of two sons, who had been looking forward to and dreaming about a better life for her children, who needed her support.

Their family moved to Tallinn, the capital of Estonia, through the 'Talents to Estonia' program that assisted them in finding an apartment and other bureaucratic requirements. Their motivation for migrating was to provide their children a better life (better education and free societal environment) and start a business in Estonia (she has an educational background in economics). Fatima seems a highly positive person outside, being humble and satisfied with her life. For her, family relations are of central importance. She has maintained a strong connection with her mother in Sri Lanka and also upholds a vision of a happy and safe life for her children. She is happy that her children are doing well at school, having integrated well into their class and acquired Estonian. Her son, although being a non-Estonian in an Estonian school, has the best grades in his class. Her husband has a job in a restaurant. They live in a nice area in the center of Tallinn. She has initiated an online community of Sri Lankan people in Estonia and has organized some cultural events.

Although it seems to be a successful adaptation story at first sight, there are also different barriers involved in her adaptation path. First, the lack of Estonian language skills has been a barrier for her from the very beginning. She is proud that her sons can be interpreters for her, helping in everyday life issues, but she admits that there are moments when it is difficult to get along without them. She took the language course as part of the national welcoming program when arriving in Estonia, but she could not fully participate, as her children were too young and she needed to take care of them. In half a year it will be possible to apply for a residence permit, as she will have been residing in Estonia for five years, but she needs to demonstrate Estonian language proficiency. She has been thinking about continuing her Estonian studies, but has postponed it for health reasons. She has been taking anti-depression pills, as she feels a lot of anxiety and depression because of missing her family (mother in Sri Lanka), and feeling bad about failing to realize her dream of building a business, which she had when she first came to Estonia. She used to have a good job in Sri Lanka, but now she has been a stay-at-home mother for almost five years in Estonia. She is active in creating a supportive network for other Sri Lankan families recently migrated to Estonia, in order to help them in adapting "as I was entirely alone when I came." She has found friends among local Sri Lankan and Indian people, forming a community in Estonia.

However, she has almost no interaction with local Estonians. The only Estonian people she knows and communicates with are the teacher from her language lessons, a doctor, and another teacher interested in the Sri Lankan culture. Nevertheless, she sees her future in a positive light, eventually hoping to start a business and organize more cultural events.

The story of Fatima is full of optimism, hope, and memories from her home country of Sri Lanka. She is open, positive, and self-confident, full of love for her children. She makes efforts to build a safe life for her two sons. She feels safe in Estonia and in her flat in the city center. However, her story involves unresolved problems, such as a lack of communication and contacts with local people, and the lack of language skills limiting her social and personal life, work, and career possibilities. She remains silent about her husband and herself as a woman, but constantly emphasizes her children in her story. Although realizing the importance of having Estonian language skills, she has not taken any concrete steps to improve them. After quitting a great job when migrating and aiming to start a business in Estonia, she did not have the necessary flexibility to find alternatives or new perspectives in her life. Moreover, she is experiencing problems with her mental health, lacking networks among the local people in Estonia that could assist in making sense of the new context, and potentially building the social capital needed to find a job or orient herself in everyday practical issues. She certainly exhibits agency in shaping the cultural life of local Sri Lankan people, but she has not fully succeeded in adapting to Estonian society.

Discussion

The findings reveal that the migration process itself usually involves the signs of transformational learning: disorienting dilemmas, incidents that cause a re-evaluation of one's previous meanings and understandings, principles, life-orientations or self-perspectives (see Figure 7.1).

The interviewees differed in terms of their stay in Estonia as a host country, ranging from a couple of months to four and a half years. However, based on the findings, the adaptation process of these migrants does not follow the same pattern and does not involve transformative learning in all cases. It is a unique and personal process, which might influence one's orientations about life as a whole. The ability of individuals to reflect, learn from situations encountered, and redesign their life-plans, tended to vary. On the other hand, it was visible that both individual resources, like self-esteem, self-reflection and agency, and the contextual factors influenced adaptation, life-satisfaction, and future perspectives.

When writing this chapter, we aimed to understand the interplay of individual resources and contextual factors shaping migrant adaptation as a transformative learning process. The stories are more than individual tales (Goodley et al., 2006, p. 195). Migrant adaptation is a social-cultural, psychological, and personal process. This process is complex, demanding, emotional, and stressful, but can also be a transformative, positive, and supportive experience.

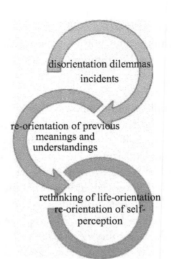

FIGURE 7.1 Transformational Learning in the Context of Migrating

The interviews provided possibilities for us as researchers to listen, understand better, and value people with migrant backgrounds, noticing their learning needs and barriers to adaptation. Adaptation through transformative learning involves transforming the personal model of reality and the frame of reference (Mezirow, 1991). Such a process is emotionally charged, stressful, demanding, and needs considerable resources. Frames of reference are part of the past and present experience, which constitute a person's model of reality offering stability, coherence, and sense of identity. Past experience structures how a person approaches a new experience and adapts in a new social context (Mezirow, 1991, p. 35).

The stories of Elias and Fatima illustrate two different paths of adaptation and learning through past, present, and future experiences. The story of Fatima serves as a difficult path of adaptation that has been, and currently is, mentally demanding and stressful. Coming back to Kuo (2014) about the necessity of personal and social resources, we observe, in the case of Fatima, a lack of those resources needed for adaptation.

In her case, her lack of Estonian language skills, inability to reorient her initial plans (start a business in Estonia), and the limited network she has in Estonia, have all become barriers for her. Although she is happy about her children's progress at school and is active in the local Sri Lankan community, she is struggling mentally. The language barrier has created the feeling that she does not fully belong in her new country. The story of Elias seems like the ideal personal success story; it is full of self-confidence and orientation towards societal transformation. Unlike Fatima, for him, problems (e.g., the need to find a job immediately in order to been able to continue his studies in Estonia) have resulted in him re-interpreting the current situation and his life-plans. Having a wide network with locals has played an important role for him.

Seeking Hope, Safety, and New Perspectives **101**

The migrants' stories reveal that the migration process certainly involves culture shock, smaller or larger barriers, and incidents causing disorienting dilemmas that can trigger critical reflection, and cause one to redefine previous experiences and orientations towards life. The case of Fatima and her story demonstrates that disorienting dilemmas might not always lead to critical reflection and transformative learning. The case of Elias and his story, on the other hand, showed that this process might have started even before the migration itself. The war has triggered him to redefine his understandings and identities, seeing himself, rather, as a global citizen and flexible to reorient his future plans if needed. In his case we can see that transformation does not involve only the transformation of individual consciousness and behavior, but is also targeted towards social transformation (Schugurensky, 2002) in terms of a more aware and less racist society.

We can see strong agentic actions in the case of Elias transforming his own life, but also contributing to a more just society. Fatima has been less agentic in terms of shaping her own life path, but has been active in building the community of Sri Lankan people in Estonia. As learning and adaptation paths are always different, she might be in the early phases of her transformative learning process. Agency is always in interplay with the structuring social context. The social context, support from networks, and relations with meaningful others play an essential role in supporting migrants in the adaptation process, assisting in sense-making of the local context and oneself in a new context. Both workplaces and adult education institutions serve potentially as valuable communities in that sense, by introducing norms, practices, possibilities, and tacit knowledge. Future research may explore the learning opportunities and support services provided for adults with migrant backgrounds by educational institutions and workplace learning contexts.

For us as researchers, this study has been a meaningful experience and it has been a privilege to meet people, listen to them, and reflect on their stories. We would like to thank all of our respondents.

Note

1 https://www.settleinestonia.ee/en/about-programme/

References

Bau, V. (2016). A narrative approach in evaluation: "Narratives of Change" method. *Qualitative Research Journal*, 16(4), 374–387.

Baumgartner, L. (2019). Fostering transformative learning in educational settings. *Adult Literacy Education: The International Journal of Literacy, Language, and Numeracy*, 1(1), 69–74.

Berry, J. W. (1997). Immigration, acculturation, and adaptation. *Applied Psychology: An International Review*, 46(1), 5–68.

Berry, J. W. (2003). Conceptual approaches to acculturation. In K. M. Chun, P. Balls Organista, & G. Marín (Eds.), *Acculturation: Advances in Theory, Measurement, and Applied Research* (pp. 17–37). American Psychological Association. https://doi.org/10.1037/10472-004.

Braun, V., & Clarke, V. (2006). Using thematic analysis in psychology. *Qualitative Research in Psychology*, 3, 77–101.

Brigham, S. (2011). Internationally educated female teachers' transformative lifelong learning experiences: Rethinking the immigrant experience through an arts-informed group process. *Journal of Adult and Continuing Education*, 17(2), 36–50.

Cappeliez, P., Beaupré, M., & Robitaille, A. (2008). Characteristics and impact of life turning points for older adults. *Ageing International*, 32(1), 54–64.

Cranton, P. (2016). *Understanding and Promoting Transformative Learning: A Guide for Educators of Adults* (3rd ed.). Stylus Publishing.

Elder, G. H. (1998). The life course and human development. In R. M. Lerner & W. Damon (Eds.), *Handbook of child psychology: Vol. 1. Theoretical models of human development* (pp. 939–991). Wiley.

Erichsen, E. A. (2011). Learning for change: Transforming international experience as identity work. *Journal of Transformative Education*, 9(2), 109–133.

Eteläpelto, A., Vähäsantanen, K., Hökkä, P., & Paloniemi, S. (2013). What is agency? Conceptualizing professional agency at work. *Educational Research Review*, 10, 45–65.

Faist, T. (2000). *The Volume and Dynamics of International Migration and Transnational Social Spaces*. Clarendon.

Giddens, A. (1976). *New Rules of Sociological Method: A Positive Critique of Interpretative Sociologies*. Hutchinson.

Giddens, A. (1984/1991). *The Constitution of Society*. Polity Press.

Golsteijn, C., & Wright, S. (2013). Using narrative research and portraiture to inform design research. In P. Kotzé, G. Marsden, G. Lindgaard, J. Wesson, & M. Winckler (Eds.), *Human-Computer Interaction—INTERACT 2013* (pp. 298–315). Springer.

Goodley, D., Lawthom, R., Clough, P., & Moore, M. (2006). *Researching Life Stories. Method, Theory and Analyses in a Biographical Age*. Routledge Falmer, Taylor & Francis Group.

Grzymala-Kazlowska, A., & Phillimore, J. (2018). Introduction: Rethinking integration. New perspectives on adaptation and settlement in the era of super-diversity. *Journal of Ethnic and Migration Studies*, 44(2), 179–196.

Hobfoll, S. (2002). Social and psychological resources and adaptation. *Review of General Psychology*, 6(4), 307–324.

Kuo, B. (2014). Coping, acculturation, and psychological adaptation among migrants: A theoretical and empirical review and synthesis of the literature. *Health Psychology and Behavioral Medicine*, 2(1), 16–33.

Lange, E. A. (2015). The ecology of transformative learning: Transdisciplinary provocations. *Journal of Transformative Learning*, 3(1), 28–34.

Mälkki, K. (2012). Rethinking disorienting dilemmas within real-life crises: The role of reflection in negotiating emotionally chaotic experiences. *Adult Education Quarterly*, 62(3), 207–229.

Mälkki, K., & Green, L. (2014). Navigational aids: The phenomenology of transformative learning. *Journal of Transformative Education*, 12(1), 5–24.

Mason, J. (2002). *Qualitative Researching* (2nd ed). Sage Publications.

Merriam, S. (2005). How adult life transitions foster learning and development. *New Directions for Adult and Continuing Education*, 108, 3–13.

Mezirow, J. (1991). *Transformative Dimensions in Adult Learning*. Jossey-Bass.

Mezirow, J. (1999). *Transformation theory: Postmodern issues*. Paper presented at the Adult Education Research Conference, DeKalb, IL.

Mezirow, J. (2000). Learning to think like an adult. Core concepts of transformation theory. In J. Mezirow & Associates (Eds.), *Learning as Transformation: Critical Perspectives on a Theory in Progress* (pp. 3–35). Jossey-Bass.

Morrice, L., Shan, H., & Spring, A. (2017). Migration, adult education and learning. *Studies in the Education of Adults*, 49(2), 129–135.

Nada, C., & Araújo, H. (2018). Migration and education: A narrative approach to the experience of foreign students in Portugal. *London Review of Education*, 16(2), 308–324.

Pitkänen, P. (2012). Introduction. In P. Pitkänen, A. İçduygu, & D. Sert (Eds.), *Migration and Transformation: Multi-level Analysis of Migrant Transnationalism*. Springer, Book Series: International Perspectives on Migration.

Portes, A. (1999). The study of transnationalism: Pitfalls and promises of an emergent research field. *Ethnic and Racial Studies*, 22(2), 217–237.

Qi, N. (2009). *Lost in transformation: Mezirow, immigrants, and identity*. Paper presented at the Sixth International Symposium on the Sociology of Music Education. https://www.aca demia.edu/8038709/Lost_in_transformation_Mezirow_immigrants_and_identity.

Qi, N., & Cesetti, D. (2019). Transformative music learning experiences: A Chinese immigrant in northeastern Brazil and his love for Música Sertaneja. *Per Musi*, (39), 1–22.

Rodrigez-Dorans, E., & Jacobs, P. (2020). Making narrative portraits: A methodological approach to analysing qualitative data. *International Journal of Social Research Methodology*, 23 (6), 611–623.

Schugurensky, D. (2002). Transformative learning and transformative politics: The pedagogical dimension of participatory democracy and social action. In E. O'Sullivan, A. Morrell, & M. A. O'Connor (Eds), *Expanding the Boundaries of Transformative Learning: Essays on Theory and Praxis* (pp. 59–76). Palgrave.

Sharpe, J. (2016). Understanding and unlocking transformative learning as a method for enabling behaviour change for adaptation and resilience to disaster threats. *International Journal of Disaster Risk Reduction*, 17, 213–219.

Taylor, E. (2000). Analysing research on Transformative Learning Theory. In J. Mezirow (Ed.), *Learning as Transformation. Critical Perspectives on a Theory in Progress* (pp. 285–329). Jossey-Bass.

Taylor, E., & Cranton P. (2013). A theory in progress? Issues in transformative learning theory. *European Journal for Research on the Education and Learning of Adults*, 4(1), 35–47.

Ward, C., Bochner, S., & Furnham, A. (2001). *The Psychology of Culture Shock*. Routledge.

Wise, A. (2005). Hope and belonging in a multicultural suburb. *Journal of Intercultural Studies* 26(1–2), 171–186.

8

ADULT MIGRANT EDUCATION AS A MEDIATOR OF DEMOCRATIC CITIZENSHIP IN POSTCOLONIAL CONTEXTS

Inferences from Adult Migrant Language Programs in Malta and Cyprus

Maria Brown, Maria N. Gravani and Carmel Borg

In recent years, the EU island states Cyprus and Malta witnessed an exponential increase in foreign nationals (Eurostat, 2018, 2019a; Statistical Service of Cyprus, 2019). At the time of the study, the main irregular migratory routes into the EU, primarily affecting Malta and Cyprus, included the Central Mediterranean and the Eastern Mediterranean route respectively (Frontex, 2019a, 2019b). At the time of the study discussed in this chapter, policy addressing migrant integration through adult education significantly differed between the two post-colonial EU island states. Cyprus was broadly monocultural, fragmented, and lacking specific and comprehensive educational provisions supporting inclusion, as adult migrants were left to their own devices (Gravani et al., 2019). In contrast, Malta's *National Lifelong Learning Strategy 2020* (Ministry of Education and Employment (MEDE), 2014) explicitly targeted increased participation of migrants and provision of specialized programs. The implementation of *Integration = Belonging: Migrant Integration Strategy & Action Plan (Vision 2020)* (Human Rights and Integration Directorate (HRID), 2017) underscored diversity of the adult-immigrant student population.

However, up to the time of writing, both countries lacked quantitative data on participation of adult immigrants in adult education programs. When considering that Cyprus and Malta are significantly challenged by the rate of 20–34-year-olds not in education, employment, or training (NEETs) (Cyprus—17.4%, Malta—10.1%) (Eurostat, 2019b); the lack of data was interpreted as an outcome of both countries prioritizing participation in further and higher education of the non-immigrant population (Brown et al., 2021). Despite the statistical dearth, qualitative observations revealed that Greek language programs for foreigners were open to all non-native Greek speakers in Cyprus, including

DOI: 10.4324/9781003124412-10

EU citizens working in Cyprus; yet were mainly attended by migrants. In Malta, adult immigrants could join state-organized lifelong learning courses, yet these educational initiatives explicitly targeted bringing back non-immigrant adults who had discontinued their studies (Brown et al., 2021). Whilst Cyprus featured absence of special provisions for adult migrants and limited educational programs, Malta's approach to migrant learning explicitly addressed integration with a more specialized attention to citizenship, language, and cultural curricula (HRID, 2017; Brown et al., 2021).

Rationalizing Micro Responses to the Challenges of Immigration

Migration and asylum policies—established in the late 1990s and early 2000s—generated hard-to-shift dependencies (Geddes, 2018). Geopolitics intensify irregular migratory dynamics and related problems (Briguglio & Brown, forthcoming). The latest *EU New Pact on Migration and Asylum* (European Commission, 2020) emphasizes efficiency (e.g., using faster asylum border crossing and technology-aided pre-screening). Yet, as well as concerns over a new 'border instrument' (Aditus Foundation, 2020), another limitation is in how the *New Pact* re-articulates 'solidarity' between member states in terms of relocating immigrants or sponsoring returns, according to gross domestic product (GDP) of the member states, their population size, and a related 'fair share' corrective mechanism. Thus, attention to immigrants' voices in related decision-making is lacking. The commitment to including immigrants' voices in policy development augurs better, although one has yet to assess the nature and range of the voices included, and the extent of impact these will have in advising the Commission.

Observations on Cyprus' and Malta's responses to the *New Pact* to date indicate that the Cypriot government reactively started working on a national plan for the integration of migrants that has not been delivered yet (Kathimerini, 2020). The Maltese government is evidently giving more attention to how the *New Pact*—as a policy—guides the dealing with new arrivals rather than what the *New Pact* offers for medium and long-term integration. Whilst acknowledging that, contrary to Cyprus, Malta's 2017 *Integration = Belonging: Migrant Integration Strategy & Action Plan (Vision 2020)* (HRID, 2017) pre-empted the 2020 *New Pact's* attention to integration policy, Malta's government's enthusiasm for the *New Pact's* relocation testifies to pressure caused by firefighting management of irregular arrivals and increased racism at national level.

Drawn by the limitations of macro approaches, this chapter discusses the extent to which a micro approach can inform long-term sustainable co-existence with migration; whilst countering a deficit-approach where migration is—primarily (if not solely)—problematic, rather than problematized. To this end, this chapter's discussion draws on select findings of a broader project[1] to tease out the potential of adult migrant classroom interactions for integration that dwells on democratic citizenship.

Theoretical Framework

Emancipatory Adult Education

Theoretically, this chapter foregrounds Emancipatory Adult Education (EAE) which has roots in the emerging need of adults to advance their life through social emancipation (Guo & Sork, 2005). EAE promotes agency for critical consciousness through action, cultural reflection, and praxis (Freire, 2001), and is deeply associated with democracy and social justice. Henry Giroux (2010) positions adult education for critical democratic citizenship as an antidote to market-driven, corporatist, and overly credentialled education. Brookfield and Holst (2011) reject the notion of migrant integration as yielding economic competitiveness within the global marketplace. Yet, the case studies discussed in this chapter have confirmed that adult migrant education systems are formally driven by employment and residency. Some evidence of emancipatory adult education dynamics transpired only when delving deeper into small scale classroom interactions—this will be elaborated later in this chapter.

This literature describes adult education as acting both *for* and *through* the practice of democratic decision-making processes and authentic dialogue (Lima, 2020) that builds trust, engages in critical dialogue, and enables the problematization of rejection whilst yielding "...a counterhegemonic response that puts right the injustices of representation" (Pisani, 2012, p. 192). In the course of this pedagogical process, dominant representations and ideologies are unpacked and problematized. In this regard, Mayo (2009)—much inspired by Freire (2001) —maintained that an education for critical citizenship is genuinely democratic when it pedagogically invites students to engage as agents of change through non-hierarchical social relations. In a similar vein, Borg (2020) argued that dialogues become real when educators assume an authoritative role without becoming authoritarian, and made the case for emancipatory learner-centered education (ELCE). ELCE fosters encounters (rather than abstract notions of migrant needs), offering migrants the opportunity to shift locationally from objects of interest to active subjects; and from recipients of professional generosity to creative, critical problem-posers, co-investigators, and co-discoverers of knowledge (Borg, 2021).

However, the literature documents challenges for democratic citizenship, especially in formal adult migrant learning settings—there is little recognition of past learning experiences (Borg, 2021); language and toolkits lack resources as these are consumed to respond to daily dilemmas and crises (Brown-Manning, 2020); participants are often deeply steeped in the 'culture of silence' and 'fear of freedom,' where pedagogical verticality is assumed as the way forward. This literature informed the understanding of nuances and ambivalences identified in the case studies informing this chapter, as will be elaborated further within this chapter.

Postcolonial, Island and Small State Dynamics

The postcolonial perspective illuminates the extent to which colonialism continues to impact the (previous) colonizers and the (previously) colonized (Jackson, 2010), whilst 'perennial' North-South structural imbalances of colonial capitalism and European imperial politics shift populations in the South "to suit imperial interests" (Mayo, 2013, p. 386). Whereas the prefix 'post' is understood as a process of ongoing transformation or change (Venn, 2006), this study unpacks possibly conflicting or contradictory layers and directions of such transformation or change in the postcolonial contexts of Cyprus and Malta—which inform critical considerations of how migrants flee hardships in their countries that are partly or largely attributable to Eurocentric, former colonial, or neo-colonial geopolitics. Additionally, the literature throws light on how adult migrant education in postcolonial contexts may catalyze a reappraisal of indigenous knowledge that counters epistemicide (Darder, 2018; Bennett, 2007), challenges the EU's position (or non-position) on migration, and describes it as a 'fortified entity' (Mayo, 2013) or as 'Fortress Europe' (Mallia & Pace, 2013; Mallia, 2012).

At micro and practical levels, adult education in island and small state postcolonial contexts often features learning spaces and human and non-human resources shared with the formal compulsory education sector (Mayo et al., 2008). Disputes transpire between those assessing adult educators' work—as based on 'relatively ineffective' (p. 249)—western models of adult non-formal education that lack the required resources (Mayo et al., 2008; Rogers, 1996), and arguments reviewing theory and practice in the global South as 'exciting and innovative' (Mayo et al., 2008, p. 249).

The relevance of the case studies discussed in this chapter can be appreciated in a literature context marked by a dearth of studies concerning adult education for immigrants in former colonies, islands, or small states. The literature is scarce (e.g., Schmidt & Schneider, 2016; Kukovetz & Sprung, 2014) and rarely contextualized in small EU island states.

Research Statement

The authors posit that in postcolonial contexts, adult migrant education's quest for authentic, self-directed integration (Gravani et al., 2019) can dwell on the diversity and multiple belongings that in postcolonial contexts are common to immigrants and non-immigrants. As a result, the authors researched the potential that adult migrant education has in mediating democratic citizenship in postcolonial contexts.

Methodology

The discussion is based on discourse and thematic analysis of qualitative data gathered from one-to-one semi-structured interviews with a total of seven interviews: five interviews with adult migrant learners, three in Cyprus, two in Malta, one adult educator in Malta, and one adult education center coordinator in Cyprus (see Table 8.1). The adult language learning programs in Cyprus and Malta were both state provided (see Table 8.2). Fieldwork took place in Spring 2017.

TABLE 8.1 Research Participants

Interviews	Cyprus	Malta
Adult migrant learners	2 females, 1 male	1 female, 1 male
Adult educators /coordinators	1 female	1 female

TABLE 8.2 Adult Language Learning Programs

Country	Program	State Provider
Cyprus	'Greek language for foreigners' Open to all non-native Greek speakers, including EU citizens (GLF)	Adult Education Center (Larnaca, Cyprus)
Malta	English as a Foreign Language Level 1 (EFL1) Maltese as a Foreign Language Level 1 (MFL 1)	Directorate for Research, Lifelong Learning and Employability Ministry for Education and Employment (2016) (Valletta, Malta)

The research questions guiding the analysis were: 1) To what extent and in what ways did the language programs under scrutiny mediate democratic citizenship, particularly for the adult migrant learners and the educators operating in the small island postcolonial contexts of Cyprus and Malta? 2) What are the contributions that formal adult migrant learning programs can make to democratic citizenship, particularly in small island states with a colonial history?

Findings

Mediation of Democratic Citizenship

This section will first present findings that inform the extent and ways that the language programs under scrutiny mediated democratic citizenship for the participating learners and educators. A search for evidence of dialogue, critical questioning, problematization, student agency, non-hierarchical relations, and ELCE, primarily guided this part of the analysis due to inferences gained from the review of emancipatory adult education literature elaborated earlier in this chapter.

The study found evidence of critical reflection among adult migrant learners and adult migrant educators. Participants asked questions that linked learners' immediate experiences to broader systemic limitations (e.g., querying assessment modes and relevance of the qualification). They critically commented on how language limitations inhibit dialogue and participation:

I say, please, change this thing with the diploma [i.e. a certificate of completing the course that is awarded to all students at the end of the year]. Not all students should get the same diploma... because then the people get the message that "Oh, if we study, or even if we don't study, the diploma will be the same." When they give me this diploma, I have more problems because the people understand that it means nothing.

(Female adult migrant learner 1, GFL, Cyprus)

... basically we are moving, always towards an exam. I think that is our greatest problem...courses that have to be exam oriented... What we do is dictated, you know, it's not my choice. They want a qualification, so you try to cater both for what they need and also for sitting an exam.

(Female adult educator, EFL1, Malta)

How can we have a dialogue? ... when the teacher asks someone to talk... they usually remain silent...in the first place because they don't understand what she said, or even if they did understand, they don't know how to express themselves in Greek.

(Male adult migrant learner, GFL, Cyprus)

Migrant learners also considered how learning is linked to broader society in economic matters such as real estate and family life:

Lessons about...for sale for the home, rent for the home. Where is your home? Where are you living? The subject is very important. And about family.

(Female adult migrant learner, EFL1, Malta)

I think after one month, after one or two months we start the class, we have subject in the story, in your country. I speak to my teacher about my country ... Subject we have: ... "Your email for my friend," "I am in Malta" ... Or this one "Where are you living?"

(Female adult migrant learner, EFL1, Malta)

Contributions to Democratic Citizenship in an Island and Small State Postcolonial Context

The second part of the findings focuses on data that inform contributions that formal adult migrant learning programs can make to democratic citizenship—particularly in small island states with a colonial history. Informed by literature on postcolonial small island state dynamics reviewed earlier in this chapter, the organization of data in this part seeks to illuminate efforts and limitations of adult migrant learners or educators in grappling with Eurocentric, former colonial/neo-colonial geopolitical, or Far Right influences.

Data analysis revealed critical and conscious juxtaposition of cultures whereby learners and educators 'revisit' their 'national' cultures with newly acquired perspectives that question matters previously taken for granted.

> [Referring to some learners]… they come from languages where even the alphabet is different, where there are language peculiarities that, many times, you're not aware of, for example, you get Japanese, Chinese, Eastern European people, Russians. They don't have the article and unless you're aware of that, you know, they keep on writing without using it. And so, you must draw their attention to that.
>
> *(Female adult educator, EFL1, Malta)*

> … for grammar it's very important you has a YouTube because in my country YouTube close—we don't have YouTube—because we can all subject found in YouTube.
>
> *(Female adult migrant learner, EFL1, Malta)*

Data analysis revealed conscious responses to difficulties experienced due to limited grasp of English or Greek (i.e., prevailing languages in the former colonies of Malta and (in the case of Greek) Cyprus). Motivations also illuminated adult migrants' desire for integration and how this was addressed—sometimes with spontaneous or organically developed tools and platforms, such as informal (virtual) networks. This took place to varying extents; thus showing that some adult migrant cohorts were integrating more successfully when compared to others:

> I couldn't speak English…but now…I have a friend, Korean friend. Very happy…It's very important for communicate.
>
> *(Female adult migrant learner, EFL1, Malta)*

> My husband when…see me I stay at home, I am alone, and he told to me, "It's better going to class. It's better because you can speak English and you can found friend."… And he go to Valletta for register school.
>
> *(Female adult migrant learner, EFL1)*

> I found good friend and we have relation with WhatsApp… Yes, on the mobile, speak, it's very good because the writing is better for me, and the speaking.
>
> *(Female adult migrant learner, EFL1, Malta)*

> [We communicate] with email…we have quite a lot communication, during and also in the break, and after on the Facebook chat as well… It helped as well… In English, although some of the students, especially the Filipinos and even the Arabs, they had some problems with English as well… So I think for them it was a bit more difficult to follow the lesson.
>
> *(Male adult migrant learner, MFL1, Malta)*

Data analysis unveiled the potential for democratic citizenship that counters Far Right discourse, because critical reflections included instances of curiosity about 'Otherness.' Triggers of curiosity varied but did not yield elitist, xenophobic, racist, or exclusionary engagement. Data show curiosity interlinked with interest, admiration, empathy, the simple pleasure of socializing, or a sense of the rewarding discovery of foreignness or minorities:

> ... a lot of people are here with their children. It's amazing! They bring their children to Malta to attend schools here and so they even start learning Maltese. They have a very hectic life because then they take them for lessons in Arabic, lessons in Russian, because they want to keep in touch with their culture. So, their life is very much full, I would say
>
> *(Female adult educator, EFL1, Malta)*

> Many times... In the lesson on occupations, for instance, we drew from the past and present profession of the learners and in the lesson on family, we did the same with their family experiences... Let's say, there is a discussion that is based on their own, personal experiences...for example, why they came to Cyprus, what they did before they arrived, what type of job they were doing in their country and so on.
>
> *(Female adult educator 1, GFL, Cyprus)*

> For example, to describe my family, as well, or what I am doing here—my work... I could talk about myself, my family, my work, the reasons why I like Malta, what I like in Malta...the first lesson was basically to know about us— about the students, about the teacher, about the place...we had to say, obviously in English—some things about us—where are we from...also a bit about the curriculum, whatever we'll work on.
>
> *(Male adult migrant learner, MFL1, Malta)*

> ... most of the people there were...extrovert...not afraid to speak up...to ask questions ... I think the teacher was tolerant and she accepted all.
>
> *(Male adult migrant learner, MFL1, Malta)*

The adult migrant learning programs under study featured self-directed learning. For instance, an adult migrant learner participating in the Cypriot case study expressed what learning Greek meant to her—namely, it allows her to fully practice her religious beliefs in the host country:

> I need to stay to this country and I need to know the language, because I need to learn Greek... I need to learn the Bible. I love Jesus, I need to bridge people... And for this, I need to know sharing the Bible.
>
> *(Female adult migrant learner 2, GFL, Cyprus)*

Further data demonstrated mediation of democratic citizenship in terms of freedom of religious association and freedom of expression:

> I am tolerant for all religions… anybody can be and believe what they want, so I respect you, you respect me.
>
> *(Male adult migrant learner, MFL1, Malta)*

Nevertheless, as can be observed in the excerpts below taken from the Malta case study, despite the critical reflections on cultural gaps, migrant learners or educators fell short of making a conscious connection or association between Malta's colonial inheritance and some learners' lack of familiarity with westernized or Eurocentric notions:

> … there is always the problem of culture…culture comes even in the name. You start realizing, for example, that names like Sue, John, mean nothing to them and to me they're So Yung… I don't know whether it's the name or the surname…it takes a while even to learn how to call them… you don't have much time—there's the time restriction.
>
> *(Female adult educator, EFL1)*

> I couldn't speak English. I [was] ashamed.
>
> *(Female adult migrant learner, EFL1, Malta)*

> In English, although some of the students, especially the Filipinos and even the Arabs, they had some problems with English as well… So I think for them it was a bit more difficult to follow the lesson.
>
> *(Male adult migrant learner, MFL1, Malta)*

In this regard, the Cyprus case study yielded more encouraging data that shed light on one educator's critical implementation of the curriculum and learning outcomes:

> I am trying to adapt their needs, but concomitantly to expand them, to push them to new directions. For example, I am not going to stick to 'καλημέρα' [good morning], just because they only need to learn how to say 'καλημέρα.' It's not that just because they need to learn the Greek words for 'good morning', or 'hello'… There are occasions when students want to play the role of the teacher, they enjoy it and different dynamics are at play. You see how dialogic communication flows between someone who is an Arab trying to teach another Arab…and trying to teach in Greek.
>
> *(Female adult educator 1, GFL, Cyprus)*

However, the Cyprus case study also revealed tribal, racist, and exclusionary dynamics between non-immigrants and immigrants, and between immigrants of different nationalities and ethnicities:

When we asked him, where are you from, he said, "From Israel" and all Arabs went like this [exclusionary gesture]! I was afraid. I sat back. Really...afraid. When he speaks, he stares like this [gesturing head down], but no problem. Inside, he is nervous. We came to Cyprus to forget this!

(Female adult migrant learner 1, GFL, Cyprus)

Adult educators spoke of their hardships in matters related to their professional status, remuneration, access to resources, and their need for continuous personal and professional development. Such data validated the limitations of adult (migrant) education provision (identified earlier in this chapter) in the postcolonial island and small state contexts of Cyprus and Malta:

You have to be a psychologist! There are occasions when students want to play the role of the teacher, they enjoy it, and different dynamics are at play. You see how dialogic communication flows between someone who is an Arab trying to teach another Arab ...and trying to teach in Greek

(Female center coordinator, Cyprus).

I try not to get influenced, because...all right, the truth is that especially people working for the state authorities when they hear that you are teaching for-eigners, they immediately say "foreigners!"... It's a bit peculiar, it's not that they are racists, but they think that teaching to foreigners is different. This is how they view it: "oh, foreigners!" But I am not influenced by these views, nor have I ever shared them. I believe that all students, all human beings have the right to learn.

(Female centre coordinator, Cyprus)

Discussion

The chapter's findings foreground the contributions that adult migrant education can make to democratic citizenship—particularly in the EU-Mediterranean region and in islands and small state contexts. The study illuminated the micro-nuanced experiences of adult immigrants and their educators in Malta and Cyprus—both former British colonies and EU island states, as they negotiate 'Otherness' and 'new us,' with evident and latent conflict and controversy.

The educational initiatives under study yielded evidence of potential, largely untapped, for emancipatory curiosity about 'Otherness' and of emancipatory democratic citizenship. Related findings echo pedagogies of liberation (Freire, 2001) where epiphanies arise organically within a learning context; thus showing adult migrant learning spaces can be added to Giroux's (2010) list (comprising the Internet and popular culture, amongst others) of "new sites of education," as part of "the realm of public pedagogy," which Giroux considers crucial to engagement with any political notion because they are the sites where people often learn and unlearn.

However, neither of the two learning communities came close to genuinely transitioning into decolonizing spaces where the protagonists, educators, and participants would counter epistemicide and subvert the politics of assimilation into a Europe that perceives itself as being invaded, and its grand cultural narrative as being attacked and diluted. Both operations were directed by an urgency to reprogram and reengineer the participants into a socio-economic and cultural milieu, with language and general acculturation, which were seen as the two main instruments of the rapid educational intervention.

As frontier countries, Malta and Cyprus continue to struggle with migrant populations who are popularly perceived as aliens that need to be re-rooted or re-cultured. With migration high on the anxiety agenda of citizens of both countries, state policies generally respond to electoral exigencies by providing uncoordinated and incoherent policies that generally reinforce alienation, rather than real integration and democratic citizenship. While remaining largely indifferent to civil society's demand for genuine economic, social, and cultural integration, the findings in this study substantiate the grand curricular narrative into which the migrants were inducted—generally answered to the anxieties of a state responding to demographic gaps in the economy. In general, the collective needs for consciousness building, mobilization, and emancipatory action were often lost in individualistic acts that bordered on what Freire (2001) would describe as 'false generosity,' or a charitable act based on dicit understanding of the 'other.' In sum, initial epistemological curiosity failed to develop into praxial initiatives that decolonize.

Epistemologically, according to Darder (2018) (following Paraskeva (2011)), the study contributes to a decolonizing interpretive approach due to its interest in a subaltern form of qualitative research practice that disrupts Eurocentric epistemicide dynamics. Additionally, the study broadens Darder's (2018) understanding of the "critically interpretive bicultural methodological tradition"—even though the study did not draw on the authors' "autoethnographic historical experiences of difference" (p. 64), yet as "members of historically colonized populations" (p. 64), the authors' "scholarly research was anchored to a decolonizing sensibility" (p. 64).

Whilst validating the key role that adult educators have in fostering democratic citizenship in a context of integration, the data analysis also illuminated the precariousness tied to the professional status of the adult educator in both countries. The movement from educators acting as functionaries of the state, through prescriptive, top-down, transmissive relationships with the migrant participants, to educators who perceive themselves as organic intellectuals of a decolonizing vision of migrant education, requires an emancipatory educational process. This would weld the ongoing interrogation of dehumanizing pedagogical practices with humanizing pedagogies that serve migrants on their own terms without—as seen in the data analysis—romanticizing and validating dubious or indefensible knowledge and practices. When committed to such objectives, the European Commission's (2020) *Pact on Migration and Asylum Action Plan 2021–2024*, concurrent to the time of writing, would comprise a golden opportunity to platform increased investment in adult educators, their professional status, and the resources made available to them.

Note

1   The project "Learner Centered education as a tool for social change in Adult Education programmes for migrants: a European comparative study" (2016–2018) was funded by the Open University of Cyprus, Cyprus.

References

Aditus Foundation. (2020, February 14). The new pact on Asylum and migration: An opportunity seized or squandered?https://aditus.org.mt/the-new-pact-on-asylum-and-migration-an-opportunity-seized-or-squandered/#.X5ARlUIzbMJ.

Bennett, K. (2007). Epistemicide! *The Translator*, 13(2), 151–169.

Borg, C. (2020). When professionals listen; Parents as co-producers of knowledge. *International Journal of Pedagogy, Innovation and New Technologies*, 7(1), 100–105.

Borg, C. (2021). Reading the migrants' world through emancipatory learner-centred education: Parting reflections on the micro pedagogical contexts. In M. N. Gravani & B. Slade (Eds.), *Learner-centred Education for Adult Migrants in Europe: A Critical Comparative Analysis* (pp. 168–181). Brill.

Briguglio, M., & Brown, M. (forthcoming). Saving migrants in the Mediterranean Sea: Interaction between states and non-governmental organizations. In M. Brown & M. Briguglio (Eds.), *Social Welfare Issues in Southern Europe*. Routledge - Europa Regional Perspectives Series.

Brookfield, S., & Holst, J. (2011). *Radicalizing Learning: Adult Education for a Just World*. Jossey-Bass.

Brown, M., Gravani, M. N., Slade, B., & Jõgi, L. (2021). Comparative cartography of adult education for migrants in the four countries. In M. N. Gravani & B. Slade (Eds.), *Learner-centred Education for Adult Migrants in Europe: A Critical Comparative Analysis* (pp. 43–53). Brill.

Brown-Manning, R. (2020). Critical Multiculturalism and Intersectionality in a Complex World (2nd ed.), *Journal of Teaching in Social Work*, 40(1), 86–88, DOI: doi:10.1080/08841233.2020.1679592

Darder, A. (2018). Decolonizing interpretive research: Subaltern sensibilities and the politics of voice. *Qualitative Research Journal*, 18(2), 94–104.

European Commission. (2020). Migration: New pact on migration and Asylum. https://ec.europa.eu/info/sites/info/files/new-pact-on-migration-and-asylum-package_1.pdf.

Eurostat. (2018). Migration and migrant population statistics. https://ec.europa.eu/eurostat/statistics-explained/index.php/Migration_and_migrant_population_statistics.

Eurostat. (2019a). Share of non-nationals in the resident population, 1 January 2018. https://ec.europa.eu/eurostat/statistics-explained/index.php?title=File:Share_of_non-nationals_in_the_resident_population,_1_January_2018_(%25).png&oldid=424544.

Eurostat. (2019b). Young people (aged 20–34) neither in employment nor in education and training, 2018. https://ec.europa.eu/eurostat/statistics-explained/index.php/Statistics_on_young_people_neither_in_employment_nor_in_education_or_training#Young_people_neither_in_employment_nor_in_education_or_training.

Freire, P. (2001). *Pedagogy of the Oppressed*. Continuum.

Frontex. (2019a). Central Mediterranean route. https://frontex.europa.eu/along-eu-borders/migratory-routes/central-mediterranean-route/.

Frontex. (2019b). Eastern Mediterranean route. https://frontex.europa.eu/along-eu-borders/migratory-routes/eastern-mediterranean-route/.

Geddes, A. (2018). The politics of European union migration governance. *Journal of Common Market Studies* 56, 120–130. doi:10.1111/jcms.12763.

Giroux, H. (2010). Rethinking education as the practice of freedom: Paulo Freire and the promise of critical pedagogy. *Policy Futures in Education*, 8(6), 715–721.

Gravani, M. N., Hatzopoulos, P., & Chinas, C. (2019). Adult education and migration in Cyprus: A critical analysis. *Journal of Adult and Continuing Education*, 27(1), 25–41.

Guo, S., & Sork, T. J. (2005). Adult education for social change: Deconstructing programs and services for adult immigrants, *Adult Education Research Conference* (online conference proceedings). https://www.semanticscholar.org/paper/Adult-Education-for-Social-Change%3ADeconstructing-Guo-Sork/d79c3c5628e4f3888881f99958c35d07d7e7f8f8.

Human Rights and Integration Directorate (HRID). (2017). Integration = belonging: Migrant integration strategy & action plan (Vision 2020). https://meae.gov.mt/en/Documents/migrant%20integration-EN.pdf.

Jackson, S. (2010). Learning through social spaces: Migrant women and lifelong learning in post-colonial London. *International Journal of Lifelong Education*, 29(2), 237–253, doi:10.1080/02601371003616657.

Kathimerini, B. (2020, September 8). EU calls on Cyprus to manage migration flows in line with EU law. https://knews.kathimerini.com.cy/en/news/eu-calls-on-cyprus-to-manage-migration-flows-in-line-with-eu-law?fbclid=IwAR2fYNSNl-RL78Zu3nxLZB5Q-m1tSn_5-5diRok1CkH3uGB3W32EpJy7TTk.

Kukovetz, B., & Sprung, A. (2014). Is adult education a 'white' business? Professionals with migrant backgrounds in Austrian adult education. *European Journal for Research on the Education and Learning of Adults*, 5(2), 161–175.

Lima. L. (2020, October 12). Together for change—Developing a more democratic society through change-oriented adult education. *European Association for the Education of Adults* Webinar. https://eaea.org/project/future-lab/?pid=13715.

Mallia, P. (2012). The disembarkation of migrants rescued at sea: Where is the "Solidarity"? In P. Xuereb (Ed.), *Migration and Asylum in Malta and the European Union: Rights and Realities 2002 to 2011* (pp. 81–101). Malta University Press.

Mallia, P., & Pace, R. (2013). The challenges of irregular maritime migration. *Jean Monnet Occasional Papers*, 4, 1–15.

Mayo, P. (2009). Foreword. In E. Lucio-Villegas (Ed.), *Citizenship as Politics: International Perspectives from Adult Education* (pp. vii–xii). Sense Publishers.

Mayo, P. (2013). Reviews: Books and other publications. *Postcolonial Direction in Education*, 2 (2), 381–386.

Mayo, P., Pace, P., & Zammit, E. (2008). Adult education in small states: The case of Malta. *Comparative Education*, 44(2), 229–246.

Ministry for Education and Employment (MEDE). (2016). Malta national lifelong learning strategy 2020. https://medecms.gov.mt/en/Documents/Malta%20National%20Lifelong%20Learning%20Strategy%202020.pdf.

Paraskeva, J. M. (2011). *Conflicts in Curriculum Theory*. Palgrave Macmillan.

Pisani, M. (2012). Addressing the 'Citizenship Assumption' in critical pedagogy: Exploring the case of rejected female sub-Saharan African asylum seekers in Malta. *Power and Education*, 4(4), 185–195.

Rogers, A. (1996). Adult continuing education in small states and islands: Concept paper. *Convergence*, 29(1), 8–21.

Schmidt, C., & Schneider, J. (2016). *Diversifying the Teaching Force in Transnational Contexts: Critical Perspectives (Transnational Migration and Education)*. Sense Publishers.

Statistical Service of Cyprus. (2019). Births, deaths, migration 1974–2018. http://www.mof.gov.cy/mof/cystat/statistics.nsf/populationcondition_21main_en/populationcondition_21main_en?OpenForm&sub=1&sel=2.

Venn, C. (2006). *The Post-colonial Challenge: Towards Alternative Worlds*. Sage.

PART III

Learning of Society as a Whole

9

EMBRACING TRANSFORMATION

Migration and Human Dignity

Tetyana Hoggan-Kloubert and Chad Hoggan

The transformation of society is deeply linked with the transformation of our imagination—with our perception of who belongs in that society and what is possible, desirable, and aspirational. This assertion has its roots in Anderson's (1983) claim that all we ever have is an 'imagined community;' we cannot ever truly know everyone in our various social circles, and therefore we imagine others' personal experiences and interpersonal bonds as members of our various communities. From this perspective, the proliferation of human mobility in and across societies is not a 'crisis' or a problem to be solved; the 'migration crisis' in Europe and the U.S. is only called such because it challenges these imaginary visions of one's (supposedly homogenous) community.[1] These images may be of an 'already perfect' society, requiring stability, resistance to change, and immobility in order to remain in such a state. Or, these images may be of a 'culturally-superior' society, with supposed linguistic, cultural, religious, and/or ethnic uniformity. Either way, these perceptions of perfect, static, or homogeneous communities are factually inaccurate. Migration is both a historical and contemporary phenomenon that affects (and has long affected) everyday life in countries around the globe; migrants have been and are an important part of almost every society (Oltmer, 2017).

An Educational Approach Based on Human Dignity

One way for people in our mobile societies to reimagine long-held images of their 'perfect, static, or homogeneous communities,' is through education, which can address the challenges of persistent cross-border movement of people in ways that embrace the reality of pluralism, allow for a more expansive imagination of what is meant by 'us,' and thereby promote a more humane society. Education is already used in many countries and in various ways to address the challenges of migration.

DOI: 10.4324/9781003124412-12

"Migration and adult learning basically belong together" (Friedenthal-Haase, 2020, p. 14, translation ours). The very fact that migrants are in a new society, often with different languages, customs, practices, and bureaucracies, means that in order to live in their new country, they must be involved in the often arduous and exhausting processes of learning. Friedenthal-Haase (2020) explains the type of learning migrants must undertake:

> Anyone who has experienced radical change and upheaval, endured displacement and flight, knows what learning in a dramatic situation means. It is a forced learning, a crisis learning, which approaches migrants of all ages, young and old, which makes inevitable demands on every single person, hard demands especially on the adults who are responsible, not only for their own survival, but also for security, health, and cohesion of the family members dependent on their care. In such life crises, people are mostly on their own.
>
> *(p. 13, translation ours)*

Adult education can play a crucial role in framing migration in human terms. We speak of the need for a more humane framing of migration because much of the current discourse speaks of migrants as in need of improvement through adaptation. Migrants are often portrayed as deficient, as not-yet-there members of their new society. To be on an equal footing they need to obtain specific skills and knowledge that, once gained (imparted by various public and private education programs), will allow them to belong.[2] Lange and Baillie Abidi (2015) explain how society often perceives the learning needs of migrants through a 'difference as deficit' perspective; a deficit society believes can be mitigated through some sort of educative process, the goals of which are often driven not by the migrant, but by the host society. Similarly, Shan and Fejes (2015) describe how the learning needs of migrants are often seen as a 'regime of skills' that society needs people to develop, turning many education programs into a "new mode of control and modulation that defines the desirability of individuals in the labor market, shapes the subjectivities, sensibility, and emotionality of migrants and workers" (p. 227).

In contrast to traditional perspectives (such as those critiqued by Lange, Baillie Abidi, Shan, and Fejes) in which migrants are seen as either a burden or a commodity rather than as individuals with personhood and aspirations, some scholars argue that policies and practices surrounding migration, especially related to education, should acknowledge migrants' agency and human dignity, and regard them with the same level of respect as others in the host society. Adult education researchers (Alfred, 2015; Hoggan & Kloubert, in press; Mecheril & Streicher, 2016; Mecheril, 2019) endorse an ethical approach to migrant education. For us, this approach needs to be grounded in the core value of honoring and protecting human dignity, acknowledging the intrinsic value of every human being.

Human dignity is featured prominently in educational discourse and serves as a consensual point of reference across wide-ranging conceptions, approaches, and societal theories. As a foundational idea of human rights, human dignity has a variety of definitions—in legal, philosophical, and theological fields. To provide a framework for understanding and discussing human dignity, we turn to Daly and May (2018), who claim that the majority of the definitions of human dignity in legal contexts contain four overlapping elements:

1.   Autonomy (possibility of determining one's own life path, 'living as one wishes')
2.   Living well (adequate living conditions)
3.   Living without humiliation (physical and moral integrity)
4.   Civic dignity (which enables the engagement in socio-political aspects of one's society)

These elements are relevant beyond just legal contexts. The first and fourth elements (autonomy, civic dignity) are within education's sphere of influence, and therefore relevant to education policy and practice. We see in this framework for human dignity the possibility for new ways for society to perceive migration, and how education might aid in the development of these new perceptions of migration, of 'us' and 'others.' From this, we envision that any societal structure for migrants, including education, would support migrants' autonomy and promote their civic dignity.

Putting human dignity at the center of educational policy and practice would demand more than just providing people with the knowledge necessary for their new environment. It would imply such imperatives as an 'ethics of recognition' (Sprung, 2013, citing Honneth); 'lifelong learning for recognitive justice' (Guo, 2010), and a 'turning to the subject' (i.e., an explicit rejection of using an instrumentalist logic towards human beings) (Hoggan & Kloubert, in press, citing Adorno). Nussbaum (2011) goes even further and demands that we apply human dignity as an ethical frame for societal development, including a list of basic human capabilities that need to be assured in any society.

Adult education has an historic and contemporary self-expectation to facilitate societal development, transitions, and upheavals (Friedenthal-Haase, 2014; Zeuner, 2020). Driven by the expectations and ideals to improve our societies (i.e., to make them more just, inclusive, free), adult education cannot be content with merely facilitating transitions into the labor market or adaptations into existing structures. Its aspirations are to anticipate changes, upheavals, and transformations, and also to support and accompany individuals and societies in overcoming the resulting challenges. Adult education does this by helping people reflect on existing conditions and to think critically in order to formulate societal alternatives where necessary (Zeuner, 2020, p. 2). Based on these principles, adult education in the context of migration would aspire not to merely inculcate specific knowledge and instill societally accepted beliefs into learners' minds, but rather to honor human dignity by supporting learners' individual agency and facilitating their transition into their host culture so they can navigate it successfully, gain sovereignty over their own lives, and become citizens in every way.

The Learning Needs of Society

Migration, as a catalyst of change, reveals the learning needs of society as a whole. In times of upheaval, there can be a tendency to adopt a pragmatic, instrumental approach to educational needs and offerings (e.g., driven solely by a one-sided, short-term logic, by which migrants are the only ones deemed to be in need of learning and change). Even if this tendency is understandable, we consider it erroneous: "[F]rom the point of view of the core values of adult education itself, it is unjustifiable to treat adult learners as means to achieve others' goals" (Kloubert & Hoggan, 2021, p. 34). From the perspective of human dignity, the interests and development of learners (not only of society) need to be at the core of any adult educational endeavor, whether migrant or native. This became clearer as we conducted research (described below) that initially was focused on understanding migrants' learning needs, but evolved in its focus into the role of educators themselves in endorsing, challenging, or modifying the educational system.

Origins and Context of Research Study

This chapter is a meta-reflection on a research study conducted by the authors in 2019–2020 with counselors and teachers who work directly with migrants (Hoggan & Kloubert, in press; Kloubert & Hoggan, 2021). The context of this study was Germany, which had recently experienced a sharp increase in its annual number of incoming migrants, making it the second highest receiver of migrants in the world (UN, 2017). With such a sudden influx, there was a sharp increase in the need to develop systems and practices to identify and address the challenges that arise in supporting such a large number of immigrants. With these new systems and practices already in place for several years, the purpose of the study was to analyze their effectiveness by inquiring into the unmet learning needs of migrants.

To this end, we interviewed ten educators and counselors in southern Germany who had been working with migrants for at least the previous four years. In the aggregate, these research participants had engaged with hundreds of migrants during their transition process and gained helpful insights into common challenges. Interviews took place between December 2019 and January 2020[3]. In the process of talking with these research participants and analyzing their interview transcripts, an unexpected insight into the learning needs of society as a whole arose: we realized that these adult educators were describing their educational practice as a well-intentioned system with a problematic underlying logic (i.e., that education for migrants often focuses solely on the needs of the host society). They talked about the tension between serving the current system that is in place to assist migrants (e. g., following established practices of pointing migrants to current employment opportunities) and feeling obligated to improve the system (e.g., questioning whether the needs of the local labor market should be the primary consideration).

The main findings of the study have already been extensively analyzed in two publications (Hoggan & Kloubert, in press; Kloubert & Hoggan, 2021). This chapter presents two overarching meta-themes, or leitmotifs, that emerged in the process of interpreting, discussing, and reflecting on the data. Based on this, we argue that learning in a migration society cannot be restricted solely to addressing migrants' learning needs; rather, as brought to the forefront by our findings, we conclude that we must also address how society as a whole is being challenged to learn and develop, and how adult education can support this process.

Two Overarching Leitmotifs

Synthesizing the overall leitmotifs that were identified in our research induces us to re-envision the role and tasks of adult education in the wake of migration. In the following, we present two major themes from the interviews and discuss their possible implications and relevance beyond just Germany. These themes correspond to the first and fourth elements of human dignity (autonomy and civic dignity). Although presented separately, these two elements are impossible to completely unravel and are therefore interwoven in both leitmotifs.

Leitmotif #1: Reinforcing Autonomy through Personal Development

Our primary insight from this study was the tacit, underlying logic of educational institutions: namely, that migrants can and should be useful for the host society. This logic is illustrated through the policies related to the local labor market and the respective educational offerings, many of which aim to integrate the migrant workers into positions where there is a scarcity of labor power, be it a high-skilled domain such as medicine or engineering, or a low paid domain such as care professions (e.g., in senior care facilities). In the words of one of our research participants:

> [F]or me it's not really the target to say: "Well, [there are] four hundred free nurse options at the university hospital. There is what you can do." ... That's not a sustainable decision in my point of view. ... [I] also offer a new aspect for the people coming to my counseling, because many of them are from the job center, and that is the only way of thinking they've learned. "What I'm interested in is not so important. What is the need of the German labor market? That is the most important."
>
> *(Wilhelm, unpublished data)*

A pragmatic approach of matching current labor market needs with migrants as workers is not necessarily bad, but it can easily devolve into an instrumental approach of seeing migrants as means to be used for the benefit of the local economy. It is against this latter approach that we argue for the logic of acknowledging and respecting human dignity, which fosters and encourages the capacity for migrants to think and act for themselves (autonomy), as well as to imagine and develop new ways of living together in a diverse society (civic dignity). The difference between these two approaches highlights the need for society as a whole to learn in the wake of migration. It requires the challenging of deeply held assumptions, including the instrumental logic of migration policies and practice. Such a learning process is, by definition, a transformative one.

If we look at migrants as learners who need to be taught in order to integrate or fit into a host society, this implies a pre-defined trajectory of transformation, which leads us to consider the distinction between educational efforts designed to transform others (a prescriptive approach) and efforts that provide knowledge, skills, and other tools that enable a learner to transform in their own way over time (a process-oriented approach), as well as with efforts that recognize that learners are enmeshed in a current process of transformation and support them accordingly (an adaptive approach) (Hoggan & Kloubert, 2020). We consider the first approach (i.e., the educational practice of seeking to transform someone else into adopting one's own worldview or culture) as problematic: "Even when educators believe their worldview is justified and laudable, it hints at indoctrination rather than emancipatory education, and anyone on the receiving end of it is justified in feeling disrespected" (2020, p. 6). Particular transformations cannot be prescribed from any group of people towards another; they should emerge from societal dialogue rather than being pre-determined.

Adult education professionals who work with migrants face an ongoing tension in their work. On the one hand, migration poses practical challenges for society and for individual migrants, and the transitional processes of migrants need to be effective in terms of both. On the other hand, there exists a core ethical commitment of adult education to privilege human dignity, which we envision to mean supporting and developing autonomy and capacities for socio-political participation, in addition to addressing pragmatic, immediate needs. Faulstich (2016), for instance, refers to this tension when suggesting that adult education engage in a permanent search for ways human beings can grow, even if the 'restricted conditions of reality' are always dictated by immediate circumstances (p. 59). He uses the term 'life-unfolding education' ('lebensentfaltende Bildung') to describe the endeavor, aiming first and foremost for personal development through a constant expanding of learners' horizons and possibilities to act (Faulstich, 2003, p.15). Personal growth and the ability to responsibly co-shape society is linked to autonomy, to "gaining increasing sovereignty over one's own life" (p. 301).

The described tension (between immediate practical needs and long-term growth) was a recurring topic in our interviews. The counseling service of the German federal labor agency, for instance, seems to operate based on the logic that laborers should meet market needs, and migrants often adopt the same logic and value system into their own thinking. In doing so, they neglect their individual aspirations out of a sense of desperation to find employment anywhere, doing anything, and adopt the desperate view that 'work is work.' One of the research participants explained this tension:

And quite often ... it was never their decision what they want to make in their professional future in Germany, but it was always the decision either of the [job center] or of friends who have a clear plan what is the best option right now here in Germany. But they never came to a point to think on their own: "What are my competencies? What is my educational background? And, what can I do with it in Germany?" … And that's one point that is very important for me at my counseling. I will step-by-step bring them to this point. Giving them a good foundation of information about the German educational system, about how it works, the structures, the processes. So, step-by-step leading them to a point where they can really make a good … sustainable decision, which doesn't plan for the next one or two years, but where do you want to be in ten years? So that we can make step by step the plans to really reach [their own] goals. Because quite often they—especially refugees—are under a huge time pressure: "We want to make money." For example, [if] the family is still living in Syria, etc., a certain income is a condition to be able to bring them to Germany. So many are under extreme pressure. Well, of course I can understand that, but I always try to [put] the focus on the long term.

(Wilhelm, unpublished data)

If adult education's role is to develop a more humane, equitable, and inclusive society, then educators and the systems they serve must do more than simply help migrants acclimate to the current societal structures:

Whether or not someone has migrated to another country has no bearing on this premise. Therefore, the task of adult education is to help learners develop their own path rather than advise them onto a path dictated solely by the needs of their new society

(Hoggan & Kloubert, in press)

On one hand, using our example of Germany, adult education needs to help migrants adapt to an already-pretty-good society: a stable political system with a (currently) successful economic system. At first glance, this is a goal worth pursuing, but it can be problematic if it neglects the development of migrants as individuals.

Too much attention on serving the perceived (short-term) needs of society can cause adult education to be an instrument solely of those in power. In contrast, a core premise of adult education as a discipline is a commitment to democratic and emancipatory values

(Kloubert, 2018), including the power to challenge authority (Hufer, 2016, pp. 13–20). It is not just a matter of serving individual interests instead of those of society at large. Rather, from this perspective, learners are treated as agents of democratic and emancipatory development, which serves both individual and societal interests. Adult education provides the means by which people can succeed within current societal structures, but also focuses on helping individuals develop the capacities to shape their own lives (autonomy) and co-shape the society in which they live (civic dignity).

The study participants also criticized the deficit-oriented (rather than asset-oriented) logic behind the design of educational and job counseling systems, which (as described earlier) aim to help migrants compensate for their deficiencies. For instance, Alexander described this approach:

> [Migrants] are people spending their lifetime with a goal that is not ... theirs. ... [I] think this is the perspective from which those programs are made, like: "OK. How do we get them to become like we want them to be, or like we need them to be?"
>
> *(as quoted in Kloubert & Hoggan, 2021, p.33–34)*

The participants in this study consistently demonstrated an orientation toward recognizing the assets of their learners: their unique histories, talents, goals, strengths, and desires. In doing so, these adult educators seek ways to modify the official system wherever possible to serve the actual needs of the migrants. They try to facilitate the personal development of their learners, to pay attention to their individual assets, while also appreciating the rationality of the labor market and society's needs that underlie most of the existing structures and inform the motivations of their migrant learners.

An important consideration is that oftentimes the migrants actually *want* or *do not mind* an instrumental approach. (This is referred to by Wilhem above and is discussed more thoroughly in the next section.) This desire can be based on a sense of urgency. They are in a new country, fully aware that there is a new language, different social norms, and unknown legal and work qualification requirements. And they come to adult education programs in search of the learning necessary to adapt to their new home. Our vision, that adult education needs to consider personal development, does not ignore the desires of these migrants. Rather, our assertion is that migrants (and all learners) should be assisted to make goals based not only on urgency or immediate demands, but also on individual attributes and aspirations. (See Faulstich, as discussed above) These goals are not mutually exclusive.

Leitmotif #2: Reinforcing Civic Dignity through Agentic & Dialogic Skills

The second leitmotif refers to Daly and May's fourth element of human dignity: civic dignity, which can be translated into the commitment of adult education to foster the ability to participate fully in socio-political processes. This can include, for instance, the development of agentic skills, e.g., exercise of agency, self-efficacy, capacity for action and, when needed, resistance. This also requires dialogic skills necessary for deliberation and communication across differences. The promotion of civic dignity in educational contexts does not presuppose or need special civic education courses or explicit political participation. Rather, for civic dignity, agentic and dialogic skills can be developed in any educational program.

One essential starting point is for people to gain an understanding of relevant systems and structures so they can build confidence in their ability to co-determine the affairs affecting their lives. As societal norms, labor market requirements, and educational systems are interwoven with each other and vary widely across cultures, an understanding of these interconnections inevitably necessitates knowledge acquisition. Knowledge of different paths and processes, institutional landscapes, gateways to certain occupations, as well as tacit knowledge inherently needed in each profession, are all things migrants must learn in order to find their 'own' place in the new society. To learn how to navigate the institutions and structures, migrants need culture-specific knowledge from both within and outside of their similarly cultured peer group. One participant described the types of culture-specific knowledge migrants need in order to take the next step towards becoming part of the host society:

> We had more and more people here who didn't know at all the German educational system, which can become a big problem if you make decisions about your future career on a wrong basis. That means on the basis of the system that you know from your home country. ... They tell me they know already what is their goal, and I show them a pathway to reach these goals. ... I try to figure out what could be the options and step-by-step we are making [them] more concrete .... At the end, it has to be always very concrete. You have to give these people a ... like a lead-map. A time lead-map. What will be the next steps, where do I have to address in order to make [the system] more transparent and in order to empower [the migrants]?
>
> *(Wilhelm, unpublished data)*

In addition to this procedural knowledge, what also emerged from our research is that migrants' efforts to integrate into a new society often intimidate them and lead to feelings of failure and inadequacy. It is not enough for migrants to pose for themselves a clear goal and to have a vision for pathways to their own possible development. On the road to this goal, a number of wrong decisions or missteps can easily be made because they do not understand the myriad systems and tacit norms of their new society; such missteps, according to our research participants, can lead to fatigue, disenchantment, and apathy.

It is understandable how migrants, feeling lost in a system they do not fully know, would desire that someone simply tell them a reasonable goal and the appropriate path to obtain it. Support systems are indeed necessary to facilitate migrants' adaptation to their new society, including for instance, learning the language, education systems, and credentialing processes. However, support systems that treat migrants as deficient or lacking autonomy can lead to migrants' incapacitation, rather than to their transition into functioning members of their new society. Migrants benefit from developing a sense of competence, agency, and self-sufficiency; all of which help them become more able to take steps to identify and realize their goals and find their way in the new society. Pedagogically, the distinction here is between developing a life path *with* people rather than *for* people. One participant described his philosophy: the best way he can help migrants is to acknowledge their role as agents in deciding what they want for themselves, and then provide them a clear path to accomplish that goal.

> People coming to Germany need clear perspectives and clear decisions. They feel disoriented and lost in an unknown context. They request instruction, a clear decision made for them by someone more knowledgeable. ... Many expect something I couldn't offer them. "You make the decision what is good for me. Tell me what would be a good future professional career in Germany." ... That's the first thing I say, "No, that's not my decision. It's *your* decision. I try to support you. I create some kind of transparency of the German educational system, of the labor market. We work out together some alternatives, some potential professional pathways." And at the end they often accept: "I [the migrant] make the decision"
>
> *(as quoted in Hoggan & Kloubert, in press)*

This is a point of tension in the learning process of migrants. Becoming overwhelmed in a system they do not know, they can be tempted to metaphorically throw up their hands and ask an educator or counselor to simply make decisions for them. Yet, an important part of their transition process is developing not only a knowledge of the system, but also a sense that they can navigate it now and in the future, in order to create and manage their life in their new country. This is described well by Friedenthal-Haase (2014): "A social integration that does not suppress the individual, but sets them free in their independence, can help to overcome hopelessness, apathy and the spirit of submission so that new things can arise" (p. 40, translation ours).

On a final note, adult education can have a special role to play in different communities where people come together, namely, to initiate and support a dialogue, and to promote dialogic competencies among adults. These are essential for civic dignity, as they allow for full participation in socio-political processes, which necessarily implies dealing with conflicts of interest and clashing worldviews. As one participant described anecdotally:

> And then there are the differences between the Arabic and the Kurdish, and that is another problem even if they [Kurds] are Yazidi. Because Muslims say Yazidi are kind of "satanic church." (laughs) Because they have a god who is a fallen angel, and this angel went back to god, and now that is their god. And the Muslims say: "Yes, we know about that angel fallen from heaven, but it never came back—and it is Satan." And sometimes there are some problems. If one says "Okay, you pray to Satan." —"No, I don't!!" This culture problem results sometimes even in the progress of learning, because there are differences.
>
> *(Alexander)*

The more heterogeneous the society, the more it demands attitudes and skills to address such plurality. It is necessary to develop skills to communicate across differences, not only between the so-called group of migrants and the host society, but even among the migrants themselves. Any heterogenous group will have such differences, and the ability to exercise civic dignity requires dialogic capacities. At the center of any society that aspires to be free and democratic must be a mutual responsibility for the shared world(s). Migrants can and should have the right to co-shape the societies in which they live, and their experiences in adult education programs can foster, rather than ignore or inhibit, the capabilities for this shared responsibility.

Discussion

Our vision is that adult education should first and foremost acknowledge and respect human dignity, specifically in this case by helping migrants develop auton-omy and civic dignity, which are necessary pre-conditions for participation in a pluralistic democratic society. If we want to live together in societies in such a way that voices are not suppressed and decisions are made fairly and deliberatively, we need to rely on individuals' ability for autonomous thinking and acting, and for participating individually and collectively in socio-political processes.

This commitment of adult education to human dignity, as discussed in this chapter, may require a constant (self-)examination by educators of the fundamental ethical orientation that influences their practices. This examination might include, for instance, considerations such as: (a) whether migrants' histories, goals, and aspirations are recognized and incorporated into the curriculum (rather than solely conveying the expectations of the host country), (b) whether the educational practices and policies are oriented towards developing agency and self-efficacy in the new society (rather than simply telling migrants what to do), and (c) whether diversity and dialogue are promoted rather than ignored.

If we consider adult education as a catalyst and facilitator of societal development (i.e., that it helps society to learn and improve, in order to become more humane and inclusive), then a temptation can arise to see adult education only in an instru-mental role, as a means of 'forming' good workers, good democrats, good citizens, etc. (and this role is sometimes even expected by the migrants themselves). Such views of adult education assume that its goal is to help migrants 'fit' into a demo-cratic, developed society. This goal is worthy only at first glance, if at all. When we take human dignity as a fundamental premise of any educational endeavor, then the practice of trying to mold someone into a preexisting form is problematic from at least two perspectives. First, such an approach bypasses the ethical commitment of adult education to hold human dignity as both an assumption and a goal. If adult education does not foster personal growth, autonomy, and self-determination in learners, then it may serve to undermine learners' long-term civic dignity, suppres-sing agency and self-efficacy in favor of filling vacancies in the workforce.

Second, from the perspective of the continual improvement of our increasingly heterogeneous migration society as a whole, the aspiration to 'help certain groups to fit' into a seemingly unalterable social/cultural system impairs the broader work that needs to be done across society: to continually learn and improve. This requires effort from *everyone,* to constantly strive to make our societies better. If education focuses all its attention on migrants' need to change, it contradicts the necessity for all members of the society to see the current state as alterable, improvable—and themselves, accordingly, as agents of desired change, as actors rather than spectators or, worse, silent sufferers.

A better framing of adult education in the wake of migration is to help people find their voice and their path, to develop effective strategies and tools to navigate their worlds, to provide opportunities and foster capacities to have a dialogue across differences: about one's own values and principles, worldviews, traditions, and cultural and personal idiosyncrasies. At a practical level, such an adult education would need to occur in public spaces, even 'counter publics' (see Finnegan, Chapter 2, this volume), where encounters with different cultural achievements are as important as the possibility to find new models and forms of living together. The type of adult education we envision neither imposes nor compels learners to simply adapt or assimilate to the status quo, as defined by economic needs or a supposed cultural homogeneity. When we speak of new imaginings for heterogeneous societies, we do, however, presuppose that they are built on premises of democracy as a sine qua non for human dignity.

Adult education as envisioned here embraces transformation as the foundation of human dignity by engaging the imagination about ourselves and our societies, dealing with questions about what is possible, desirable, and aspirational for society. Who belongs? Whose norms and heritages are accepted? Who is authorized to co-shape the evolving nature of the society? The corresponding adult education would facilitate transformation, not from a 'prescriptive' approach (dictating how migrants need to change), but from both an 'adaptive' (recognizing the transformational challenges migrants are facing), as well as a 'process-oriented,' approach (fostering dialogue and critical reflection in a constant pursuit of better ways of thinking and interacting). It is an engagement with society as a whole to imagine new possibilities for living together in an increasingly diverse world.

Adult education plays a role in shaping societal responses to migration. From the perspective of this chapter, it would of necessity promote heterogeneity and dialogue, as well as reject uniformizing, incapacitating, and instrumentalizing tendencies. Such an approach would entail, inter alia, the imperative that no person may be used as a means to achieve someone else's ends, and that no person's dignity is of less value than any other's in the society. This is essential because the implicit and explicit messages embedded in educational policies and practices shape perceptions about such issues as whether all people inherently possess human dignity, regardless of their status as 'migrants' or 'natives.'

Notes

1 We refer here to concerns voiced over a diluting of the (imaginary) native culture (e.g., German *Leitkultur*), including the xenophobia usually implied. However, we recognize that there are also concerns about potential economic challenges due to the need to

provide adequate living conditions and employment for large numbers of incoming people. We would also contest the legitimacy of these latter concerns as a 'crisis,' but do not do so here, as that is a separate issue.

2 Such 'belonging' might be overstated, as, taking the German example, the official categorization for migrants as 'citizen with migration background,' applies not only to the migrants themselves, but to their next two generations.

3 Research participants were given the option to respond in German or in English; they all chose to speak in English.

References

Alfred, M. V. (2015). Diaspora, migration, and globalization: Expanding the discourse of adult education. *New Directions for Adult and Continuing Education*, 146, 87–97.

Anderson, B. (1983). *Imagined Communities*. Verso.

Daly, E., & May, J. (2018). A Primer for Dignity Rights (September 20, 2018). *International Juriste*. Available at SSRN: https://ssrn.com/abstract=3252694.

Faulstich, P. (2003). *Weiterbildung: Begründungen lebensentfaltender Bildung*. Oldenbourg.

Faulstich, P. (2016). Das Politische in der Bildung. In K.-P. Hufer & D. Lange (Hrsg.), *Handbuch politische Erwachsenenbildung* (pp. 52–61). Wochenschau Verlag.

Friedenthal-Haase, M. (2020). Emigration und Remigration im Blickpunkt der Erwachsenenbildung. In T. Kloubert (Ed.), *Erwachsenenbildung und Migration* (pp. 13–32). Wiesbaden.

Friedenthal-Haase, M. (2014). Einleitung der Herausgeberin (Introduction by editor). In F. Borinski (Ed.) *The German Volkshochschule: An Experiment in Democratic Adult Education Under the Weimar Republic*. Julius Klinkhardt.

Guo, S. (2010). Toward recognitive justice: emerging trends and challenges in transnational migration and lifelong learning. *International Journal of Lifelong Education*, 29(2), 149–167.

Hoggan, C., & Kloubert, T. (2020). Transformative learning in theory and practice. *Adult Education Quarterly*, 70(3), 295–307.

Hoggan, C., & Kloubert, T. (in press). Migration and human dignity: Rhetoric and practice in Germany. In M. Alfred, P. Robinson, & E. Roumell (Eds.), *Advancing the Global Agenda for Human Rights, Vulnerable Populations and Environmental Sustainability: Adult Education as Strategic Partner*. Information Age Publishing.

Hufer, K. P. (2016). *Politische Erwachsenenbildung: Plädoyer für eine vernachlässigte Disziplin*. wbv.

Kloubert, T. (2018). Mündigkeit in "postfaktischer" Zeit. *Hessische Blätter für Volksbildung*, 2018(3), 217–226.

Kloubert, T., & Hoggan, C. (2021). Migrants and the labor market: The role and tasks of adult education. *Adult Learning*, 32(1), 29–39.

Lange, E., & Baillie Abidi, C. (2015). Rethinking social justice and adult education for welcoming, inclusive communities: Synthesis of themes. *New Directions for Adult and Continuing Education*, 2015(146), 99–109.

Mecheril, P. (2019). Pädagogik der Migrationsgesellschaft. In M. Stein, D. Steenkamp, S. Weingraber, & V. Zimmer (Hrsg.), *Flucht. Migration. Pädagogik. Willkommen? Aktuelle Kontroversen und Vorhaben* (pp. 41–56). Klinkhardt.

Mecheril, P., & Streicher, N. P. (2016). Politische Erwachsenenbildung in der Migrationsgesellschaft: Handbuch Politische Erwachsenenbildung. In K.-P. Hufer & D. Lange (Eds.), *Reihe Politik und Bildung* (pp. 163–172). Wochenschau Verlag.

Nussbaum, M. C. (2011). *Creating Capabilities: The Human Development Approach*. The Belknap Press of Harvard University Press.

Oltmer, J. (2017). *Migration, Geschichte und Zukunft der Gegenwart*. wgb.

Shan, H., & Fejes, A. (2015). Editorial: Skill regime in the context of globalization and migration. *Journal of Continuous Studies*, 37(3), 227–235.

Sprung, A. (2013). Adult education in migration societies and the challenge of 'Recognition' in Austrian and German adult education. *Studies in the Education of Adults*, 45(1), 82–98.

UN (United Nations Department of Economic and Social Affairs). (2017). International migration report. https://www.un.org/en/development/desa/population/migration/publica tions/migrationreport/index.asp.

Zeuner, C. (2020). Krisen?–Nachdenken über Bildung als Gegenbewegung. Humanismus und Freiheitlichkeit: Stolpersteine am Weg zu einer demokratischen Bildung und nach- haltigen Gesellschaft? *Magazin erwachsenenbildung.at*, 39(2020), 1–13.

10

BUILDING THE 'HERE' AND 'THERE' IN DIFFERENT SENSESCAPES

Embodied Dialogues among Refugees and Natives

Laura Formenti and Silvia Luraschi

In this chapter, we present a specific *embodied* method appropriate for research on migration using the conducted research to illustrate the application of this method. The experience was a part of a larger research project conducted in Northern Italy and involving a wide array of people: refugees and asylum seekers, young native citizens, professionals, and researchers[1]. All of them were involved as insiders of the experience of migration. Through a dynamic and dialogic co-construction, we wanted to explore with them the layered and complex representations of space, of migrants' inclusion, and the struggles it involves. We wanted to learn from their everyday experiences, memories, and different perspectives.

In order to do that, we used a panoply of qualitative and participatory methods, over a period of a year and a half. Here, we will refer to a part of the study, using an embodied narrative methodology—the sensobiographic walk (Järviluoma, 2021)—which is not only apt to 'gather data,' but also to generate new ideas and knowledge in order to enhance dialogue and a deeper understanding of human experience. We proposed the walks to pairs of young adult natives and asylum seekers, about the same age, since we knew from previous phases of our research that these two groups of people have very rare occasions to meet, let alone to talk to each other.

According to the Organization for Economic Co-operation and Development (OECD, 2018), refugees and native-born citizens may experience many kinds of separation and disconnection, including 1) physical and symbolic walls, invisibility, and parallel worlds; 2) absence of reciprocal communication and knowledge; 3) reciprocal misunderstandings due to a lack of shared cultural codes; 4) occasional or repeated conflict, escalation, and more hidden forms of refusal; and 5) prejudice, reciprocal distrust, or fear powered by negative narratives, representations, and generalizations.

DOI: 10.4324/9781003124412-13

In the Italian context, radicalization and the reification of difference between migrants and Italians is very strong—not just in the political and public discourse. 'Unexpected subjects'—our project's title—is a quote from an Italian feminist, Carla Lonzi (1970), who wrote of women as unexpected subjects in the 1970s public scene. Newcomers may be subjects who voice their condition and their desire, given the proper context. Challenging objectification and categorization of the other is a task for adult education and for biographical research.

As researchers whose aim is 'making a difference' (Formenti & West, 2016) by opening possibilities and imagining new forms of co-existence, we try to offer ways to challenge the dominant discourse of education and social intervention aimed at 'integration' or 'inclusion' of new migrants in the local community, to propose research as a learning context that aims to enhance dialogue, critical thinking, reciprocity, and a generative culture contact (Formenti & Luraschi, 2020).

Space, Belonging, and Research as a Learning Experience

The (post)migration society is in transition, and all citizens are constantly negotiating the boundaries of belonging. If we are all 'migrants,' the task of adult education goes far beyond supporting migrants and refugees in their integration process: it can offer a framework to develop a new inclusive social model, grounded in diversity and multiple belongings. For these reasons, we focus on space as learnt and constructed by multiple interactions in a 'more-than-human world'—a physical and symbolic space for possibilities, where old settlers and newcomers must learn how to co-exist. The narrative construction of the 'here' and 'there' is constitutive in telling lives (Horsdal, 2012) and building a sense of 'belonging' in the effort to make one's life livable. In our view, this deserves attention since it can pave the way to innovative ideas and actions in education, as well as fuel new forms of participation and solidarity.

In this chapter, we tell some stories from four sensobiographic walks involving Silvia as a walking biographic researcher with four companions of experience: Matteo and Chiara (young adults from Brianza, Province of Lecco, Italy), Asad (an adult from Pakistan), and Samakè (a young adult from Mali). From their conversations during the walks, we want to offer examples of the method, its appropriateness for research on migration and its potential in sustaining reciprocal learning. We chronicle some epiphanies that emerged from this human, embodied, and dialogic experience of sharing a path, memories, and perceptions in a physical space that becomes 'unexpected' because migrants—in dialogue with native-borns—are invited to imagine a common place and to co-create new meanings of living (Formenti & Luraschi 2020).

We see the local theory of the 'here' and 'there' (Horsdal, 2012) developed in the walks, an embodied narrative construction—a narrative of the physical world—as crucial in the establishment of a sense of 'belonging' (Formenti et al., 2019). The symbolic connection of here and there heals difficult feelings, sustains the painful process of identity transformation entailed by migration (Anderson, 2019), and opens possibilities for new subjective and relational politics of space (Darling, 2009) where the physical space is re-imagined through lived experience (Massey, 2005).

As researchers of adult education and learning, we aim to celebrate the learning potential of diversity and dialogue based on the Batesonian concept of information as a difference that makes a difference (Bateson, 1979). We leverage differences among migrants and natives—their experience of space is shaped by their bodies, biographies, cultural values, and frameworks of meaning. So, by creating this unconventional and non-typical contact, we hoped to cast some light on their experience (Formenti & Luraschi, 2020).

The first pair is Asad and Matteo. For them, this is an unprecedented relationship.

> Asad, a 37-year-old man from Pakistan, has been living in Lecco for 4 years. He is a refugee for religious reasons. During our first walk, he told Matteo some episodes from his life in Islamabad. He had a business, selling and distributing medicinal products before he decided to escape due to the fear of being killed in a terrorist attack like his father in 2015. He maintains contact by telephone with his wife and two children, who are still living in Islamabad. Prior to entering the SPRAR project[2], he worked as a warehouseman in a Chinese shop in Italy. Now, he is looking for a job as kitchen assistant and tries to improve his scarce Italian with the desire to live in Lecco with his family in the future.
>
> Matteo is a civil servant in a library, living in Brianza since his birth. He is 20, and recently had a lot of reflection about his future: he took a year off education after realizing that maybe he was not really interested in what he was studying. Doing his work among books in the tiny library of Sirtori—the village where his youth's cultural association is based—he discovered a passion for psychology, so he is now preparing for the admission test at a university.
>
> *(Transcription of Silvia's field notes, 24th June 2019)*

Asad and Matteo are different—albeit not in every respect. The former is a newcomer (at least this is how others, and maybe himself, still see him after four years); the latter was born in this place, though we do not know whether or not he feels a sense of belonging here. Both are struggling for their future in a different and uncertain way. Asad is struggling with a new country, language, and social relationships and being separated from his wife and his children. Matteo, on the other hand, is struggling with uncertainty—he could become a migrant himself, given that many Italian young adults are going abroad. The press names this 'the brains' escape' (commonly termed 'brain drain' in the U.S.). More simply, they are looking for better opportunities elsewhere. The degree of their struggling is different because Matteo—like many Italians who decide to migrate—starts from a position of privilege compared to the migration out of persecution for religious reasons that Asad has lived. Their biographies, though, invite their minds to expect the unexpected that they still do not know how to deal with.

Their biographies shape their perspectives, including their use of senses and movement. Their narratives thus are also shaped by their actions and perceptions. This is a circular entangled process—movements create actions that design perceptions and are shaped by biographies that generate narratives and vice versa. The theory of embodiment and enactivism (Varela et al., 1991) defines this reciprocal coupling of perception and action as a process that constantly feeds daily life: it provides information about our resources, obligations, and basic needs (e.g. food, housing, learning, work) and shapes our values, desires, and hopes. We transform little by little, unknowingly. As biographical researchers, we are especially interested in the stories that are not or cannot be told, since the development of a sense of place, identity, belonging, and possibility mainly happens unconsciously. Meeting the other creates an unprecedented possibility for telling the untold story, hence producing reciprocal learning and understanding.

Our idea at the start was to investigate the circular interconnection of migrants' perception of space and their movements within the territory hosting them—inside and outside the hosting centers, in public spaces, in urban, in rural areas, and within different landscapes. In fact, the embodied construction of space, 'sensescape,' (Howes, 2005) is different for subjects who live in the 'same' territory but do not have the same experience. Howes defines sensescape as "the idea that the experience of the environment and of the other persons and things which inhabit the environment. Sensescape is produced by a particular mode of distinguishing, valuing and combining the senses in the culture under study" (Howes, 2005, p. 143). We connect this idea with an embodied and embedded narrative methodology (Formenti et al., 2014) and see it as an evolution of biographical methods in adult learning research that embraces the relevance of both the material and the unconscious in biographical telling, beyond what can be said or thought (Evans, 2016; Formenti & West, 2018). From a systemic perspective, biography always refers to *concrete*, embodied, and lived knowing (Varela, 1992).

Sensobiography is also a way to disrupt dominant narratives. The most common way of telling stories of migration and adult learning marginalizes the body, objectifies the physical context, and categorizes human beings (West, 2016). Besides, there is a risk of hidden colonization in overly psychological accounts of migrants' experience, especially when we use categories that are alien from their cultures and epistemologies (Fanon, 1961; Papadopoulos, 2007). The body brings us to celebrate the *sensible* (Bois, 2001; Bois & Austry, 2007; Lachance et al., 2018), "a force capable of endlessly altering everything that comes in contact with it" (Bois, 2001, p. 114).

The Walks: An Embodied Methodology

Sensobiographic walks (Järviluoma, 2021, 2017; Murray & Järviluoma, 2019), developed in the framework of a new anthropology of senses, belong to the wide interdisciplinary field of sensory studies. Two different subjects (e.g., a young and old person, an artist and non-artist, a local and a newcomer) walk together in a place of choice—one tells the other his/her present and past perceptions of this space. They walk together and share perceptions and memories. The researcher facilitates the dialogue, listens, and documents by recording, taking notes, pictures or videos. They can propose further questions after the walk.

It is an embodied method; walking radically changes the context of narration and incorporates the space and non-human world more evidently into the relationship. According to Solnit, "Walking shares with making and working that crucial element of engagement of the body and the mind with the world, of knowing the world through the body and the body through the world" (Solnit, 2000, p. 29).

The method values the double nature of space—concrete and symbolic—and its construction emerges from the ongoing interactions. It mirrors the double feature of the human as a living organism and an observer (Maturana, 1978); this is a main tenet of complexity theory, backing our epistemological and methodological choices. Movement is crucial in human existence, and it is a necessity for survival indeed. We can only know a place by moving through it, pausing, choosing a direction, looking around us at the larger landscape as well as details, and using all our senses, including touching, smelling, feeling foot contact with the ground, etc. This is also our limit—we will not know what is selected out from our perception in action.

Walking together is a trigger of learning—"Walking with others or asking others to represent their own experiences through walking offers an inspiring route to understanding" (Pink et al., 2010, p. 3). In the sensobiographic walk, we are invited to use words and share with the other, point and name objects, remember, tell stories, make connections, etc. Our senses appreciate the quality of the environment, while our talking develops meaning, sometimes in very unexpected ways. Weaving together movement, perception, communication, and thought, a local embodied theory emerges from the ongoing relationship, and sometimes the presence of the other is the occasion for an epiphany.

In this process, all kinds of feelings and emotions emerge constantly in relation with the participants' perception and construction of meaning, illuminating the ongoing experience and the presence of the other. The sensobiographic walk fosters and somehow documents a constant and dynamic process of multiple interactions with the other, with the environment and its objects, and with oneself. Walking together is a way of giving space to interrelation and interdependencies in the complexity of human life. When walking while telling a story about our experience or biography, *present and past* and *here and there* are also linked. The levels of knowledge multiply and interconnect—the individual subjective experience (micro level) is weaved in the relational and communicative process between the participants (meso level) to create a sense of 'us,' and constant explicit and implicit reference is made to the larger social and cultural system (macro level).

Walking-with in the Place of the Heart

We realized twelve sensobiographic walks with six male refugees from different countries included in local programs for 'integrated reception' and six native young adults (three male and three female). The latter confessed they never had a conversation with a refugee in their lives; they are members of an association—Rethink the Future with Youths—and we decided to invite them into the project after field observation that revealed a gap of interaction between refugees and same-age natives. Six pairs of difference were formed to walk together in a place of choice, which we named 'the place of the heart.' In order to mitigate the strangeness of our request for refugees, natives led first by telling their story of past and present experience in the place they had chosen, while the refugee and the researcher followed, listened, commented, and asked questions. In the second walk, it was the turn of the refugee to choose his place of the heart and become the teller. Sounds, smells, and other sensuous perceptions were the core of both conversations—Silvia's role was to invite them to share at this level.

Among the many observations that emerged from the walks, we want to highlight the quality of the relationship (as an intercultural experience of dialogue) and the construction of the 'here' and 'there' (as an emerging pattern that seemed to offer a frame to organize meaning).

In proposing the walks, we hoped to be able to create a 'good enough' space, in Winnicott's (1971) language, where the strange would be made familiar (West, 2016) and participants would be able to open themselves to new possibilities. Within an unprecedented relationship, embarrassment could dominate. In intercultural exchanges, there are many reasons for conflict and wariness due to the clash of cultural frameworks (Sclavi, 2003). However, our hopeful expectations about the relationship were exceeded during the experience. As an example, in their first walk, Matteo brought Asad to his place of the heart (a scenic spot), and Asad's reaction was surprising:

MATTEO: (after a short walk uphill) Here we are, this is my place of the heart. From here we can admire...
ASAD: ... together Islamabad!
SILVIA: What?
ASAD: We are in Islamabad, it's the same there.
MATTEO: Really?
ASAD: Yes, if you Google Islamabad, look at the photographs and you will see it is the same (Figure 10.1).
MATTEO: I didn't know, I am amazed.
SILVIA: Really? It should be told more that Brianza (Figure 10.2) looks like Islamabad. Do you feel at home?
ASAD: Yes.(see Luraschi, 2020, pp. 45–46)

Asad showed pictures of Islamabad on his smartphone. Since then, he regularly shares with Silvia beautiful images of his and her country (see Figure 10.1 and Figure 10.2).

By comparing the two places, Asad is suggesting a concept and a feeling of 'familiarity' by finding similar patterns in the landscape. His perception connects

FIGURE 10.1 Islamabad, Pakistan. Picture sent by Asad

FIGURE 10.2 Montevecchia Brianza, Italy. Picture sent by Asad

body and mind in creating a link between 'here' and 'there.' There are many examples of familiarity in our walks, epiphanies where our subjects remember something from the past. Hence, the 'now' and 'then' meets the 'here' and 'there,' time connects to space, and the autobiographic narrative connects to the body (Horsdal, 2012; Formenti et al., 2014).

Sometimes familiarity is suggested by the eye, as in this case; in other occasions, familiarity is suggested by smell (the scent of jasmine flower), flavors (blackberry), touch (wind, heat), or movement itself. Also, more links surely happen unconsciously since the landscape acts as an 'evocative object' (Bollas, 2009).

A good enough learning space creates the conditions for an atmosphere of reciprocity (Tillmann-Healy, 2003) (see another pair of walkers, Chiara and Samakè, in Figure 10.3 and 10.4).

> Chiara is a 22 student with a BA in Philosophy, strongly involved in the project. At our first meeting, in the local youth association for cultural promotion, she quoted Segre, the Italian woman and Senator survivor of the Holocaust[3]: "Liliana Segre always says that love was the unique reason pushing her to put one foot in front of the other, in those troubled times."
>
> Samakè is a 27 young man born in Mali, with—Chiara says—"a round, smiling and sincere face." He has been living in the Province of Lecco since

FIGURE 10.3 The first sensobiographic walk of Chiara and Samakè

FIGURE 10.4 The second sensobiographic walk of Samakè and Chiara

2014 and works as a storekeeper in a supermarket. His program within the reception project has just finished: during the summer he moved to an apartment with another African friend.

(Transcription of Silvia's field notes, 27th June 2019)

About their second walk, Silvia wrote in her notes:

Samakè guides us into the woods and we walk together for more than two hours: he and Chiara talk as if they knew each other a long time, so I feel the need to listen silently. Walking, as maintained by Le Breton (2012), opens us to feeling the world. To me, while I walk, the ground under my feet is alive and talking.
[...]

SAMAKÈ: People are what changed me. Since, if you don't want to let them in, but they want to enter anyway, what can you do? By force, isn't it? So, I have already changed, this way, slowly, bit by bit.
CHIARA: That is, others started to talk to you, then you opened up a little more.
SAMAKÈ: Yes, that's it.

[...]

SAMAKÈ: I have changed now. Even if people don't talk to me, I talk to people. Now. Because I have changed. Not before. Before I just greeted. Since I came with that. From my country: if you see someone, you greet them. Even if you don't know them, greet them.

SILVIA: In Italy, we do not do that…

SAMAKÈ: No, you don't. If you greet them, they do not answer. But they look at you: why are you greeting me?

SILVIA: It is different…

SAMAKÈ: It is too different.

CHIARA: The only place with this rule, in Italy, is just the mountains. There, you must greet the people passing by.

SAMAKÈ: With us always, knowing or not, you must greet.

(Transcription of second sensobiographic walk with Chiara and Samakè,
4th July 2019, our translation)

From Silvia's notes:

On our way back to the car, we pass close the reception center where Samaké has been hosted for some time, in the past; here, a black-skinned young man walks towards us.

Later, Chiara will write to me an e-mail about this meeting:

We met an African boy just like Samakè in the woods. I said hello but he struggled to answer and didn't even make eye contact. I imagined seeing Samakè three years ago in his place, same position and same attitude. I also thought that even the unknown boy will soon or later find a job, a home, some stability. And I would have talked to him too, to know his story, since people's stories are all different.

(Transcription of Silvia's field notes, 6th July 2019)

This fragment is an example of the relationship, experiences, resonances, imagination, and new concepts that might emerge from a sensobiographic walk. We consider this experience of *walking-with* as a form of solidarity, unlearning, and critical engagement with situated knowledge (Springgay & Truman, 2017, p. 11). Research does not need to be neutral and objective. When we research lives and learning, we are responsible for the processes we create; objectification and false neutrality may bring hidden colonization and exclusion, or it will be balanced by active subjectivation, recognition, friendship, and curiosity.

Aesthetic Participation and Reflexivity: Signs of Transformation

SAMAKÈ: […] I wandered in Lecco but never went out.

SILVIA: Are you happy with that or would you prefer to hang out more?

SAMAKÈ: If I must go, I go, but then I come back here. Since where I live, in Lomagna, I know many people, do you see? I know many in the province of Lecco. But, if I go elsewhere, I become a new one, as a person.

CHIARA: Of course.

SAMAKÈ: And I don't like it.

SILVIA: You don't like to be a stranger?

SAMAKÈ: Yes, I don't.

(Transcription of the first sensobiographic walk with Chiara and Samakè, 27th June 2019, our translation)

After a few days, Chiara wrote an email to Silvia where she makes her own theory of the sensobiographic experience. This is a beautifully reflexive passage, connecting her perceptions and feelings with Samakè's experience:

It was really very hot when we started to stroll in the fields. An 'African hot' on which we made jokes, but then again, I can't remember a single time when I did not suffer, on that lane, from the burning sun. A dirt road, winding its way among corn fields, is the perfect place for a long conversation between friends: it puts you at ease and in a good mood. I consider this place almost as mine, as home, and I know every bush and tree like my own pocket, and yet, in its extreme simplicity, I appreciate the beauty of a country lane identical to other hundred thousand. One among the others, but this one only is mine. Appropriation and affect towards one place, among infinite undifferentiated places: after all, this is what happens to us, at birth. We find ourselves already assigned to this family, to this city, to this Country by a crazy turning roulette wheel, discarding other alternatives, equally likely. Samakè told me a story about a snake living with his family, about monkeys making jokes of you and beating you with a stick in the forest, about the sweet fruits in the land where he was born.

(Fragment of Chiara's e-mail, 30th June 2019, our translation)

Another reflective text came from Matteo the day after the second walk with Asad (see Figure 10.5):

It was evident that Asad knew and liked the places that he made us visit—especially the Kennedy Bridge! [in Lecco] He made me also understand that he loves to go swimming in the lake—especially in Malgrate [a small-town facing Lecco, on the opposite shore of the lake: Kennedy Bridge is a way there]. I enjoyed when he talked about his cousin, living in Caen [France] who owns an ethnic restaurant named 'Benazir' to honour the first woman President of Pakistan, and I was especially surprised when he said that he would never go away from Italy, neither to work in France (to his cousin), since he likes Lecco. [...]. Asad gave me his number, we promised each other to meet again in Lecco—if not in the summer, next autumn.

(Fragment of Matteo's e-mail, 15th July 2019, our translation)

FIGURE 10.5 Asad and Matteo are looking toward Lecco from Malgrate during their second sensobiographic walk

What about the refugees? Silvia kept contact with some of them since technology can be a mediator of relationships at a distance. Asad sends videos and photos of Islamabad and Lecco, while Samakè talks about his new home in a place where he doesn't know anybody for now. Silvia discovered the unexpected pleasure of staying in company with refugees. They took care of her—Asad prepared Kheer (a traditional rice pudding) and brought fruits to her and Matteo; Samakè made tea with a lot of sugar and promised to invite her and Chiara for a dinner at the new apartment. This experience pushed her to visit ethnic grocery stores near home more frequently and try new ingredients. Now, her favorite is okra, a vegetable of disputed origins used in West Africa, Ethiopia, and South Asia, and even in Crete, as she found during holidays. In this case, the idea of 'here' and 'there' is expressed in food—dishes and flavors are a site of connection between different places and people. (Luraschi 2021; Cottino & Luraschi, 2021)

We tried to celebrate the learning potential of sensobiographic walks in creating unprecedented relationships and conversations, fueling a sense of friendship, familiarity, and curiosity—far beyond the rhetoric of agency and empowerment narrowing down adult education to the compensation of vulnerability. In the walks, we witnessed the emergence of another identity in the newcomers—from the passive, needing, and vulnerable subjects depicted by the narratives that are dominant in the so called 'inclusive' programs (Però, 2007), to expert, active, and caring guides.

Adult education in a (post)migration society entails the creation of new spaces for dialogue where everybody—newcomers and natives—can learn about the context where they live, the 'here' and other places 'there'—not least the newcomers' place of origin and transition. The sensobiographic walks offer a space for discovery, inviting participants on both sides to see the place through the other's eyes. This can bring them to recognize their habits, reciprocal stereotypes, and perspectives. Living in a (post)migration society needs critical research *with* rather than *about* migrants; this demands theoretical and methodological creativity.

Creativity is linked to our capacity to rely on imaginative resources—like our participants did—to communicate and access each other's social worlds. By walking together, we brought dialogue and learning in the public space, and by doing this kind of sensitive biographical research, we fuel our own capacity to see, feel, reflect and develop our creative resources for thinking, feeling, and acting in new ways towards a participatory society.

Notes

1 'Unexpected subjects' (October 2018 – March 2020), Department of Human Science for Education University of Milano Bicocca. Research founded by Fondazione Alsos.
2 Protection System for Asylum Seekers and Refugees, https://www.sprar.it/english.
3 http://www.memorialeshoah.it/liliana-segre/?lang=en

References

Anderson, B. (2019). New directions in migration studies: Towards methodological de-nationalism. *Comparative Migration Studies*, 7, 36. https://doi.org/10.1186/s40878-019-0140-8.
Bateson, G. (1979). *Mind and Nature: A Necessary Unity (Advances in Systems Theory, Complexity, and the Human Sciences)*. Hampton Press.
Bois, D. (2001). *Le Sensible et le Mouvement [The Sensible and the Movement]*. Éditions Point d'Appui.
Bois, D., & Austry, D. (2007). Vers l'émergence du paradigme du Sensible [Towards the emergence of the paradigm of the sensible]. *Réciprocités*, 1, 6–22.
Bollas, C. (2009). *The Evocative Object World*. Routledge.
Cottino G., Luraschi, S. (2021, in review). Farsi casa attraverso le pratiche alimentari. Voci di richiedenti asilo e operatori nelle province di Cuneo e Lecco. *Mondi Migranti*, https://www.francoangeli.it/riviste/Sommario.aspx?IDRivista=149.
Darling. J. (2009). Thinking beyond place: The responsibilities of a relational spatial politics. *Geography Compass*, 3(5), 1938–1954.
Evans, R. (Ed.). (2016). *Before, Beside and After (Beyond) the Biographical Narrative*. Nisabaverlag.
Fanon, F. (1961). *Les Damnés de la Terre*. Éditions Maspero.
Formenti, L., & Luraschi, S. (2020). Migration, culture contact and the complexity of coexistence: A systemic imagination. *RELA – European Journal for Research on the Education and Learning of Adults*, 11(3), 349–365, 10.3384/rela.2000–7426.ojs1711.
Formenti, L., Luraschi, S., Osman, A., Thumborg, C., & Bron, A. (2019). Symposium: Belonging to a place or not - immigrants' perception of place as space for learning. In *ESREA 9th Triennial European Research Conference Adult Education Research and Practice:*

*Between the Welfare State and Neoliberalism, Book of Abstracts*Institute for Pedagogy and Andragogy, Faculty of Philosophy, University of Belgrade.

Formenti, L., & West, L. (Eds.). (2016). *Stories that Make a Difference. Exploring the Collective, Social and Political Potential of Narratives in Adult Education Research*. Pensa Multimedia.

Formenti, L., & West, L. (2018). *Transforming Perspectives in Lifelong Learning and Adult Education: A Dialogue*. Palgrave Macmillan.

Formenti, L., West, L., & Horsdal, M. (Eds.). (2014). *Embodied Narratives. Connecting Stories, Bodies, Cultures and Ecologies*. University Press of Southern Denmark.

Horsdal, M. (2012). *Telling Lives: Exploring Dimensions of Narratives*. Routledge.

Howes, D. (2005). *Empire of the Senses: The Sensual Culture Reader*. Bloomsbury Academic.

Järviluoma, H. (2017). The art and science of sensory memory walking. In M. Cobussen, V. Meelberg, & B. Truax (Eds.), *The Routledge Companion to Sounding Art* (pp. 191–204). Routledge.

Järviluoma, H. (2021, in press). Sensobiographic walking and ethnographic approach of the Finnish School of Soundscape Studies. In G. Stahl & P. Mark (Eds.), *The Bloomsbury Handbook of Popular Music and Place*. Bloomsbury.

Lachance, J., Edmond, G., & Vinit, F. (2018). Learning to be a sensitive professional: A life-enhancing process grounded in the experience of the body. *Adult Education Quarterly* 69 (1), 24–41.

Le Breton, D. (2012). *Marcher (Elogedeschemins et de la Lenteur)*. Métailié.

Lonzi, C. (1970). *Let's Spit on Hegel* (transl. V. Newman). Secunda.

Luraschi, S. (2020). Il gelsomino e la mora selvatica. Le passeggiate sensobiografiche in una ricerca pedagogica con giovani rifugiati/richiedenti a Lecco. In P. Ascari (Ed.), *Oggetti Contesi: Le Cose Nella Migrazione* (pp. 37–52). Mimesis.

Luraschi S. (2021, in review). Exploring the space of conviviality with newcomers and host communities. *Adult Education Discourses*, http://www.dma.wpps.uz.zgora.pl/index.php?journal=DMA&page=index.

Massey, D. (2005). *For Space*. Sage.

Maturana, H. R. (1978). Biology of language: The epistemology of reality. In G. A. Miller & E. Lenneberg (Eds.), *Psychology and Biology of Language and Thought: Essays in Honor of Eric Lenneberg* (pp. 27–63). Academic Press.

Murray L., & Järviluoma H. (2019). Walking as transgenerational methodology. *Qualitative Research*, 20(2), 229–238, https://doi.org/10.1177/1468794119830533.

OECD. (2018), International Migration Outlook 2018. OECD Publishing. https://doi.org/10.1787/migr_outlook-2018-en.

Papadopoulos, R. K. (2007). Refugees, trauma and adversity-activated development. *European Journal of Psychotherapy and Counseling*, 9(3), 301–312.

Però, D. (2007). *Inclusionary Rhetoric / Exclusionary Practices: Left-wing Politics and Migrants in Italy*. Berghahn Books.

Pink, S., Hubbard, P., & O'Neill, M. (2010). Walking across disciplines: From ethnography to arts practice. *Visual Studies*, 25(1), 1–7.

Sclavi, M. (2003). *Arte di Ascoltare e Mondi Possibili*. Mondadori.

Solnit, R. (2000). *Wanderlust: A History of Walking*. Penguin.

Springgay, S., & Truman, S. E. (2017). *Walking Methodologies in a More-than-human World: WalkingLab*. Routledge.

Tillmann-Healy, L. M. (2003). Friendship as method. *Qualitative Inquiry*, 9(5), 729–749.

Varela, F. J. (1992). *Ethical Know-how: Action, Wisdom, and Cognition*. Stanford University Press.

Varela F. J., Thompson E., & Rosch E. (1991). *The Embodied Mind: Cognitive Science and Human Experience*. MIT Press.

West, L. (2016). *Distress in the City: Racism, Fundamentalism and a Democratic Education*. Trentham Books.

Winnicott, D. (1971). *Playing and Reality*. Routledge.

11

TRANSFORMATIVE CIVIC LEARNING WITHIN VOLUNTEERING IN REFUGEE RELIEF

Brigitte Kukovetz and Annette Sprung

Migration is an interdisciplinary field which provides analyses of highly diverse phenomena and perspectives. The main focus of theoretical and empirical research around migration issues in educational sciences—especially in the German speaking context—is on challenges related to the so-called integration of newcomers in the host countries. Accordingly, many publications in adult education (and also programs in the field of practice) deal with educational support for migrants—for example—with regard to language learning or labor market participation (Öztürk, 2014; Sievers & Grawan, 2017; Altenburg et al., 2019; Schmidtke, 2020). Very few studies address topics, such as racism, the question of belonging, and related democratic challenges in migration societies (Sprung & Kukovetz, 2018; Kloubert & Dickerhoff, 2020).

This chapter seeks to explore how civic learning is realized in a specific social context—volunteering in refugee relief. A general interest behind this approach lies in reflecting on possibilities for the development of solidarity in times of increasing global interconnectedness, (new and old) inequalities in pluralistic societies, and current risks for democracies. Since we conceive civic learning as a (potential) transformation of both thinking about and acting in the world, we use theories of transformative learning for an analysis of learning processes in the field of civic engagement. We discuss how civic learning can be realized, exemplified—mostly informally—by an empirical study on the learning of volunteers who have supported refugees since 2015/2016. Our research was conducted in Austria, where a relatively high number of refugees (compared to the overall population of 8.8 million) have been hosted since 2015. Between 2015 and 2019, Austria counted 182,000 applications for asylum. Due to restrictive policies and border controls, the number of refugees has decreased during this time from 88,000 applications in 2015 to 13,000 in 2019 (Statistik Austria, 2020).

DOI: 10.4324/9781003124412-14

In the first section of the chapter, we give a short description of the background and methodology of our study. Later, we discuss theoretical approaches of civic and transformative learning theories. Then, we return to the analysis and discussion of selected empirical results and explore the above-mentioned questions. Our data shows that having personal experience of migration (or not) seems to be relevant for some differences in the learning processes in refugee relief. This is why we also look at possible disparities in the learning of volunteers with and without experience of migration. At the same time, we take a careful approach to the respective interpretations, as we are aware of the problematic implications of making this sort of distinction—in terms of *othering* (Said, 1991). Finally, we conclude with some reflections on transformative learning in connection with civic learning and active citizenship.

"Learning Solidarity (?)"—A Brief Project Outline

Although more than five years have passed since large refugee movements (mainly from Syria and Afghanistan) challenged politics and public discourse in Europe in an unprecedented way, the images of many thousands of people marching along motorways or railway tracks in search of a safe place have remained vivid in the memory of many Europeans. The European Union recorded 2.5 million applications for asylum in 2015 and 2016 alone. Germany, Sweden, and Austria were amongst the countries with the highest number of newly arrived refugees in these years (EU Open Data Portal, 2019). In Austria, where our research is situated, the administration was not properly prepared to host the refugees as they arrived. Consequently, civil society began to engage in refugee relief. Numerous volunteers either worked in established relief organizations or set up new groups and initiatives, often organized by means of social media. The volunteers took on a wide range of short-term activities in the first phase, such as providing food, clothing, transportation and accommodation, translation services, etc. Many activists also engaged in long-term support, such as counseling, educational programs, cultural exchanges, or political activism around migration issues. The volunteers in Austria were—generally speaking—of diverse ages and social backgrounds, but they were predominantly female, well-educated, and many of them had experience of migration themselves (Kukovetz & Sprung, 2020).

After a pre-study on volunteering in the context described, we set up a research project entitled 'Learning Solidarity', which looked at the learning of volunteers who were still engaged at the time of our research in 2018 and 2019.[1] Volunteering within refugee relief is mostly associated with informal learning experiences. We analyzed these learning processes by focusing on *civic* learning and the development of attitudes and actions of solidarity on the part of the volunteers. Our theoretical background was driven by research on informal learning within social movements, and we used grounded theory in our research methodology (Strauss & Corbin, 1996). We conducted thirteen qualitative problem-centered interviews with volunteers and one group discussion with five coordinators of volunteers. Five out of the thirteen volunteers in our sample and one of the coordinating volunteers of the group discussion had migrated. Two volunteers still had the legal status of asylum seeker at the date of the interview. Furthermore, we analyzed the public representation of a group of activists on Facebook, which was used by these activists as a primary media platform. The research project was complemented by a philosophical analysis of the term *solidarity*.

For this chapter, we selected two empirical results, which we will interpret newly under these specific theoretical lenses: civic learning according to Gert Biesta (2014) and transformative learning theory.

Theoretical Approaches to Transformative Civic Learning

In this chapter, we use Gert Biesta's concept of civic learning. Biesta (2014) suggests a distinction between a *socialization* versus a *subjectification* conception of civic learning. While the socialization conception aims at supporting people to participate in the existing social and political order, the subjectification conception means that individuals exert political agency, and they are learning in and through their engagement in the 'ongoing experiment of democracy' (Biesta, 2014, p. 6). According to this concept, learning is an open process and cannot be (pre-)defined by clear *skills* that should be acquired. Pertinent learning processes can involve a transformation of the subject. Biesta is referring to Rancière when he writes:

> If … the moment of democracy is a moment of dis-identification with the existing sociopolitical order and if it is the case that it is in this moment that the democratic subject emerges, then the position and nature of the learning involved change.
>
> *(Biesta, 2014, p. 6)*

Our research findings indicate that Biesta's approach is useful in framing the learning experiences—which we interpreted as potentially being transformative (or as showing resources for transformative learning). The concept of transformative learning, mainly coined by Jack Mezirow (1997/1991), focuses on the consideration and re-interpretation of former experiences. It is precipitated by a 'disorientating experience' (Fuhr et al., 2017b, p. x), in other contexts also described as a 'disorientating dilemma.' This experience leads learners to question meanings that were previously taken for granted, and ultimately to integrate alternative meanings into their life (Fuhr et al., 2017b, p. x). Different specifications of transformative learning theories can be subsumed under a metatheory of transformative learning (Hoggan, 2016a, 2016b) with the following definition: "Transformative learning refers to processes that result in significant and irreversible changes in the way a person experiences, conceptualizes, and interacts with the world" (Hoggan, 2016a, p. 77).

To analyze empirical data through the lens of transformative learning theory, it is useful to differentiate between the object of transformation (What is changed?), the causes (What triggers the transformation?), and the conditions for transformation (Koller, 2012). According to Koller, who analyzes transformative learning processes in Germany, transformative learning is not a completed process of the replacement of one established concept of the world and oneself by a new one. It is a process of questioning the existing orders with an open outcome (Koller, 2012, p. 31). We consider two aspects of transformative learning theory as of specific relevance for the analysis of our empirical data. First, transformative learning processes result not only from reflection and through new insights, but that transformation is also a process of communication and interaction (Koller, 2012; West, 2017; Mejuni, 2017). Secondly, the newly acquired perspectives are not totally different from the old assumptions, but emanate from them (Fuhr et al., 2017a, p. 366). Transformative learning seems indispensable in pluralistic societies which are characterized by rapid change. People need to be able to reflect on challenging experiences critically—to adapt to new situations and to be able to participate actively within processes of change (Illeris, 2017).

The idea of the recognition of differences, central to pluralistic democratic societies, implies learning, and unsettling experiences that trigger learning processes make this approach interesting for the field of migration studies. Transformative learning theories were already used by many scholars to understand the experience of migration (Eschenbacher, 2020, p. 371). It is not only appropriate to explore disorienting dilemmas due to the process of migration, but also for analyzing the learning of volunteers in refugee relief. It seems even more suitable, since transformative learning theory was originally developed to describe (individual) learning processes that lead to social change (Hoggan, 2016b). As Hoggan (2016a) points out, like Jack Mezirow, there are many authors who believe that transformative learning is not only a new perspective on learning, but also includes a new form of action. This facet is especially relevant, because one of our aims is to analyze how people develop actions of solidarity while they are volunteering.

In the following presentation and discussion of some empirical results—especially focusing on the relevance of the migration experience for the volunteers—we will ask how transformative civic learning takes place within volunteering in refugee relief. First, we will illustrate the impulses triggering the learning processes, and then we will present and discuss the learning processes themselves. As non-transformative learning is often a necessary precondition for transformative learning, we will also touch on the connection between non-transformative and transformative learning.

Impulses for Transformative Learning within Volunteering in Refugee Relief

Volunteers in the field of refugee relief gained a lot of experience that led to an increase in knowledge—e.g., about refugees' living conditions, administrative procedures, and legal framework. The respective results of our research have been described elsewhere in more detail (see Sprung et al., 2017; Kukovetz & Sprung,

2019). It is challenging to ascertain from the interviews whether, and under what circumstances, these experiences have transformative effects. Therefore, we first looked at the volunteers' disorientating experiences as possible impulses for transformative learning and how they perceived and described these situations. Based on the qualitative analysis of the data, we now present four main experiences of crisis of which especially the first two—pressure of justification, as well as the questioning of the Austrian state—can be regarded as typical of engagement in the field of migration and asylum. The third, emotional involvement, might also be found in other areas of volunteer work for disadvantaged groups. The fourth and last, personal experiences as migrants, is in fact typical in the field of migration, though it is not normally connected to volunteering. Emotional involvement and being a migrant are of course not necessarily experiences of crisis, but they might have a potential connection to it, as we will show.

Pressure of Justification

One volunteer said of the start of her engagement for refugees:

> So, in 2016, a lot of things occurred to me—things I would have never thought of before. It was a kind of 'outing' … I perceived it directly as a division. In my case, it was directly within the family.[2]
>
> *(VS 108–113)*

People who advocated for refugees found that they had to justify and defend their activities in their social environment. Sometimes neighbors made derogatory remarks, and sometimes these controversies even occurred within their family. The volunteers perceived these tensions as real divisions in the family, city, or region where they live. A coordinator of volunteers explained:

> … because a lot of people [volunteers] had the feeling they wanted to withdraw their engagement or that you had to be ashamed of it [of supporting the refugees], that their neighbors should not know about it.
>
> *(AM 214–217)*

Not only in Austria, but also in Germany, that hostility is commonly found in the direct surroundings of the volunteers and on a very personal level (Hamann et al., 2016, p. 49). A quantitative study showed that 24 percent of German volunteers faced hostility or insults due to their engagement for refugees (Institut für Demoskopie Allensbach, 2017, p. 37f).

Volunteers who had migrated themselves did not bring up incidences of hostility because of their work for refugees. They experienced hostility as persons themselves (e.g., one of the volunteers spoke about discriminatory experiences in his job), or they shared stories about hostility directed at the refugees they were supporting, or which they had observed in their surroundings (e.g., in their neighborhood or instances on public transport). For volunteers who have no experience of migration, this pressure of justification seemed to enhance (transformative) learning—for example, they developed strategies for responding to these incidents of hostility. This was not found in our sample with regard to volunteers who themselves had migrated.

Questioning Austria as a Functioning Constitutional State

"What concerns you most is the injustice—that in Austria, the procedures are that unjust" (LB 288–289), said one volunteer who reported on a deportation that her lawyer had classified as illegal. Later, she said about this deportation: "And this was *my* state and it treats you this way, and I would have never thought, that this always affected me badly, this terrible injustice" (LB 293–296).

In many of the interviews, it became apparent that *before* their engagement, the volunteers had perceived Austria as a well-functioning constitutional state. Due to their new and negative experiences with the asylum system, the volunteers were shocked to discover that Austria's legal system did not seem to work correctly. This was—to give another example—the case when a father was treated as a criminal in front of his son, or when officers raised the refugees' hopes for no reason. The interviews at the *Bundesamt für Fremdenwesen und Asyl* (Federal Office for Immigration and Asylum) were partly considered "catastrophic" (UH 579). The volunteers were especially shocked by the lack of due process when they realized that deportations were illegal, or when they simply could not understand why the court deemed an asylum seeker whom they had accompanied, not credible.

We found this newly gained awareness of the lack of constitutional legality of administrative actions only in the interviews with volunteers who had not migrated to Austria themselves. Those with their own experiences of migration were critical about some political conditions, such as the lack of recognition of competences or the indifference of police officers towards the exploitation of refugees. But as far as the interviews reveal, the volunteers do not talk much about possible disappointments in the public administration, so their accounts cannot be interpreted as triggering enduring transformative learning processes.

Emotional Involvement

Emotional shock—in response to the hardship and misery of the refugees—was one of the main motives prompting volunteers to engage in refugee relief. Strong emotions played a significant role in this field. Volunteers were affected by the experiences and vulnerability of the refugees—both on their arrival in Austria and along the escape routes. In the interviews, they also demonstrated a high level of emotional closeness towards the refugees and their experiences in Austria. This became visible when they shared their stories about deportations. Their emotional involvement and burden were also expressed by the fact that many interview partners began to cry (or were close to tears) during the interview. We interpreted this as a reflection of their intense emotional involvement with the refugees. Although the volunteers spoke about the burdens, they nonetheless saw their close personal relationship with the refugees as something that greatly enriched their lives. Conversely, the populist and racist statements of politicians from the far right and the media reporting on migration politics were considered far more stressful than other emotional strain—due to some difficult situations in their support of the refugees, for example. Many interviews clearly revealed that this emotional connectedness had triggered educational processes. The significance of emotions in learning processes corresponds to previous research regarding the relation of learning and emotions (see Klika, 2018).

Various disorientating experiences occurred for volunteers with their own experience of migration. They did not report that they felt the need to justify their engagement to their family members or their social environment. Neither did they refer to the poor functioning of the asylum system. However, some had similar 'experiences of crisis' that also indicated the relevance of their emotional involvement. This was the case for a volunteer who told a story about a refugee woman who had lost her child, and her ensuing search for him through a refugee camp. He further shared his observations that newly arrived refugees were exploited by people of their own national origin, who pretended to help them. These incidents shocked him and changed his self-perception in such a way that he became aware of his capacity to help these people.

The Migration/Flight Experience as Disorienting Crisis

For those volunteers who were themselves refugees, their experience as refugees was more important and affected the subjects far more than their work as volunteers. One volunteer responded to the question as to whether his engagement as a volunteer had changed his thinking as follows: "Not really, but the journey I would never repeat." (LL 352–353). This indicates that his most disturbing experience was his own flight, and nothing about his volunteering work seemed comparable.

For another volunteer who had migrated to Austria years before from a European but non-EU country, her own migration experience also seemed to be more important than the volunteering itself. When she was asked what she had learned for the future from her volunteering, she talked about her own experiences as a migrant in Austria, and how important it was to know the language. She argued that it can only be understood by having a similar experience—that as a refugee without German language skills, you were somewhat invisible, and you could not speak about yourself. As a result, 'we' (the host society) did not know anything about them.

Since our study focused on the learning that arose from volunteering, the data provided little evidence of the learning processes resulting from these disorientating crises connected to people's personal experiences as migrants/refugees. At the same time, it is possible that because the volunteers had confronted precarious situations, that's why they tend to have different perspectives and new ways to reflect on their own migrant biography.

Learning Processes of Volunteers

For many of our interview partners, volunteering for refugees had triggered learning processes that can be described as transformative—there was a change in how they conceptualized and interacted with the world (Koller, 2012; Hoggan 2016a).

First, volunteers expanded their horizons of experience and reflected on their own social position. They gained new insights into armed conflicts, political structures, and developments of other countries, including their way of living, family and working structures, different religions, and e.g., Muslim customs. These were, in part, non-transformative learning processes, but the experiences prompted the volunteers to reflect on their own (privileged) position in the world and their way of living. Some started to also reflect critically upon their own prejudices and moral concepts.

Second, the volunteers had to acknowledge that not all of their ideas and concepts were suitable for the refugees. Moreover, migration policies changed rapidly, and the volunteers had to adapt their proposals. Consequently, they altered their actions. In some cases, we can assume that this also entailed a change of perspective, that is, when they reflected on why their plans were not embraced by the target groups—for example, because the volunteers did not talk to the refugees enough and did not ask them about their real needs. But in general, social relations between volunteers and refugees were seldom subjected to critical consideration, especially since this concerned paternalistic attitudes towards the refugees. These attitudes can be seen in the volunteers' aim of 'educating' refugees and/or trying to foster their emancipation (Kukovetz et al., 2019).

Finally, the volunteers developed a critical understanding of political contexts. Volunteering did not dramatically change political attitudes, but "small adaptations [took place], or … you start[ed] to be more interested in certain topics" (SK 608–609), as one coordinator of volunteers put it. She continued: "… and that you go a bit further with your opinions, attitudes that you question yourself, and so on" (SK 611–613). This interpretation fits with Koller's concept of learning (Bildung) as a constant challenging of existing conditions with an open end.

Some volunteers developed democratic and civic competencies, for example when they expanded their activities and started to sensitize the resident population to topics of antidiscrimination and intercultural encounters. They also acquired individual strategies on how to respond to hostility, or developed political strategies for protesting against deportations or specific migration policies.

In some interviews, the volunteers indicated changes with regard to both their thoughts and their actions. However, since this was not a long-term study, such as would be required to identify enduring impacts, it is only possible to speak of the *potential* for transformative effects in the long run. Personal experience of migration seems to have had an impact on the topics that concerned the volunteers. The learning processes described above were found predominantly in the interviews of volunteers who had no experience of migration. Although these findings cannot be generalized, possible reasons could be that migrant volunteers are already culturally sensitized. Moreover, those with their own flight experiences or those being acquainted with other refugees, might know the needs of refugees better, and are already aware of the migration and integration politics in Austria due to their own experiences before they had started volunteering. Regarding the volunteers' attitudes towards politically hegemonial concepts, volunteers with no experience of migration often spoke about the concept of 'integration' and how 'integration' was defined. For volunteers *with* experience of migration, it was instead their understanding of belonging to a community that they mentioned. One volunteer said, for example, that her perception of "who belongs to this society or does not, or to this country" (JS 596–597) has changed. She specified that she had a fairly excluding attitude towards refugees in her own country before she herself had to flee to Austria. After her own migration, she realized how much refugees could contribute to a country, and that they should be considered a member of a country just like everyone else. Interview partners who had not migrated themselves also reflected on their understanding of community. Whereas here perspectives were changed by joint activities with refugees (and sometimes the interview itself seemed to trigger their first consideration of this issue); volunteers with experience of migration indicated that their change in perspective was initiated by their own experiences of flight.

Analysis of the interviews with volunteers in refugee relief revealed that volunteering produced diverse and complex learning processes. Many of them can be regarded as the acquisition of competencies and might not be seen as transformative. Despite this, non-transformative learning is often connected to—or provides impulses for—transformative learning. This was, for example, the case for one volunteer who herself had experience of migration. Thanks to her volunteering, she discovered that it was possible to earn a living as a social worker in Austria. As a result, she decided to study social work. In this case, the volunteering experience was important to her, and was interrelated with her experience of being a refugee. Through volunteering, she first gained the knowledge that this work was a good fit for her, and then it became her possible profession here (unlike in her home country where one could not earn money as a social worker). This example shows that the knowledge that social work is an approved and paid job in Austria—together with her volunteering experiences—triggered a transformation in her perspectives.

Implications for Civic Learning

Our empirical study took place in the field of civic engagement around the topics of flight, migration, and belonging. We were especially interested in the civic learning of 'active citizens' (Ross, 2012), the development of democratic agency, and the processes of political subjectification. As we know from research on social movements (Duguid et al., 2013; Trumann, 2013) and on volunteering (Düx et al., 2009), people acquire diverse civic competencies through their engagement, and also transformative learning can take place. We identified the desire and also several concrete attempts—by volunteers—to change the existing political order in terms of migration, asylum, and integration policy, which they perceived as deeply inhuman and unfair. It was in the process of engagement for refugees that they developed a more differentiated and critical understanding of how integration is predominantly defined in Austrian society. Apart from a change in attitude and awareness, some volunteers also adapted their actions accordingly—at this point, it should be mentioned that learning took place not just individually, but also in collective ways together with other volunteers (Sprung et al., 2017). To give just one example, people who had started their engagement by providing individual support for refugees, gradually extended their agency towards activities aimed at changing existing structures—through protest activities or by organizing public events—to raise awareness of the situation of refugees and to fight racism by addressing a broader public. These activities were mainly developed in group settings.

Active citizenship can lead to transformative learning, but this is not automatic. Apart from the predominantly informal mode of learning, some volunteers also had the opportunity to attend educational programs, and thus to reflect on their activities while guided by professionals (e.g., in the form of coordinated meetings, supervisions, or non-formal educational courses). These volunteers tended to deliberate more on their convictions and actions (Kukovetz & Sprung, 2020, p. 69). We conclude that adult education can contribute to political subjectivation (Biesta, 2014) by accompanying an ongoing democratic engagement of citizens and by opening up spaces for critical reflection and pertinent learning processes. We assume that these spaces and opportunities can neither be 'designed' in advance, nor are the outcomes predictable. Civic learning within the horizons described should instead work with open and experimental approaches to enable self-directed ways of possible transformative learning.

We have seen that civic engagement in solidarity with refugees includes many learning processes, triggered by disorientating dilemmas, that have transformative impacts on the individual volunteers, and that can be categorized as civic learning corresponding to the subjectification conception of civic learning by Gert Biesta (2014). Learning concerns, for instance, reflecting one's own social position, adapting the volunteers' services for and their relations with refugees, developing a critical understanding of political contexts and the hegemonial concept of 'integration' and involvement in political and awareness-raising activities. Thus, civic engagement does not only mean to act in solidarity, but also to reflect and to learn how solidarity—as one basic value of democracies (e.g., Haarmann et al., 2020, p. 1)—can be lived, which socio-political conditions are relevant, and how the individual person is affected by this form of civic engagement.

Notes

1 The research project "'Learning solidarity': The potential of volunteering for civic education in migration societies" (3/2018–12/2019) was carried out by the Institute of Educational Sciences of the University of Graz, in cooperation with the Institute of Philosophy of the University of Graz, the Institute of Social Work of the University of Applied Sciences Joanneum, Volkshilfe Steiermark and the Department of Education and Integration of the City of Graz. The project was funded by the Federal State of Styria and the City of Graz.
2 Originally, all quotes were in German. They have been translated into English for this chapter.

References

Altenburg, F., Faustmann, A., & Czaika, M. (Eds.). (2019). *Migration & Integration 7: Dialog zwischen Politik, Wissenschaft und Praxis*. Edition Donau-Universität Krems.
Biesta, G. (2014). Learning in public places. Civic learning for the twenty-first century. In G. Biesta, M. De Bie, & D. Wildemeersch (Eds.), *Civic Learning, Democratic Citizenship and the Public Sphere* (pp. 1–11). Springer.
Duguid, F., Mündel, C., & Schugurensky, D. (2013). *Volunteer Work, Informal Learning and Social Action*. Sense Publishers.
Düx, W., Prein, G., Sass, E., & Tully, C. (2009). *Kompetenzerwerb im freiwilligen Engagement*. Springer VS.
Eschenbacher, S. (2020). Transformative learning theory and migration: Having transformative and edifying conversations. *European Journal for Research on the Education and Learning of Adults*, 11(3), 367–381.
EU Open Data Portal. (2019). Asylum and first time asylum applicants—annual aggregated data (rounded) [TPS00191]. Eurostat. https://data.europa.eu/euodp/en/data/dataset/qXxvM2WbUmPxz8GTwOcuQ.
Fuhr, T., Laros, A., & Taylor, E. W. (2017a). Afterword. Transformative learning meets Bildung. In A. Laros, T. Fuhr, & E. W. Taylor (Eds.), *Transformative Learning Meets Bildung: An International Exchange* (pp. 364–384). Sense Publishers.
Fuhr, T., Laros, A., & Taylor, E. W. (2017b). Transformative learning meets Bildung: Introduction. In A. Laros, T. Fuhr, & E. W. Taylor (Eds.), *Transformative Learning Meets Bildung: An International Exchange* (pp. ix–xvi). Sense Publishers.
Haarmann, M. P., Kenner, S., & Lange, D. (2020). Demokratie, Demokratieiserung und das Demokratische. Aufgaben und Zugänge der Politischen Bildung. Eine Hinführung. In M. P. Haarmann, S. Kenner, & D. Lange (Eds.), *Demokratie, Demokratisierung und das Demokratische. Aufgaben und Zugänge der Politischen Bildung* (pp. 1–6). Springer VS.
Hamann, U., Karakayali, S., Wallis, M., & Höfler, L. J. (2016). *Koordinationsmodelle und Herausforderungen ehrenamtlicher Flüchtlingshilfe in den Kommunen*. Bertelsmann Stiftung. https://www.bertelsmann-stiftung.de/fileadmin/files/BSt/Publikationen/GrauePublikationen/Koordinationsmodelle_und_Herausforderungen_ehrenamtlicher_Fluechtlingshilfe_in_den_Kommunen.pdf [01. 04. 2019].
Hoggan, C. (2016a). A typology of transformation: Reviewing the transformative learning literature. *Studies in the Education of Adults*, 48(1), 65–82.
Hoggan, C. (2016b). Transformative learning as a metatheory: Definition, criteria, and typology. *Adult Education Quarterly*, 66(1), 57–75.
Illeris, K. (2017). Transformative learning as change and development of identity. In A. Laros, T. Fuhr, & E. W. Taylor (Eds.), *Transformative Learning Meets Bildung: An International Exchange* (pp. 179–190). Sense Publishers.

Institut für Demoskopie Allensbach. (2017). *Engagement in der Flüchtlingshilfe. Ergebnisbericht einer Untersuchung des Instituts für Demoskopie Allensbach*. Berlin. https://www.bmfsfj.de/blob/122010/d35ec9bf4a940ea49283485db4625aaf/engagement-in-der-flue chlingshilfe-data.pdf [9. 1. 2019].

Klika, D. (2018). Bildung und Emotion. Historisch-systematische Zugänge. In M. Huber & S. Krause (Eds.), *Bildung und Emotion* (pp. 75–89). Springer VS.

Kloubert, T., & Dickerhoff, I. (2020). Learning democracy in a new society: German orientation courses for migrants through the lens of Buber's dialogical education. *European Journal for Research on the Education and Learning of Adults*, 11(3), 275–291.

Koller, H.-C. (2012). *Bildung anders denken. Einführung in die Theorie transformatorischer Bildungsprozesse*. Kohlhammer.

Kukovetz, B., & Sprung, A. (2019). Questioning power relations: Learning processes through solidarity with refugees. In F. Finnegan & B. Grummell (Eds.), *Power and Possibility: Adult Education in a Diverse and Complex World* (pp. 131–142). Brill Sense.

Kukovetz, B., & Sprung, A. (2020). *Solidarität lernen (?) Das Potenzial freiwilligen Engagements für politische Bildungsprozesse in Migrationsgesellschaften*. Forschungsbericht. Graz.

Kukovetz, B., Moser, E., Sprung, A., Stelzer, H., & Stuart, A. (2019). Zwischen Solidarität und Paternalismus. Das Potenzial freiwilligen Engagements für eine kritische Bildungspraxis. *Schulheft*, 176, 22–32.

Mejuni, O. (2017). Sustaining collective transformative learning: Informal learning and revision. In A. Laros, T. Fuhr, & E. W. Taylor (Eds.), *Transformative Learning Meets Bildung: An International Exchange* (pp. 205–216). Sense Publishers.

Mezirow, J. (1997[1991]). *Transformative Erwachsenenbildung*. Schneider-Verlag.

Öztürk, H. (2014). *Migration und Erwachsenenbildung*. W. Bertelsmann Verlag.

Ross, A. (2012). Education for active citizenship: Practices, policies, promises. *International Journal of Progressive Education*, 8(3), 7–14.

Said, E. (1991). *Orientalism*. Penguin Books.

Schmidtke, B. (2020). *Bildungs- und Berufsberatung in der Migrationsgesellschaft. Pädagogische Perspektiven auf Beratung zur Anerkennung im Ausland erworbener Qualifikationen*. transcript Verlag.

Sievers, I., & Grawan, F. (Eds.). (2017). *Fluchtmigration, gesellschaftliche Teilhabe und Bildung*. Brandes & Apsel.

Sprung, A., & Kukovetz, B. (2018). Refugees welcome? Active Citizenship und politische Bildungsprozesse durch freiwilliges Engagement . *Zeitschrift für Weiterbildungsforschung*, 41 (2), 227–240.

Sprung, A., Kukovetz, B., & Tinauer, R. (2017). Solidarität' und informelle Bildungsprozesse Freiwilliger im Kontext der aktuellen Fluchtbewegungen nach Österreich. In L. Karasz (Ed.), *Migration und die Macht der Forschung. Kritische Wissenschaft in der Migrationsgesellschaft* (pp. 179–192). ÖGB Verlag.

Statistik Austria. (2020). Asylanträge 2000–2019. https://www.statistik.at/web_de/statistiken/m enschen_und_gesellschaft/bevoelkerung/wanderungen/asyl/022914.html [16. 12. 2020].

Strauss, A. L., & Corbin, J. (1996). *Grounded Theory: Grundlagen qualitativer Sozialforschung*. Beltz.

Trumann, J. (2013). *Lernen in Bewegung(en)*. Transcript.

West, L. (2017). Love actually: Transformative learning meets Bildung, and the psychosocial concept of recognition. In A. Laros, T. Fuhr, & E. W. Taylor (Eds.), *Transformative Learning Meets Bildung: An International Exchange* (pp. 217–232). Sense Publishers.

12

LEARNING BEYOND THE OBVIOUS

Holocaust Education, Historical Education, and Remembrance in a Plural Society

Elisabeth Beck

Migration is a human form of action that has existed throughout all history. It has always initiated and promoted social changes and innovations and fostered the sharing, mixing, and (ex)changing of languages, knowledge, experiences, and views (Mecheril, 2016b; Mecheril, 2010). Similarly, biographies, stories, memories, and narratives migrate(d); they were and are on the move. Not only is migration as a phenomenon a matter of fact in a globalized world; so also is the plurality of (migration) stories, histories, and memories due to various backgrounds, experiences, and origins. They are part of the plural world in which we live. At the same time, diversity and difference in memory are considered challenging, as they confront specific images of belonging and identity, defined (solely) through nationality and (re-)produced mainly through (national) remembrance. Through migration, the imagination of (national) homogeneity, due to one common history that provides orientation and identification, is called into question. It provokes the myth of a unitary vision of national history and questions and confronts assumed entities of nation, memory, and identity. Hence, explicit references to origin, 'one' common history, and belonging do not (or not any longer) reflect the reality of diverse memories of different individuals and groups. Thus, migration as an articulation of changing societies is continuously presented as a challenge for remembrance and, therefore, historical education.

Society has changed and still changes—besides various transformation processes—inter alia because of ongoing migration processes. The given diversity expands the "space of remembrance" (Terkessidis, 2019, p. 176). Furthermore, globalization processes open up exchange possibilities of histories and stories, experiences, and approaches. In Terkessidis' conception, the diversity of people and society results in different *spaces of remembrance*, which arise, develop, also merge, and yet do not always coexist harmoniously. Taking a closer look at a highly institutionalized 'memory culture,' which, of course, also changes because of

DOI: 10.4324/9781003124412-15

migration and the resulting diversity of society, Terkessidis asks: "Whose memory counts? What is remembered? How is it remembered? And why?" (Terkessidis, 2019, p. 175) It is essential to ask these questions in a globalized world, where ideas, goods, capital, knowledge, and histories, with humans, also migrate. Firstly, it is essential in order to understand the phenomenon of plural migration societies, to which, of course, also the multiplicity of memories belong; and secondly, to discover responses to the simultaneity of shared, divided, marginalized, conflicting, and even forgotten memories of individuals, groups, and collectives. The diversity of society is, of course, reflected in the plurality of references to history. The so-perceived challenging diversification of memories can be seen not exclusively, but especially in Germany, where the remembrance of the National Socialist (Nazi) history is strongly linked to 'the German' identity and self-conception (see Theile, 2009, p. 8). The recognition of diversity allows to point to the fact that alongside the primary memory of National Socialism and the Holocaust as the *caesura*, the "rupture of civilization" (Diner, 1998), other stories, histories, narratives, and memories are likewise valuable and essential, and belong to a memory culture of a plural society. Diversity in memory, however, is not only addressed in memory culture and (memory) politics, but also in education. The educational context offers a wide space to learn, negotiate, and remember these different stories, histories, narratives, and memories.

Focusing on the interface of migration, remembrance, and education, the purpose of this chapter is: (1) to point out the relevance of remembrance and 'memory culture' in a plural society by using the example of the Holocaust, (2) to explore educational approaches in historical education in the context of migration and its transformative potential, and (3) to identify possibilities of how adult education based on 'the' past, especially the Holocaust, can be enriched by also taking into account different (migrant) stories, histories, and memories. All the mentioned considerations are embedded in the basic assumption that migration is a matter of fact, as it has "led to an empirically measurable changed, pluralized composition of societies" (Foroutan et al., 2018, p. 11). The aim of this contribution is to investigate a picture of adult education about the past in a contemporary plural society that takes people's heterogeneity—not only regarding their members' origin but also age, gender, sexuality, and religion—into account and is 'beyond the obvious.' This means an (historical) education for and with migrants that directs not exclusively toward teaching language and professional skills with the aim of social or job 'integration,'[1] but also opens spaces and possibilities to deliberate a multiplicity of (historical) perspectives, which reach beyond a national-state defined remembrance, belonging, and identity.

Commemoration, Memory Culture, and Holocaust Remembrance in a Plural Society

Both individual and collective memory (Halbwachs, 1985/1925) are essential for forming, constructing, and further developing an identity. For Halbwachs, remembrance is always simultaneously individual and social, because—following

Assmann—every 'me' is connected to a 'we.' This 'we' is not an entity, but is multi-leveled and marks partly intertwined, disparate, and juxtaposed horizons of reference. Hence, multiple belongings to different groups with divergent memories are possible. Memories, as well as identities, are (re-)constructed within these groups (see Assmann, 2008); collective memories are historically developed and serve the purpose of visualizing the group's past in order to construct membership and belonging. In this conception, the relation between memory and identity is highly intertwined; it is circular: Memory strengthens both an individual and group identity and vice versa. Nevertheless, the concept of identity remains imaginary (Terkessidis, 2019, p. 184), fed by the belief in an imagined national-collective that results from telling and sharing 'one' national history (see Lücke, 2016, p. 357). The strong interconnectedness of memory, nation, and identity is thus increasingly called into question in a globalized world.

When considering memory and remembrance, it can be seen that public and official, but also personal, remembrance is related to a national-state oriented history. Therefore, there are numerous memory cultures in different nation-states focusing on different stories and narratives in order to create cohesion, social integration, and identification (see, for example, Smith, 1991). The National-Socialist past, which affected significant parts of the world, plays an especially central role in Germany. The Nazi-past, with its scale and extensive effects, is considered *the* master narrative of German identity. It is the often-stated perpetual task of Germans[2] to take responsibility for the past and defend the high value of humanity and human rights (see, for example, Maas, 2018). Of course, a multitude of stories, memories, and histories, which are not or just remotely related to National Socialism and the Holocaust, are remembered individually and collectively by various people and groups. Nevertheless, within a highly institutionalized cultural memory[3], (only) specific stories and histories are remembered. Public and private, individual and collective memory (see Halbwachs, 1967, 1985/1925) are always specifically linked to or expressed within a so-called 'memory culture' (see, for example, Assmann, 2006; for an overview see further, for example, Wagoner, 2017; Tota & Hagen, 2016; Erll & Nünning, 2010). Memory culture means a "loose collective term for the totality of the not specifically scientific use of history in public" (Hockerts, 2001, p. 16); it can be described as a "general term for all possible forms of intentional remembrance of historical events, personalities and processes" (Cornelißen, 2012). Memory culture(s)—as they can be defined in a broad sense—are diverse; they are constantly (re-)constructed and (re-)produced by certain societies or groups. Consequently, not only an institutionalized memory culture, but also the formation of memory, is dynamic and processual. Thereby the remembered stories serve a particular purpose: only these stories and histories are remembered, which can (be) connect(ed) to a current frame of reference (Hein, 2009, p. 53) and a particular self-image of the respective society. Accordingly, 'the' past is constructed from the present, and references to 'the' past are changeable and dependent on current interests (pp. 53–54). This is why there are various constructed and negotiated pasts, and why there are different cultures of memory, which can overlap but also contradict each other in their approaches to the past(s). The representation forms of different past(s) become increasingly complex due to numerous players from politics, media, science, and of course, civil society in general; everyone—consciously or unconsciously, directly or indirectly—is involved in (re-)constructing past(s) and their remembrance, by telling specific stories and leaving others out.

Alongside national references in remembering past(s), transnational historiography and forms of memory are becoming increasingly important (Sznaider, 2016). Levy and Sznaider (2006) analyzed the different forms of collective memories in the age of globalization. They developed the concept of 'cosmopolitan memory' to explain the transition from national to cosmopolitan memory cultures, using the example of the Holocaust. This example is intentionally chosen, as the Holocaust "is not considered as a German–Jewish tragedy but as a tragedy of reason or of modernity itself" (Levy & Sznaider, 2002, p. 88). They "suggest that shared memories of the Holocaust … provide the foundations for a new cosmopolitan memory, a memory transcending ethnic and national boundaries" (p. 88). As the concept of 'collective memory' is firmly connected to the nation-state, which "is in the process of slowly being cracked" (p. 88), the cosmopolitan memory concept seeks to make remembrance beyond national frames possible. Transnational memories become part of the national remembrance and, still, memories are rather transformed than erased due to processes of globalization. The combination of global and national narratives results in every memory culture in something different, in something new. Such changing—national and transnational—representations of 'the' past have fostered the emergence of cosmopolitan memories. Such memories are both the result of worldwide processes of globalization[4] and, at the same time, catalysts for further developments of a global and transnational identity. Such contemporary references to history are, of course, highly relevant in memory work and historical education.

Migration, Holocaust Education, and its Transformative Potential

As already mentioned, the Holocaust past is considered a prime example of a cosmopolitan memory. Consequently, it is the objective of the International Holocaust Remembrance Alliance to "strengthen, advance and promote Holocaust education, research and remembrance" (International Holocaust Remembrance Alliance (IHRA), 2018). The international organization's activities aim at "a world that remembers the Holocaust. A world without genocide." Holocaust *education* is the first goal the IHRA notes, embedded in an international context. This shows the overall importance, not only of globally remembering the Holocaust as an event in history, but also of teaching and learning about the atrocities and crimes committed against humanity. Thus, the aim is a historical-political learning, too, giving a democratic and ethical orientation for present and future action (Werker, 2016, p. 159). Remembrance and education are closely connected. It appears uncontroversial that learning lessons from history is an educational task; this demand for coping with the past through education can be described as the "pedagogization of remembrance" (Meseth, 2007, p. 97). Shortly after the end of the Second World War, pedagogical thinking and acting were considered a resource to solve social problems, to overcome the negative past, and develop an optimistic and democratic vision of the future after the Holocaust[5]. Therefore, dealing with past(s) in an educational setting is always linked to specific moral expectations regarding tolerance, openness, respect, and democratic values (compare critically Hartmann, 2020). At the same time, "education as an effective coping strategy" (Meseth, 2007, p. 116) faces the difficulty of contributing to the formation and development of certain and high moral values among (adult) learners, without overloading it with too many expectations. Therefore, historical and especially Holocaust education goes beyond merely remembering what took place over 75 years ago. Heyl (1997) distinguishes between forms of teaching and learning about the Holocaust. He differentiates between "education *after* Auschwitz" and "teaching *about* Auschwitz." While teaching *about* Auschwitz has the topic Holocaust, education *after* Auschwitz extends beyond the historical event. Education *after* Auschwitz was first formulated by the philosopher Theodor W. Adorno (1998/ 1969). In his famous essay, he clearly emphasizes the central importance of education in preventing atrocities in the present and future. He writes: "The premier demand upon all education is that Auschwitz not happen again. … Every debate about the ideals of education is trivial and inconsequential compared to this single ideal: never again Auschwitz" (Adorno, 1998/1969, p. 191). Due to this fundamental statement, Adorno's lecture is one of the main points of reference in German discourse on remembering and teaching about the Holocaust (Heyl, 1999, p. 4). This poses a great challenge and a wide expectation of historical education: both teaching the historical events, remembering the victims, and creating ethical imperatives for present and future.

Although Germany's memory culture is influenced by globalization and migration processes and associated manifold stories and narratives, the focus of remembering still lies on the Holocaust[6]. Attempts at drawing comparisons and analogies with other atrocities in history are often accused of shortening, narrowing, decontextualizing, and, consequently, instrumentalization and generalization (see, for example, Hartmann, 2020). There are educational approaches that open and offer space for finding access to history in the context of a plural society, in which individual, family, and collective references can be highly diverse. For example, the international organization and network *Facing History and Ourselves* "address[es] racism, antisemitism, and prejudice at pivotal moments in history" (Facing History and Ourselves, 2021). It promotes student reflection by dealing with historical events, choices made in the past, and their relevance and consequences for today's democracy, justice, and human rights, so that "students will be more deliberate and social in their own decision making" (Nelson, 2015, p. 116). Within their educational program, Facing History and Ourselves, the focus is not only on the Holocaust, but also on other forms of mass violence and genocide; for example, the Armenian and Cambodian genocides. This enables broadening perspectives and historical references by creating space for possible connections to and memories of these historical events; this implies accepting such connections as an expression of the multiplicity of (historical) experiences and stories in a migration society.

These connections do not apply exclusively to historical, but also to contemporary events. Considering the concept of genocide—which develops in both successive and simultaneous stages and processes (Stanton, 2021/1996)—it becomes clear that numerous contemporary conflicts in the world can, to various degrees, be described as genocide, (political) mass murder, ethnic cleansing, or genocide-like crimes (see Genocidewatch, 2021; for an overview see Bloxham & Moses, 2010). In the present-day world, where more than 80 million people have been forcibly displaced due to (civil) war, tyranny, and terror (The UN Refugee Agency (UNHCR), 2020), individual, family, and collective references to historical and current tragedies play a crucial role in remembrance and historical-political education. This facilitates the recognition and integration of various references to alternative historical and current events. In doing so, it seems reasonable to take the Holocaust as a cosmopolitan memory as a direct or indirect frame of reference,[7] in order to be able to understand and interpret historical and ongoing crises, developments, and events. The Holocaust can be perceived as a 'paradigmatic genocide' (International Holocaust Remembrance Alliance (IHRA), 2021), and in the context of dealing with it, a key concern in education is the question of addressing other genocidal events or crimes against humanity, which are perpetrated today. There are important reasons why it can be valuable to address the Holocaust and other genocides comparatively in order to offer further learning opportunities (2021): In analyzing historical events, attention is drawn to both similarities and differences as well as to historical singularities[8]. This can initiate and promote a deep dialogue of historical references and narratives on an equal footing.

Historical stories and narratives about the Holocaust that diverge from an assumed *master narrative* are still negotiated controversially and still considered problematical or at least challenging in education. A common notion is that—especially migrant—learners who do not at first glance have a family connection to the history of National Socialism have difficulty approaching the subject or are hostile to it (Gryglewski, 2020, p. 259). Even further, assumptions have been made that special attention must be paid to persons with a 'Muslim migration background,' as they were particularly susceptible to anti-Semitism and would bring it to Europe (Diekmann, 2018). Consequently, learners see themselves confronted with the assumption that migrant participants—or rather learners that are identified and marked as migrants—are an educational difficulty, or even a problem in teaching about 'the' past (Gryglewski, 2020, p. 260). Therefore, migrants are often addressed as a particular 'target group' with specific needs in historical learning[9]. However, one of the central aspects in dealing with historical-political education in a plural society is the temporal and generational distance between the historical event and today's learners (Hartmann, 2020, p. 244), and not the question of particular deviant or migrant memories and remembrance.

Certain approaches in education try to reach beyond the assumption that migrants lack democratic attitudes and require a specific pedagogy in order to get to know, adopt, and internalize a particular (German) way of remembrance (see, for example, Kloubert & Dickerhoff, 2020). Such assumptions are often unreflectively connected to a particular imagination of 'integration' in an assimilative sense (Beck & Gelardi, Chapter 3, this volume), and reproduce the notion of belonging and national membership through 'proper' remembrance, as can be seen from the example of Felix Klein, the anti-Semitism commissioner of the German federal government. He stated: "If you want to live successfully in Germany, you have to know our history—even if you personally have nothing to do with it. Knowledge of German history is important in order to integrate here and to understand our values" (Gillert, 2018). Here, questions of formal membership in a society become apparent in discussing who does and does not belong to an assumed 'us' and 'our' remembrance community; who does and does not share 'our' collective memory (Assmann, 2006; Halbwachs, 1985/1925). Such still existing assumptions of *one* remembrance community and collective memory evoke the question of a contemporary conceptualization of historical education in a plural society. These considerations are closely connected to the question of who do 'we' want to be, which image of 'ourselves' is reflected in what and how we remember, and in what way 'our' identity is affected by different narratives about 'the' past (see, for example, Czollek, 2018). Controversies and conflicts over ambivalent narratives also occur where a national self-perception is based on certain historical narratives and is then confronted with contradictions. This is impressively demonstrated, for example, in the debate between Poland and Israel (Yad Vashem) over the question of collaboration or complicity in Nazi crimes (Welle, 2018). The central issue here is the question of the interpretative authority over history (Ellmenreich, 2020) and whether an identity-forming Polish national narrative can be (legally) protected from contradictions, even though this might hide historical realities.

Globalization and migration processes contribute to make the *space of remembrance* more conflictual and contradictory. For example, the postcolonial perspective (see Beck & Gelardi, Chapter 3, this volume) is based on the assumption that there is more than just *one* past. As already mentioned, there are numerous past(s). The term 'past(s)' refers to an alternative perspective on historical events and assumes that there is not only one 'real' past or one history[10], but that—due to certain processes of knowledge production—different global and local past(s), stories, narratives, and histories are intertwined and remembered by various people and groups; sometimes in the same way and sometimes differently. This affects how historical (adult) education can be conceptualized in a plural society: Learners can relate to various accounts of past(s) and position themselves in different ways. Such positioning can be manifold, contradictory, and also conflictual. Therefore, (adult) education can foster questions and encourage discussions and self-reflection, instead of merely providing historical knowledge. Thus, it can teach learners not to uncritically adopt general and taken-for-granted assumptions about 'the' past (see, for example, Nelson 2015).[11] Historical-political education can then "be an emotionally difficult process that challenges core beliefs and assumptions" (Stevick & Gross, 2014, p. 67). In doing so, learners can confront and reflect on how they see the world they live in, and even themselves. Historical learning can then be transformative. Learners have the opportunity to construct and embrace "new and revised interpretations of the meaning of an experience in the world" (Taylor, 2008, p. 5), and likewise realize the potential for a significant change in their lives. They can draw attention to different and alternative historical narratives they did not know before; they change, extend, and develop their ways of observing 'the' past and begin to negotiate a broader perception of different past(s) of diverse groups and people. Additionally, they can explore that with telling a story and remembering a past a certain—educational, political, or social—purpose is connected. Education and learning can then be transformative and emancipatory when a space for encounter and dialogue is opened, in which appreciation and recognition for the learners themselves and their individual relations are expressed. This

> ... does not mean that every statement and every behavior should be accepted without comment. Especially in view of ... the responsibility for history, young people and adults must be clearly disagreed with when relativizing, anti-Semitic or racist statements are formulated.
>
> *(Gryglewski, 2020, p. 264)*

At the same time, it is necessary to identify if questions and remarks are formulated, for example, due to ideological beliefs or a historical lack of knowledge.

After all, peoples' (historical) socialization takes place in a specific geographical, social, and political framework. In general, adults have already—although under various circumstances—heard and learned about the Holocaust. They have adopted and developed certain assumptions, beliefs, habits of mind, stereotypes, images, and narratives about this part of history, not always depending on the knowledge about the historical event, but instead on the remembrance policy agenda of different nation-states. In adult education, which takes place in a migration society, it is necessary to take these existing frames of reference shaped by family, friends, teachers, peers, state, religion, and the so-called 'culture' into account and address them in discourse. Transformative learning processes are initiated by a 'disorienting dilemma' (Mezirow, 1978)[12] emerging from a "critical event in the subject's life" (Vinciguerra, 2017, p. 353). Being confronted with disturbing historical events, (civil) war, the Holocaust, mass murder, or genocide can be such a disorienting dilemma and reveal transformative potential. Then, once adult learning unfolds this transformative potential, the learners can develop into critical thinkers who are capable of becoming more liberated, autonomous, socially responsible, and critically reflective (Mezirow, 2000); they can change the way they experience the world and how they see themselves in relation to others and the world (Hoggan, 2016, pp. 77–78); they can prevent injustices and atrocities from happening again. Such learning processes can also result in a transformation of how one sees 'the' past and perceives a globalized world generally and a migration society in particular.

Learning Beyond the Obvious: Historical Education in the Migration Society

"We live in the age of migration" (Mecheril, 2016a, p. 105). It is a human phenomenon and reflects societal normality; at the same time, it shapes society (see, for example, Hansenjürgen, 2013). Unlike an *immigration* society, which means focusing only on one-time and one-directional movements from one national-state to another (Mecheril, 2016b, p. 13), a migration society is characterized by societal processes of change due to mobility. Thereby, migration can be perceived as an ambivalent phenomenon. On the one hand, society as a whole is changed by new lifestyles, biographies, languages, and narratives; migration restructures society and is, therefore, also the origin and motor for processes of transformation and modernization (Mecheril, 2010; Foroutan & Ikiz, 2016). On the other hand, migration also confirms and modifies the known and existing, in contrast to the construction of the 'other' (Broden & Mecheril, 2007, p. 7). Processes of *othering* occur (Said, 1999; Beck & Gelardi, Chapter 3, this volume). From a migration pedagogy approach, simple group-thinking distinguishing between migrant and non-migrant learners is problematized and questioned. Considering the diversity of memory in education, the *space of remembrance* can be extended for different narratives and past (s) that diverge from a conventional *master narrative,* which is limited to the (constructed) borders of a nation-state and nationality. Historical education embracing different historical experiences and references can open new horizons and new perspectives, including other stories. This can result in a transformation in perceiving 'the' past and can lead to the insight that an imagined 'our' past is the product of the passing on of particular stories, and the neglect, ignorance, and marginalization of 'other' stories (see, for example, Attia, 2015). Since migration and past(s) are permanently (re-) constructed and repeatedly interpreted through discourse,[13] they are changeable through the way we think and talk about them, also in education. Changing the way of addressing *one* assumed past and taking into account the processes of how knowledge about past(s) is produced, learning can unfold its transformative potential.

Learning in a migration society aims at transformation instead of skill acquisition (Mecheril, 2016b, p. 23). From a migration pedagogy approach, learning processes are initiated by crisis-related experiences and events that result in irritations of previous images of oneself and one's values. Thus, education can be described as transformative cultivation and differentiation of self-perception and world-perception (Koller, 2018). Thereby, learners can become critical, independent, autonomous, socially responsible, and reflective thinkers. They can negotiate which purposes serve specific past(s) in constructing 'our' past and 'our' identity. In doing so, 'nation-racial-culturally' (Mecheril, 2018, p. 121) coded orders of belonging and how these are negotiated through memory can be identified and questioned.

The objective is to reach beyond the reproduction of 'our' past and 'your' past, in order to foster the pluralization of memory and the visualization of connections between different past(s) (Attia, 2015, p. 76). Such a postcolonial perspective objects that alternative stories, experiences, knowledge systems, practices, or modes of action are marginalized or even made unthinkable in the prevailing colonial world view (Purtschert, 2017). To overcome narrow perceptions of 'one' past, in education learners are challenged with their experiences, knowledge, and narratives about the Holocaust and other nation-state-oriented interpretations of 'the' past. Holocaust education that extends the *space of remembrance* for various past(s) in a plural society can contribute to constructing and negotiating a more integral, more globalized, and more accessible approach to history. The intention of reaching beyond typical aims in education in the context of migration and 'integration'— that is, learning the language of a so-called 'receiving' country, forming usable vocational and professional skills, and finding a job – is fostering a more democratic and fairer society and world (Dirkx, 1998; McGregor, 2004).

After all, Holocaust education deals with universal and human rights; therefore, it is always connected to democratic ideals. Learners who are involved in historical-political education, experiencing that their opinions matter, and that they can make a difference between the 'is' and the 'ought,' can become reflective, responsible, and active citizens (Nelson, 2015, p. 118). In the sense of civic education, such learning experiences are what a strong democracy requires to prevent atrocities in the present and future. Unquestioningly, the history of Nazi crimes and the Holocaust in its singularity needs to be remembered. Besides this cosmopolitan memory including a master narrative, there is still place in the *space of remembrance* for other stories, narratives, and past(s); stories about the violation of human rights, genocide, ethnic cleansing, displacement, and forced migration, which all belong to a migration society in a globalized world.

Michael Rothberg has, therefore, introduced the concept of 'multidirectional memory' (2009) in order to enable an interdisciplinary and transnational analysis of memory (cultures). To overcome the model of collective memory and deconstruct the clear connection between memory and identity, Rothberg proposes a concept that shows ways of understanding the complex interplay between different past(s). He writes: "Against the framework that understands collective memory as competitive memory—as a zero-sum struggle over scarce resources—I suggest that we consider memory as multidirectional: as subject to ongoing negotiation, cross-referencing, and borrowing; as productive and not private" (Rothberg, 2009, p. 3). He describes the discursive space—within which memories are negotiated and articulated—as always containing "elements of alterity and memories of those whom we consider as 'other'" (Becker, 2016, p. 309). Rather than different victim groups competing for public predominance in the memory culture, he highlights with his concept the relations and interactions between different past(s) and "reveal[s] the familiarity of ostensibly disparate memories" (p. 309). Rothberg illustrates the global memory of the Holocaust as something that does not hinder different victim narratives, but rather serves their articulation. In doing so, the references between different stories and past(s) can be drawn beyond a temporal and spatial location. This is what Rothberg calls 'multidirectional.' Different events that took place before the Holocaust, such as the Armenian Genocide, or after, such as the Rwandan Genocide, are remembered publicly; and at the same time, references are made between them. This allows both a remembrance of the Holocaust and, simultaneously, an appreciation of social references to different past(s).

Migration is a matter of fact; it is no special case, but rather a societal normality (Foroutan, 2015). Migration "can be studied and understood as phenomena in which new knowledge, experiences, languages, and even perspectives have been introduced into different social contexts, which have in turn been rearranged, modernized, and renovated" (Mecheril, 2018, p. 122). With humans, knowledge and also new perceptions and interpretations of the past have migrated and are still migrating. They contribute to the pluralization and globalization of memory. So, the existing plurality of society can be seen in the various references to history. Experiences, memories, stories, and narratives are highly diverse; they exist side by side and with one another, intertwined and yet separate. They can be shared and also conflicting. This is why plurality in remembrance and historical education is still perceived as a problem, first and foremost in Holocaust education, which deals with the historical event understood as a "generalized symbol of human suffering and moral evil" (Alexander, 2002, p. 6). Nevertheless, pluralization due to migration is reality, and the diverse society is normality, although there are continuing political and social debates and negotiations concerning the reality of migration (Foroutan, 2019, p. 73). In this context, at the interface of migration and historical education, it is crucial to discover a conceptualization of adult education concerning the various past(s) in a contemporary plural society. Such an adult education considers the heterogeneity of people regarding their backgrounds and experiences with discrimination, exclusion, and violation of human rights—currently or historically.

To find responses to the question of the conceptualization of contemporary historical-political education, in this contribution the relevance of remembrance and memory culture in a plural society was explored. Following this, educational approaches in historical education in the context of migration and its transformative potential could be identified. There the central relevance of education for promoting both: (1) knowledge about past violence, its causes, circumstances, dynamics, and consequences, and (2) skills, values, and attitudes in order to prevent future group-targeted violence, genocide, and atrocities were shown. Such a historical-political education preserves, fosters, and strengthens democratic and egalitarian values. Consequently, an idea could be formulated of how adult historical-political education could be enriched by including different (migrant) stories, histories, and past(s). Participation in teaching and learning about the past, taking the Holocaust and other identity-related past(s) into account, can foster the transformative potential of learning. Thereby, both individual and collective transformation, due to the broadening of relations to past(s) and the development of 'multidirectional memories,' can contribute to a social transformation aiming at a more plural, more open-minded, and fairer society, with critical and reflective thinkers or citizens.

Notes

1 Compare, for example, the critical examination of the concept of 'integration' in Foroutan (2015), Mecheril (2016b).
2 This responsibility—often unreflected—is linked to an image of national membership.
   The task of an enduring remembrance of the past often addresses only 'Germans' (see
   Lücke, 2016). In doing so, it is not always explicit who exactly is meant and addressed; thus,
   again, inclusion and exclusion processes of an imagined community become evident.
3 Jan Assmann describes "cultural memory" as "a collective term for all knowledge that
   controls action and experience in the specific interaction framework of a society and is
   intended to be repeatedly practiced and taught from generation to generation" (Assmann,
   1988, p. 9).
4 At the same time, however, stronger references to nation-states and nation-state thinking
   can be observed (Kraemer, 2018) which emerge as a social counter-reaction to a highly
   controversial pluralization of societies (see Foroutan, 2018, p. 269).
5 For example, as part of the reeducation policy of the Allies after the Second World War,
   German citizens were to be re-educated to become mature democrats. The goal was to
   change the attitude of the German people through education (see Meseth, 2007, p. 100;
   Friedenthal-Haase, 1988). At this point, it must be emphasized that different allied
   powers pursued distinct goals.
6 The school curriculum is a clear illustration of this logic, i.e., schoolbooks reflect contemporary history mostly from the perspective of Germans as the dominant group
   (Lässig, 2012), which leads to a strong emphasis on the Holocaust.
7 Using the Holocaust as a decontextualized icon or symbol, see critically Hartmann,
   2020; Bauer, 2011; Sznaider, 2008.
8 On the tensions between particularism and universalism in Holocaust remembrance, see
   Sznaider, 2008.
9 On the question of target group orientation in adult (migrant) education in the field of
   Holocaust education, see Meilhammer & Matthes, 2020, pp. 206–207.
10 For the interwoven histories of colonialism and the Holocaust, see Castro Varela &
   Dhawan, 2020 or Klävers, 2019.
11 Georgi (2003) describes in her study "Borrowed Memory" (German: "*Entliehene Erinnerung*"), however, that for students with a migration background in Germany, dealing
   with the National-Socialist past is a core topic in the negotiation of identity and
   belonging in the German immigration society. She describes that dealing with the past is
   considered a kind of "entrance ticket" into the so-called 'majority' society. Thus, if
   belonging is negotiated through memory, there is little space for finding 'own' answers
   and going beyond existing interpretations of history.
12 In Mezirow's conception, a disorienting dilemma, a construct highly influenced by
   Freire (1970), represents the first phase or step in a learning process.
13 Discourse means the dynamic and constant production of information about a certain
   issue (Mecheril, 2016b, p. 10). Hence, a subject of discussion—for example, migration,
   'the' migrant, past(s)—emerges within the discourse and, at the same time, forms it.
   Knowledge generated by discourse creates social reality (Mecheril, 2018).

References

Adorno, T. W. (1998/1969). Education after Auschwitz. In T. W. Adorno (Ed.), *Critical Models: Interventions and Catchwords* (pp. 191–204). Columbia University Press.

Alexander, J. C. (2002). On the social construction of moral universals: The `Holocaust' from war crime to trauma drama. *European Journal of Social Theory*, 5(1), 5–85.

Assmann, A. (2006). *Der lange Schatten der Vergangenheit. Erinnerungskultur und Geschichtspolitik*. Beck.

Assmann, A. (2008). Gedächtnis-Formen. https://www.bpb.de/geschichte/zeitgeschichte/geschichte-und-erinnerung/39786/gedaechtnisformen.

Assmann, J. (1988). Kollektives Gedächtnis und kulturelle Identität. In J. Assmann & T. Hölscher (Eds.), *Kultur und Gedächtnis* (pp. 9–19). Suhrkamp

Attia, I. (2015). Geteilte Erinnerungen. Global- und beziehungsgeschichtliche Perspektiven auf Erinnerungspolitik. In I. Attia, S. Köbsell, & N. Prasad (Eds.), *Dominanzkultur reloaded. Neue Texte zu gesellschaftlichen Machtverhältnissen und ihren Wechselwirkungen* (pp. 75–88). transcript.

Bauer, Y. (2011). Reflektionen über den Holocaust: Das Verhältnis von Text und Kontext. *Der Holocaust und wir.* https://www.yadvashem.org/de/education/newsletter/1/bauer.html.

Becker, B. (2016). Review of Rothberg, Michael. Multidirectional memory: Remembering the Holocaust in the age of decolonization. *Kritikon Litterarum*, 43(3–4),308–313.

Bloxham, D., & Moses, A. D. (Eds.). (2010). *The Oxford Handbook of Genocide Studies.* Oxford University Press.

Broden, A., & Mecheril, P. (2007). Migrationsgesellschaftliche Re-Präsentationen. Eine Einführung. In A. Broden & P. Mecheril (Eds.), *Re-Präsentationen. Dynamiken der Migrationsgesellschaft* (pp. 7–28). IDA-NRW.

Castro Varela, M. d. M., & Dhawan, N. (2020). *Postkoloniale Theorie: Eine kritische Einführung* (3rd ed.). transcript.

Cornelißen, C. (2012). Erinnerungskulturen. https://docupedia.de/zg/Erinnerungskulturen_Version_2.0_Christoph_Corneli%C3%9Fen#cite_ref-2.

Czollek, M. (2018). *Desintegriert euch!*Carl Hanser Verlag.

Diekmann, K. (2018). Zum Holocaust-Gedenktag. Wir Täter schulden es den Toten. *Der Tagesspiegel.* https://www.tagesspiegel.de/meinung/zum-holocaust-gedenktag-wir-taeter-schulden-es-den-toten/20898480.html.

Diner, D. (Ed.). (1998). *Zivilisationsbruch: Denken nach Auschwitz.* Fischer.

Dirkx, J. M. (1998). Transformative learning theory in the practice of adult education: An overview. *PAACE Journal of Lifelong Learning*, 7, 1–14.

Ellmenreich, M. (2020). Es geht um "die Herrschaft über die richtige Geschichtserzählung."https://www.deutschlandfunk.de/streit-zwischen-russland-und-polen-es-geht-um-die.691.de.html?dram:article_id=468490.

Erll, A., & Nünning, A. (Eds.). (2010). *Cultural Memory Studies: An International and Interdisciplinary Handbook.* de Gruyter.

Facing History and Ourselves. (2021). About us. https://www.facinghistory.org/about-us.

Foroutan, N. (2015). Brauchen wir den Integrationsbegriff noch?https://www.bpb.de/gesellschaft/migration/kurzdossiers/205196/brauchen-wir-den-integrationsbegriff-noch.

Foroutan, N. (2018). Was will eine postmigrantische Gesllschaftsanalyse? In N. Foroutan, J. Karakayali, & R. Spielhaus (Eds.), *Postmigrantische Perspektiven. Ordnungssysteme, Repräsentationen, Kritik* (pp. 269–299). Campus Verlag.

Foroutan, N. (2019). *Die postmigrantische Gesellschaft: Ein Versprechen der pluralen Demokratie.* transcript.

Foroutan, N., & Ikiz, D. (2016). Migrationsgesellschaft. In P. Mecheril (Ed.), *Handbuch Migrationspädagogik* (pp. 138–151). Beltz.

Foroutan, N., Karakayali, J., & Spielhaus, R. (2018). Einleitung: Kritische Wissensproduktion zur postmigrantischen Gesellschaft. In N. Foroutan, J. Karakayali, & R. Spielhaus (Eds.), *Postmigrantische Perspektiven. Ordnungssysteme, Repräsentationen, Kritik* (pp. 9–16). Campus Verlag.

Freire, P. (1970). *Pedagogy of the Oppressed.* Continuum.

Friedenthal-Haase, M. (1988). Britische Reeducation: Struktur und Aktualität eines Beispiels interkultureller Erwachsenenbildung. *Neue Sammlung*, 28(2), 221–230.

Genocidewatch. (2021). Our mission. https://www.genocidewatch.com/copy-of-our-mission-1.

Georgi, V. (2003). *Entliehene Erinnerung. Geschichtsbilder junger Migranten in Deutschland.* Hamburger Edition.

Gillert, S. (2018). Besuch in KZ-Gedenkstätten sollte für Schüler zur Pflicht werden. https://www.welt.de/politik/deutschland/article180991032/Antisemitismus-Besuch-in-KZ-Gedenkstaetten-sollte-Pflicht-werden.html.

Gryglewski, E. (2020): Didaktische Ansätze der Gedenkstättenarbeit in der diversen Gesellschaft. *Bildung und Erziehung,* 73(3), 259–272.

Halbwachs, M. (1967). *Das kollektive Gedächtnis.* Enke.

Halbwachs, M. (1985/1925). *Das Gedächtnis und seine sozialen Bedingungen.* Suhrkamp.

Hansenjürgen, B. (2013). *Demokratische Migrationsgesellschaft: Zusammenleben neu aushandeln.* https://www.bpb.de/apuz/156770/demokratische-migrationsgesellschaft-zusammenleben-neu-aushandeln?p=all.

Hartmann, D. (2020). Geschichte und Gegenwart, eine komplexe Beziehung. Jüdische Perspektiven und Verbindungslinien zur historischen Erfahrung der Shoah. *Bildung und Erziehung,* 73(3), 242–258.

Hein, D. (2009). *Erinnerungskulturen online: Angebote, Kommunikatoren und Nutzer von Websites zu Nationalsozialismus und Holocaust.* UVK.

Heyl, M. (1997). *Erziehung nach Auschwitz—Eine Bestandsaufnahme: Deutschland, Niederlande, Israel, USA.* Krämer.

Heyl, M. (1999). "Holocaust Education." Internationale Tendenzen im pädagogischen Umgang mit der Geschichte des Holocaust. *Schriftenreihe Probleme des Friedens. Band 1: Zivilisationsbruch Auschwitz, 1/1999.* Idsein, 27–43.

Hockerts, H.-G. (2001). Zugänge zur Zeitgeschichte: Primärerfahrung, Erinnerungskultur, Geschichtswissenschaft. Aus Politik und Zeitgeschichte B28. https://www.bpb.de/system/files/pdf/737XU4.pdf [21.01.2021].

Hoggan, C. D. (2016). A typology of transformation: Reviewing the transformative learning literature. *Studies in the Education of Adults,* 48(1), 65–82.

International Holocaust Remembrance Alliance (IHRA). (2018). A world that remembers the Holocaust. A world without genocide. https://www.holocaustremembrance.com/index.php/.

International Holocaust Remembrance Alliance (IHRA). (2021). The Holocaust and other genocides. https://www.holocaustremembrance.com/resources/educational-materials/holocaust-and-other-genocides.

Klävers, S. (2019). *Decolonizing Auschwitz? Komparativ-postkoloniale Ansätze in der Holocaustforschung.* de Gruyter.

Kloubert, T., & Dickerhoff, I. (2020). Learning democracy in a new society: German orientation courses for migrants through the lens of Buber's dialogical education. *European Journal for Research on the Education and Learning of Adults,* 11(3), 275–291.

Koller, H.-C. (2018). *Bildung anders denken. Einführung in die Theorie transformativer Bildungsprozesse* (2nd ed.). Kohlhammer.

Kraemer, K. (2018). Sehnsucht nach dem nationalen Container. Zur symbolischen Ökonomie des neuen Nationalismus in Europa. *Leviathan,* 46(2), 280–302.

Lässig, S. (2012). Repräsentationen des "Gegenwärtigen" im deutschen Schulbuch. *Aus Politik und Zeitgeschichte,* 62(1–3).

Levy, D., & Sznaider, N. (2002). Memory unbound. The Holocaust and the formation of cosmopolitan memory. *European Journal of Social Theory,* 5(1), 87–106.

Levy, D., & Sznaider, N. (2006). *The Holocaust and Memory in the Global Age.* Temple University Press.

Lücke, M. (2016). Erinnerungsarbeit. In P. Mechril (Ed.), *Handbuch Migrationspädagogik* (pp. 356–371). Beltz.

Maas, H. (2018). Zukunft braucht Erinnern. Ansprache vom Bundesminister des Auswärtigen am 20. https://www.stiftung-20-juli-1944.de/reden/zukunft-braucht-erinnern.

McGregor, C. (2004). Care(full) deliberation: A pedagogy for citizenship. *Journal of Transformative Education*, 2, 90–106.

Mecheril, P. (2010). Migrationspädagogik. Hinführung zu einer Perspektive. In P. Mecheril, M. d. M. Castro Varela, & İ. Dirim (Eds.), *Bachelor/Master Migrationspädagogik* (pp. 7–22). Beltz.

Mecheril, P. (2016a). Es bleibt anders. Kämpfe um die (Pädagogik der) Migrationsgesellschaft. In M. Ziese & C. Gritschke (Eds.), *Geflüchtete und kulturelle Bildung. Formate und Konzepte für ein neues Praxisfeld* (pp. 101–106). transcript.

Mecheril, P. (2016b). Migrationspädagogik: ein Projekt. In P. Mecheril (Ed.), *Handbuch Migrationspädagogik* (pp. 8–30). Beltz.

Mecheril, P. (2018). Orders of belonging and education. Migration pedagogy as criticism. In D. Bachmann-Medick & J. Kugele (Eds.), *Migration: Changing Concepts, Critical Approaches* (pp. 121–138). de Gruyter.

Meilhammer, E., & Matthes, E. (2020). Holocaust Education in der Migrationsgesellschaft. *Bildung und Erziehung*, 73(3), 203–211.

Meseth, W. (2007). Die Pädagogisierung der Erinnerungskultur. Erziehungswissenschaftliche Beobachtungen eines bisher kaum beobachteten Phänomens. *Zeitschrift für Genozidforschung*, 2, 96–117.

Mezirow, J. (1978). Perspective transformation. *Adult Education Quarterly*, 28(2), 100–110.

Mezirow, J. (2000). Learning to think like an adult. In *Learning as Transformation: Critical Perspectives on a Theory in Progress* (pp. 3–33). Jossey-Bass.

Nelson, P. (2015). Facing the Holocaust and ourselves: The need to personalize the history of the Shoah. In E. Matthes & E. Meilhammer (Eds.), *Holocaust Education in the 21st Century* (pp. 116–123). Julius Klinkhardt.

Purtschert, P. (2017). Postkolonialismus und intellektuelle Dekolonisation. https://www.bpb.de/geschichte/zeitgeschichte/postkolonialismus-und-globalgeschichte/240817/intellektuelle-dekolonisation.

Rothberg, M. (2009). *Multidirectional Memory: Remembering the Holocaust in the Age of Decolonization*. Stanford University Press.

Said, E. (1999). Die Konstruktion des "Anderen". In C. Burgmer (Ed.), *Rassismus in der Diskussion* (pp. 27–44). Elefanten Press.

Smith, A. D. (1991). *National Identity*. Penguin Books.

Stanton, G. H. (2021/1996). The ten stages of genocide. https://www.genocidewatch.com/tenstages [17. 01. 2021].

Stevick, D., & Gross, Z. (2014). Research in Holocaust education: Emerging themes and directions. In K. Fracapane, M. Haß, & The Topography of Terror Foundation (Germany) (Eds.), *Holocaust Education in a Global Context* (pp. 59–76). The United Nations Educational, Scientific and Cultural Organization.

Sznaider, N. (2008). *Gedächtnisraum Europa: Die Visionen des europäischen Kosmopolitismus. Eine jüdische Perspektive*. transcript.

Sznaider, N. (2016). Gedächtnis im Zeitalter der Globalisierung. Prinzipien für eine neue Politik im 21. Jahrhundert. *Aus Politik und Zeitgeschichte*, 66(3–4), 10–15.

Taylor, E. W. (2008). Transformative learning theory. *New Directions for Adult and Continuing Education*, 119, 5–15.

Terkessidis, M. (2019). *Wessen Erinnerung zählt? Koloniale Vergangenheit und Rassismus heute*. Hoffmann und Campe.

Theile, E. E. (2009). *Erinnerungskultur und Erwachsenenbildung*. Wochenschau Verlag.

The UN Refugee Agency (UNHCR). (2020). UNHCR's refugee population statistics database. https://www.unhcr.org/refugee-statistics/.

Tota, A. L., & Hagen, T. (Eds.). (2016). *Routledge International Handbook of Memory Studies*. Routledge.

Vinciguerra, M. (2017). Narrating migration. The result of transformative learning. In A. Laros, T. Fuhr, & E. W. Taylor (Eds.), *Transformative Learning Meets Bildung. An International Exchange* (pp. 353–362). Sense Publishers.

Wagoner, B. (Ed.). (2017). *Handbook of Culture and Memory*. Oxford University Press.

Welle, D. (2018). Israel: Polen soll Geschichte des Holocaust aufarbeiten. https://p.dw.com/p/2vwmf.

Werker, B. (2016). *Gedenkstättenpädagogik im Zeitalter der Globalisierung. Forschung, Konzepte, Angebote*. Waxmann.

PART IV

Reflective Dialogues

13

WHERE IS HOME? MIGRATION, TRAUMA, AND ADULT EDUCATION

A Dialogue

Stefan Alexa and Linden West

Estragon: All the dead voices.
Vladimir: They all speak at once.
Estragon: Each one to itself...
Vladimir: What do they say?
Estragon: They talk about their lives.
Vladimir: To have lived is not enough for them.
Estragon: They have to talk about it.

(Beckett, 1982)

Our chapter is grounded in a developing dialogue and a quest. A quest as to where home is, one that can vary in importance at different times in our lives—some more poignantly and painfully than others. The question is pertinent for migrants, especially those forcibly displaced, longing for safety and a new home. The longing however cannot disguise the ambivalence inherent in loss and journey: remembering that what is left behind, even in extremis, was never all bad. It may once have been a place of beauty, solace, comfort, familiarity, and security; a home of books and family archives and reaching back generations. But it might now be destroyed or altered beyond recognition. Working through lost reality, and recognizing impossible longing, is part of the psychological work we must do. Questions of where is and was home, where and how new homes can be created, and on what terms, are fundamental to the quest, which might also have the deepest implications for adult education among migrants and their hosts.

Dialogue, a serious deepening dialogue, weaving shared understanding and mutual recognition, is hard won. This takes time—even a lifetime—to nurture and sustain; this requires a particular quality of space to encompass conflicting moods, confusion, longings to return, and the desire and resistance to progress. Dialogue

DOI: 10.4324/9781003124412-16

requires a transitional space, in the language of psychoanalyst Donald Winnicott (1971), where risks are taken with who we are, pauses are allowed, and authenticity becomes possible as heart, body, mind, and memory are exercised in building what Molly Andrews calls 'the narrative imagination' (2014).

This chapter is grounded in dialogue shaped by our two histories and present preoccupations. Our relationship and dialogue began in a doctoral program where Linden was supervisor, and Stefan a student. The process started with Stefan's questions about trauma in the life of someone dear to him, in Romania, where Stefan was born. They embraced Islamic fundamentalism. The question of "Why did they do this?" haunted him. Stefan was energized by Linden's research on the rise of various fundamentalisms—Islamic and fascist—in the city of Stoke-on-Trent in the English Midlands, where Linden was born; a place suffering from 'post-industrial' distress, like similar communities across the world (West, 2016). Linden's writing encouraged Stefan on a migratory journey into his own family and relational history: geographically located in a border country at the edge of an Empire—a place once constituting a multi-cultural tolerant space—but it is a space that degenerated into barbarity, murder, and denial in which families were implicated, not least his own. It is a space where communism succeeded Nazism, and forced smiles and clownish compliance became the norm. A place called Bukovina, divided nowadays between Romania and Ukraine. Boundaries shift—nothing stays the same in this part of Europe, including borders.

History Matters Greatly in Psychic Life

Stefan's imaginative journey into family archives and repressed memories of life and death affected Linden. There are traces of Linden's autobiography in our text, of a lost home and culture, and of migration over the contours of the English class system. However, much of the narrative is left aside for reasons of space. Linden's migration encompassed the rejection of home and a lifetime's struggle for self, identity, authenticity, narrative truth, and imaginative return (West, 1996; 2016; Formenti & West, 2018). Stefan's eclectic writing also inspired Linden in his work for dialogue and peace among Jews and Palestinians. The idea of trauma and of where home and healing lie infuse Stefan's history and the stories of many Jews and Palestinians too.

So, Linden will introduce his teaching and research among Israeli Jews and Palestinians as a backcloth to Stefan's quest for home and the truth of lives. Linden's work consisted of developing auto/biographical workshops and research within a European Union financed project to cultivate democratic values and active citizenship in Israeli teacher education (Bainbridge & West, in press). The project was haunted, however, by questions of trauma and injustice in a bitterly contested geographical and imagined place. The question of where home and security lie haunts Palestinians as well as Jews. In the stories, for instance, of someone we call Hanna, a Palestinian Christian, and Jewish Elie, whose family migrated from North Africa. They are partly fictional characters, composites of various stories told by a number of people. They are intended to convey narrative truth about the interplay of past, present, and future, the personal and political, in difficult migrations. The stories, and their novelistic quality, were stimulated by Stefan's imaginative doctoral writing, in particular his use of characters to represent aspects of his inner turmoil. His characters are called Arke and Aezra. Arke, as it were, never left Bukovina as Stefan and his immediate family migrated to the United Kingdom. Arke is a kind of playful and questioning part of the self who is determined to explore what is not said about family history, including death and violence. But he is no nomad and has stayed in one place. Aezra is the learned, nomadic self in search of depth, wisdom, and historical parallel. He is the traveler, the cosmopolitan, the sage who 'leads his people home.' They enter our dialogue to help create narrative truth crafted in a present context of Brexit and Covid-19, which disturbed Stefan's family tranquility in London.

The award-winning novelist Hilary Mantel (2020) has observed that fictional forms give access to history's unconscious. To moment-by-moment experience—as the tides of past and present ebb and flow—to what isn't on the record and never really could be in conventional history. It is not about fact, but plausibility. Our various characters traverse, in Raf Zreik's (2017) words, the folds of silence in individual and collective lives. Fictionalization (Clough, 2002; Fraser, 2017) evokes a playful and creative spirit when seeking to illuminate the complexity, nuance, and trauma of lives, and the quest for home. The chapter occupies a border country between fact and fiction, research and teaching, therapy and education, adult education and life stories. Part of our shared quest is for greater experimentation in a therapeutic, narrative, and dialogical form of adult education which can humanize the other as well as self—a place of synthesis of life stories, therapeutic process, and adult education. We eventually settle, imaginatively, in a space representing Stefan's Grandma's kitchen in the beautiful Bukovina where dialogue between past and present, an Israeli Jew and a Palestinian, and different dimensions of self and generations, is possible, even when it asks not less than everything.

When the Holocaust Met Al Nakba

Linden: Lebanese writer, Elias Khoury (2017) has written that the Jew and Palestinian can become mirror images of human suffering if they rid themselves of the delusion of exclusionist, nationalist ideology. The oppressed Jew in Nazi Europe is not simply the mirror image of the Palestinian, but of human suffering everywhere—just as the Palestinian represents the mirror image of the refugee tragedy being played in seas of suffering. The Jewish people suffered of course the catastrophe of the Holocaust, while Palestinians suffered their own trauma —Al Nakbah—in the forced displacement of the 1948 war, through to the present day. Our question was whether and if so, how, it becomes possible to recognize the other as traumatized and hurting too as a basis for some dialogue. How can dialogue and self/other recognition begin as part of a quest for peace and justice? What quality of space is needed for such work?

The Holocaust is often understood as a historically unique trauma, but this can silence the other's story of Al Nakba. Palestinian suffering, so a dominant Israeli argument proceeds, pales into insignificance in comparison. Moreover, Palestinians, Israelis often insist, left home voluntarily, on the instructions of Arab commanders. The State of Israel regards the 1948 War as an unambiguous triumph and the realization of a safe Homeland. But if Palestinian suffering continues, the Holocaust is not simply history either, but plays out, in a psychoanalytic perspective, as unresolved trauma over generations (Rose, 2017)—trauma that fuels Israel's colonialism and continuing oppression of Palestinians. The wounds on all sides are, in this sense, unhealed. 'Arabs,' in this colonialist narrative, live in shabby villages and towns as well as inhabiting misogynistic cultures. They are backward, anti-modern, undemocratic, Eastern, and deserving of their fate, unlike the relatively egalitarian 'us,' Jews in our shining modernist cities with gleaming apartments and glittering swimming pools. The cultural and psychological damage is ubiquitous.

Hanna and Elie—or the characters from whom they derive—participated in the project on cultivating democratic values and active citizenship. Auto/biographical narrative workshops and research were used to chronicle experiences of citizenship, but also family trauma, hurt, and insecurity. For Hanna, Palestinian and Christian, colonization encompasses a lost home, forced family migration, and the death of a grandmother, alongside feelings of continuing humiliation. For Israeli Jews, like Elie, the other (Hanna) is a potential terrorist. Elie's family migrated from North Africa, where they were made to feel unwelcome as Islamism, and before that pan-Arabism, reared their heads.

There were interviews and week-long workshops in Canterbury. A typical workshop involved up to 16 people with an opening round in which participants shared an object of biographical significance, like a photograph, poem, drawing, a piece of music, or even a fountain pen. There was a theoretical and methodological introduction to auto/biographical and narrative methods, with agreement reached over ground rules, and followed by a role play of a narrative interview in which one of us, as facilitators, told stories of learning to be a citizen while a colleague modelled good listening. The whole group discussed the experience, agreed upon the interview protocol, and moved into small deliberately diverse groups of four. Participants interviewed each other and then experimented with being interviewees, interviewers, and observers in turn. Over the course of a week, oral material was developed into written auto/biographical accounts of how they became citizens and/or politically conscious. Written accounts were produced individually and/or in small groups; everyone presented their writing, and we considered how such methods could be applied in the schools, colleges, and universities where they worked.

The work touched deep sensitivities, evoking frustration and anger among particular Palestinians. Ethically, the process was troubling, despite us laying down explicit ground rules of mutual respect, non-abusive behavior, of listening, equality, and the right to speak or stay silent. Themes of injustice, silencing, and the difficulty of raising issues in the wider group were drawn to our attention privately, as facilitators, by specific individuals. Power was asymmetrical, they said, and there could be negative implications back 'home' if they were seen as troublemakers. Israeli Jews held the power. The Israeli Jewish novelist, Amos Oz, likens the position of Palestinians and Israelis to two traumatized characters adrift on a piece of wood in a raging ocean (Hari, 2018). While both desire safety, each party wants the other to let go. However, one party has more power to decide who lets go. The Palestinians live within the State of Israel and have learned how to be silent or to adjust their stories under the gaze of power. One Palestinian we interviewed, later, outside the program, thought that we were asking Palestinians in the workshops to tell a story while the other, the Israeli Jew, held a metaphorical gun to their heads.

Hanna introduced herself, in Canterbury, as working in an Arab College of Higher Education near Nazareth. She was an active citizen, working in the field of cultural studies for the preservation of Palestinian history and culture. Later, outside the workshop, she talked about her family's forced migration, when the Jewish Hagenah (terrorists, in this perspective) came to their town of Haifa in 1948. Her family had lived and worked there for generations, including on the railways built by the British. Her immediate family now lives in Nazareth. She told of her family's desperate search for safety in 1948 and about relatives lost, homes seized, and communities abandoned. The family fled to Nazareth with other relatives who were escaping a nearby village, Saffuriyya, being 'ethnically cleansed.' "Surely, Jewish forces would not desecrate a place full of Christian churches, for fear of losing Western support?", Hanna's forebears asked. They were right. She talked too of present humiliations, with a relative living in Gaza not being allowed to finish her degree studies in Bethlehem. They were arrested by Israeli defense forces on the way back to Gaza: handcuffed, blindfolded, and left waiting for hours in ritual humiliation.

Hanna described her family's lost home in Haifa and concluded with a question:

> Do you know the novel by Ghassan Kanafani, *Returning to Haifa*? It's about a couple who did go back to their apartment. They arrived at their old home to find a Jewish Polish family living there. Who in fact had adopted a son they left behind? But they cannot communicate, any of them. There is a wall of silence.

Elie, an Israeli Jew, told a story of Jewish people in North Africa. Persecution, anti-Semitism, and poverty, combined with the 'Arab struggle' and later Islamist fundamentalism, provoked his family's exodus. But his father was a bully and there was abuse in the family home.

> He pretended to be nice, when others were there, but he was a bully to me, and bullied my mother. I hated him for it, I felt abused. I tremble now as I tell this story. Things were getting bad anyway and we eventually went by boat: when we landed in Israel, I felt so strongly that at last I was safe.

FIGURE 13.1 An abandoned Palestinian apartment in Haifa

Later, like everyone else, Elie was conscripted into the military, deployed to deal with 'terrorist infiltration.' He might have been the person responsible for the abuse of the young student from Gaza. But his military experience brought abuse of self again from sadistic authority figures, and Elie quit the military:

> I was instructed to beat up someone I knew. Not to hold back. That I needed to act like a psychopath. I tried. I put my fists to his face, like a boxer. I breathed deeply but began to tremble. It was not good. I couldn't hit him. He was much smaller than I was. Get out the Commander said, you are no use to us. This is not a f— kindergarten.

What difference might an experiment in dialogical adult education and research make? Can we really create open and in-depth forms of storytelling in which a shared 'narrative imagination' is possible for people like Hanna and Elie? Can this kind of narrative work offer sufficient glimpses of the other's humanity, and thus some degree of self/other recognition (in the language of critical theorist Axel Honneth (2007)), where the other learns to listen respectfully and is able to tell their story too? Hannah Arendt (2006), in her book *Eichmann in Jerusalem*, draws a distinction between evil acts and evil doers. There are far fewer of the latter. Israeli troops are not angels, but they are not all demons either. Maybe, if Hanna knew more of Elie's story, a dialogue of reciprocity and self/other recognition is possible. What do you think, Stefan?

Stefan: The cycle of victims and victimizers seems to continue relentlessly with trauma, traversing generations and geographies. A perpetual inflicting of suffering on the other, whose existence bothers us and always inhibits any unifying tendencies in encountering with the other. "The internalized aggression of persecutions that have not been worked through reappear as displaced aggression towards Palestinians" (Bar-On, 2008, p. 196), those who can easily be labelled terrorists. Within every one of us, there are biographies of others shaped by past aggression, violence, and trauma. Are we doomed to repeat the destructive cycles over again? Maybe that's too close to home for me—with a someone-very-dear-to-me seduced by fundamentalism and a family that has suffered violence, silencing, and repressed history.

I want to introduce that family, talk about a picture, and share an imaginary conversation that I have with my grandparents. It is partly an imaginary dialogue around a photo, which disappeared at some point from the family's photo albums; its loss bothered me. It signified a repressed story of a family at war, where some were seduced by the Nazi-inspired Iron Guard, and others, Jewish, were murdered. Arke, my Bukovinian self, says about the picture:

> It was showing women dressed in white, long clothes with what appeared to be some vertical faded lines... they were standing in front of a building's set of stairs; they were there to work... in 1941 at a 'labour camp' (Arbeitslager) at Bad Sulza... some of them returned, but others could not, they were moved to other camps and then... no one knows anything of their existence any more... I can sense bitterness and profound sadness in my grandma's voice and appearance... not sure what else she was thinking about, but she snapped at my grandpa when he tried to add that "it was what it was"... "Do you like your soup?" the question came briskly and without a chance for a reply and the photo was put back in the cupboard... Afterwards I had one more chance to take a closer look at it in the living room; grandma moved all her photos in the library cabinet and started to categorize them and cluster them in a more logical way, e.g. by events, family gatherings, trips etc. After seeing it once more and then asking my grandmother again about it, I had a strong feeling of unease, a growing void and struggle to understand what really happened during those years.
>
> *(Alexa, 2020)*

There is also an old photo hanging on the wall. It shows a world long gone, with my grandma in the middle and my great grandmother and great grandfather flanking her. I am here, 'home,' right now, and the picture is behind me in my grandma's room, which became my room for a short time after I finished my first degree. I am here, 'home'... this is what my head seems to say. Arke confirms this, he who never left 'my Bukovina.'

This picture (Figure 13.2) was taken twenty years ago when Bukovina joined Romania from the Habsburg Empire. My Grandmother, Lucia (Lutzi), is in the

FIGURE 13.2 Family photo taken during the Second World War (presumably around
            1939–1940) in my birth town, Suceava, in Bukovina

middle, and her two brothers, father, and my great grandmother, Rosa (born
Schley), are on the left. Suddenly, I feel that this on-the-border place is now only
of my imagination. This is still my birthplace, and so is the house I am in at
present. Beyond is the city of Suceava and the historical region of Bukovina, but
the way I look at them now is different—more from the perspective of memory.
It is fragmentary and broken, with missing elements. A silent and dusty whisper
fills the narrow high space of the room. It certainly starts to feel like home in the
first four days since our recent arrival from London, but for us being there was
difficult, emotional and unsettling, especially for my parents who weren't really
ready to have us in their space. It was unsettling for us, too, as a family. I see my
arrival 'home' as a journey to a land invested with projections and desires,
derived from fragmented memory. One should not mistake these for 'real facts,'
which can be 'touched' again (Eakin, 1992). But then, in a profound sense, they
are real too.

The account of my going-back-home is novelistic in style, of memory and about memory, where facts are blurred and fragmented, but equally important. Maybe unconscious, too, which demands a 'narrative imagination' to illuminate the obscurity of lives (Andrews, 2014) and to understand motives for 'going-back-home.' Maybe this is close to Freud's narrative truth—not to do with events per se, but when we seek to make meaning from them.

Grandma's Kitchen...

As a part of my doctorate (Alexa, 2020), I staged a 'fictional family gathering' in 'Grandma's Kitchen.' I grew up in it and witnessed its magic as people came to share stories, interact, cry, laugh, dream, remember or forget a past, and re-imagine a future. My 'Grandma's Kitchen' was a remarkable space, and now it only exists in memory. However, it has become a 'place' in which the 'narrative imagination' can develop. I am aware that Grandma's Kitchen is not simply a place of dialogue and positive things, but where the uncanny is manifest and past trauma haunts. It is a journey into an 'immediate irreality' (Blecher, 2015). Such 'kitchens' exist in many geographies and cultures, in borderlands, liminal spaces, from Stoke-on-Trent, to Suceava, to Haifa; however, one must 'beware of thresholds,' as Anatolian elders advise. They see "such a point of transition as the domain of the djinn, creatures made of smokeless fire, famous for their fickleness. ... in their unwritten culture" (Shafak, 2020, p. 198). A threshold is a domain of elusiveness, obscurity, precariousness, and danger (2020). It is not surprising that I felt compelled to invite into Grandma's Kitchen not only family members, but philosophers, and two prominent djinni from a Salman Rushdie book (2015): *Two Years, Eight Months and Twenty-Eight Nights*.

> The squeaking doors to the past felt so heavy; Arke's voice is the language of the past and memory, we are tormented by dust, we are squeaking from birth, oh my dear, don't you know that here on the border the past can only squeak in the present? Between six minutes to and six past midnight, you have about twelve minutes when memories squeak back in torment, bring unhealed pain, this is when the midnight voids squeak back in, this is a capsule of time on the border when dust happens, when dust comes back to life, when the voids of people and their actions and reactions reemerge into reality... I heard my mum saying, "it's almost midnight, do you want a cookie, it is homemade, a recipe you know from your great grandmother, Rosa". Rosa and Arke added in chorus: "Here is no torment, no nostalgia, and also no pain."
>
> (Alexa, 2020)

What seems certain is that along the way—in 'on-the-border' places—stories collide to create illusion, and a collective pretense or a struggle for truth and solidarity across geographies, time, and generations. They can reveal human interconnectedness—a 'common humanity' (Rushdie, 2012, p. 12)—coupled with awareness of the striking fragility of all migrations, the loss of home and the uncertainty of arrival.

Brexitland

2020 was a year of 'migration' for my family too. The lockdown since March, on top of worries over the post-Brexit realities of anti-intellectualism and antagonism towards multiculturalism—in parts of England—combined eerily to mirror the 1930s. It has drawn me to look back at 'people and books' (Paul Celan, in Manea, 2012) and old photos, and to read without apparent direction and purpose. I have feelings of insufficiently looking back, not reading enough, which have joined other daily anxieties.

I was shielding for my wife and eldest daughter—both are having respiratory problems. Spending time with my wife and daughters brought us closer and made us think about our families, and of the past and future in a Covid-dominated present. Surprisingly, the virus brought—beside danger—the opportunity to learn of ourselves, to remember and dream; and for me, there were unusual, troubling dreams to which I paid insufficient attention. Until one night, a dream made me feel frightened and grateful at the same time. Dreams are part of the 'narrative imagination.' In this dream, the picture on the wall came vividly to life. I was in the picture, while my grandma was being told off by her mother for using foul language during a photoshoot. My grandma thought this was only meant to relax and put smiles on everybody's faces. Her dad, two brothers, and her mum were unamused and found the joke vulgar and unnecessary. It was a reference to a 'bird' ('pasarica' in Romanian—this word is used by photographers who want to attract attention. The word also has sexual connotations, referring to female genitals). The whole metaphor is revolting. It was meant to be a serious photo-experience, guided by ancient Habsburg formality. Arke saw me and became cross because I was supporting and encouraging Grandma in her transgressive utterance. Suddenly, Grandma was old, wrinkled, severe and looked at me with fixed, serious blue eyes, as if saying "it is your fault... look, they are all gone... my brothers, my mum, my dad; they are upset because of you... and, what you are doing there, you have lost your senses. I am upset to see you like this, wake up and come 'home'..., it is not in the past, it is still here and waiting for you".

Arke recited the mantra: "the past is a foreign country; they do things differently there" (Hartley, 2015). Salman Rushdie, in his *Imagining Homelands*, reflects on the possibility of going home in relation to 'his India.' He concludes that "it's my present that is foreign, and that the past is home, albeit a lost home in a lost city in the mists of lost time" (Rushdie, 2012, p. 9). I feel differently to Rushdie and, surprisingly, from my old self, Arke. It seems that something has happened to me. A nomadic self has emerged, anchored in a continuous present without the possibility of pinning down a clear linear beginning or end. My journey back-home is surprisingly understood by Arke too, while Grandma appealed to my nomadic part to 'swim (back) home' (Baden... Heim), a reference to Aharon Applefeld's novel *Badenheim 1939* (1980).

This story of going-back-home must be told by a new character, capable of telling a tale of being lost in migration, and the confusing relationship between time past and present, trauma now and then. This second character is invested with Biblical qualities of a 'scribe leading his people home.' It is Ezra who becomes a scribe of daily experience of going-back-home, to a land on-the-border, to an 'imaginary home.' In a way, an imaginary home does not negate the reality of an 'original home,' but it is an expression of it in its absence. Hence, my narrator's name derives from the so-called 'alpha privative.' The prefix 'a' before vowels is used in Greek to express negation or absence. I have added the privative 'a' to an ancient Biblical name: A to Ezra, to name my nomadic self, Aezra. This is to emphasize the metaphysics of presence and absence. Arke and Aezra will team up—I hope—to express my story of going-back-home, my migration, my 'swimming (back) home' shaped by tensions between Heimlich and Unheimlich, between the homely and the uncanny, presence and absence, in an emerging narrative imagination.

Aezra says to my grandma and Arke: "Our journey, our ongoing pilgrimage" (Formenti & West, 2018) "can be towards life or death" (Alexa, 2020). Our journey is physical, mental, and temporal, toward an imagined space 'on-the-border,' where time is suspended in deep-crypts. "I would like to help illuminate your path(s) in different ways from Arke," says Aezra, "as now everything seems foreign, distant and uncomfortable. I will help you dive into your few air-deprived experiences, the borderlands between sanity and madness, history and now, filled with unexpected things." My car was filled in London with 'books and people'—full and heavy on the suspension, and the space between the tail-end and asphalt was only a few inches... We travelled surprisingly speedily towards Eastern Europe and to a small point on the map where 'people and books once lived...,' as the German-language poet of Bukovinian origin, Paul Celan (Manea, 2012), depicted.

Linden: I wonder if your home is found imaginatively in the old Habsburg empire? Or maybe in the 2nd World War and the fascist Iron Guard Legion of Archangel Michael? Maybe it's in Nicolae Ceausescu's Romania and the comic circus of Marxism-Leninism. Maybe really significant learning and adult education require a deep narrative imagination and the capacity to weave stories encompassing contested history and longed-for healing. Maybe the good enough story is an aesthetic achievement stimulated by old photographs and includes the uncanny, the inchoate, yet potentially meaningful. The ordinary can sometimes hide the unspeakable, the erased, the unheard (Solnit, 2017).

Stefan: Those words make me tremble. I am shaken by the realization that my encounter with 'home' is both ordinary and troubling, despite expectations of a dream-like perfect-fit, of a recovered essence and tranquility in migration. A shiver goes down my spine as I write these lines: where have so many people gone? When reflecting on my imaginary home, 'my Suceava,' 'my Bukovina,' you are right, I feel: 'home' is not just from my childhood experience in Ceausescu's communist Romania and the White Clown's communist circus, as the author and co-citizen Norman Manea (1993) frames it. But it is a way of life, too, and stories from long ago, during and long before World War Two. Grandma's tale of a lost cultural space, of harmony between peoples and ethnicities, where 'people and books' were invited to settle and participate in a diverse, democratic, and prosperous society, the will of a Habsburg emperor, Franz Joseph (Hirsch & Spitzer, 2011).

I was 'formed through the deformations' of the communist circus (Manea, 2012). Many of us were taught to be clowns and to repress sadness—through a display of hideous, fake smiles. Clowns willing to be beaten up and humiliated. Arke has these elements inside him, combined but 'sweetened' by the place on-the-border—the past 'sweet Bukovina.' He longs for a lost welcoming experiment in building a liberal multicultural society. But Arke witnessed the horrors of World War Two and still searches for 'lost ones': family members like Maria and Emma but Arke also embodies the sad smile of an Augustus, a type of clown (Manea, 1993) who learned to receive beatings from the grandiose Clown of communism.

The Iron Guard's Nazi ideology continued into the Communist era with false unifying narratives of homogeneity and rejection of the Other. Grandma's stories stayed alive as a kind of 'tribal' memory. The stories taught me how 'my Bukovina' was subject to an Empire, the Austrian-Hungarian (Bar-On, 2008, p. 195). Previous generations' exposure to empire as well as later darkness does not disappear at the cultural or psychic level. The loss of the good lingers, mixed with bad secrets in crypts that haunt (Abraham & Torok, 2005). I guess this is true for many migrants. Migrants searching for home, longing for home, and some resolution of past and present—a resolution that may be found in storytelling and witness, in some kind of psychological and cultural recognition and integration.

So where is home?

So where do these stories of seeking home lead us? Themes of insecurity, violence, death, silence, and silencing stand out. History leaves its mark: Coronavirus, Brexit, the Holocaust, the Palestinian exodus and colonialism, the Habsburg Empire, fascism and Communism. Many of the Hagenah fighters 'ethnically cleansing' Haifa were themselves traumatized victims of the Holocaust. Violent fathers haunt as can long dead grandmothers. Trauma travels unpredictably with migrants except we can eventually progress, if a little, in internal as well as relational narrative journeys. Life stories potentially represent royal roads to reconciliation in ourselves and others.

Storytelling demands good listeners and open hearts. Linden talks of auto/biographical narrative research and therapy, and of therapeutic education. Where stories are shared and the other is listened to, despite our own traumas, and common humanity is evoked. But working through trauma is hard, like the forced abandonment of precious homes. Someone else has taken over, someone who also tyrannizes here and now, and there is anger to feel and mourning to do. All of us need courage to speak truth spanning generations, grounded in humanity and social justice. If this can be done, however, we might create home in our hearts, minds, and bodies—a home where we distinguish between evil acts and the flawed humans perpetuating them.

Every home could have a kitchen like Grandma's, on a border between generations, history and the present, oppression and justice, and conscious and unconscious life. It can become a transitional space for an imaginative, thoughtful, therapeutic, narrative adult education: a threshold for care-full-ness, listening, and witness. A precarious but potentially beautiful space, where the other can migrate towards self and vice-versa. Perhaps, we require many more Grandma's Kitchens where people and characters—real and imagined—meet and eventually enrich the collective and individual 'narrative imagination.' This could be a place: 1) for Hanna to talk of lost apartments in Haifa and the abuse of a relative studying in Bethlehem; 2) where Elie could come alongside, apologize, and the two cry together; and 3) where Arke and Aezra are reconciled and psychic integration is possible. This is no space for power games or clowning, but for the experiment of imagining worlds through another's eyes. A multi-disciplinary space where therapists might work alongside adult educators, historians with novelists. A demanding place, on a border between truth and denial, learning and therapy, silence and voice, power and powerlessness, life and death.

References

Abraham, N., & Torok, M. (2005). *The Wolf Man's Magic Word: A Cryptonymy.* University of Minnesota Press. https://market.android.com/details?id=book-fBMu-EeV9ZIC.

Alexa, S. (2020). *Terrorism-affected Biographies Within Us: 'Terrorist Learning' as Pilgrimage Towards Death.* PhD. Canterbury Christ Church University. https://repository.canterbury.ac.uk/item/8qyyw/terrorism-affected-biographies-within-us-terrorist-learning-as-pilgrimage-towards-death (Accessed: 9 August 2020).

Andrews, M. (2014). *Narrative Imagination and Everyday Life.* OUP USA. https://market.android.com/details?id=book-RfVMAgAAQBAJ.

Appelfeld, A. (1980) *Badenheim 1939.* David R. Godine Publisher. https://play.google.com/store/books/details?id=TNXEZy7R8aUC.

Arendt, H. (2006). *Eichmann in Jerusalem: A Report on the Banality of Evil.* Penguin. https://play.google.com/store/books/details?id=yGoxZEdw36oC.

Bainbridge, A., & West, L. (in press). Conflict and the struggle for dialogue, learning and peace among Israeli and Palestinian Educators. In A. Bainbridge, L. Formenti, & L. West (Eds.), *An Ecology of Life and Learning.* Brill/Sense.

Bar-On, D. (2008). *The Others Within Us: Constructing Jewish-Israeli Identity.* Cambridge University Press. https://market.android.com/details?id=book-Oam2AH2hY8QC.

Beckett, S. (1982). *Waiting for Godot: A Tragicomedy in 2 Acts.* Grove Press. https://play.google.com/store/books/details?id=9ukKq4MTYosC.

Blecher, M. (2015) *Adventures in Immediate Irreality.* New Directions. https://market.android.com/details?id=book-liFrBgAAQBAJ.

Clough, P. (2002) *Narratives and Fictions in Educational Research.* Open University Press. https://market.android.com/details?id=book-eBMiAQAAIAAJ.

Eakin, P. J. (1992). *Touching the World: Reference in Autobiography.* Princeton University Press. https://market.android.com/details?id=book-_VPccnom34cC.

Formenti, L., & West, L. (2018). *Transforming Perspectives in Lifelong Learning and Adult Education: A Dialogue.* Springer International Publishing. https://market.android.com/details?id=book-D3JtuAEACAAJ.

Fraser, W. (2017). *Seeking Wisdom in Adult Teaching and Learning: An Autoethnographic Inquiry.* Springer. https://play.google.com/store/books/details?id=UTU7DwAAQBAJ.

Hari, J. (2018). A life in focus: Amos Oz, Israeli literary colossus and lifelong advocate of a two- state solution. *The Independent* Obituaries, 31st December.

Hartley, L. P. (2015). *The Go-between*. Penguin. https://play.google.com/store/books/deta ils?id=Z2ZaBgAAQBAJ.

Hirsch, M., & Spitzer, L. (2011). *Ghosts of Home: The Afterlife of Czernowitz in Jewish Memory*. University of California Press. https://market.android.com/details?id=book-ybowDwAAQBAJ.

Honneth, A. (2007). *Disrespect: The Normative Foundations of Critical Theory*. Polity Press.

Khoury, E. (2017). Foreword. In B. Bashir & A. Goldberg (Eds.), *The Holocaust and the Nakba: A New Grammar of Trauma and History*. Columbia.

Manea, N. (1993). *On Clowns: The Dictator and the Artist: Essays*. Grove Weidenfeld. https://ma rket.android.com/details?id=book-HlC4LVvVPFMC.

Manea, N. (2012). *The Fifth Impossibility: Essays on Exile and Language*. Yale University Press. https://market.android.com/details?id=book-7q3kOJDzKqUC.

Mantel, H. (2020). Being a novelist is no fun. But fun isn't high on my list. *The Observer*, The New Review, 4th October.

Rose, J. (2017). Afterword: The Holocaust and Al Nakba. In B. Bahir & A. Goldberg (Eds.), Op. Cit. (pp. 363–384).

Rushdie, S. (2012). *Imaginary Homelands: Essays and Criticism 1981–1991*. Random House. https://play.google.com/store/books/details?id=y385XCOrVZIC.

Rushdie, S. (2015). *Two Years, Eight Months and Twenty-Eight Nights*. Random House. https://ma rket.android.com/details?id=book-9h8rCQAAQBAJ.

Shafak, E. (2020). *How to Stay Sane in an Age of Division: The Powerful, Pocket-sized Manifesto*. Profile Books. https://play.google.com/store/books/details?id=cTbIDwAAQBAJ.

Solnit, R. (2017). *The Mother of all Questions: Further Feminisms*. Granta Books. https://play. google.com/store/books/details?id=dNslDwAAQBAJ.

West, L. (1996). *Beyond Fragments: Adults, Motivation and Higher Education*. Taylor and Francis.

West, L. (2016). *Distress in the City: Racism, Fundamentalism and a Democratic Education*. Trentham Books, UCL Institute of Education Press.

Winnicott, D. (1971). *Playing and Reality*. Routledge.

Zreik, Z. (2017). Writing silence: Reading Khoury's novel Children of the Ghetto: My name is Adam. In B. Bahir & A. Goldberg (Eds.), Op. Cit. (pp. 307–328).

14

A DIALOGUE ON MIGRATION, CRITICAL AUTO/BIOGRAPHICAL RESEARCH AND TRANSFORMATIVE EDUCATION

Silvia Luraschi and Fergal Finnegan

This chapter aims to present a crossed perspective between two researchers having different experience in biographic research with migrants in Italy and Ireland. We use a dialogic form of writing for questioning the transformative potential of exploring stories about migration. We hope that readers can follow our dialogue to reflect with us about the use of auto/biographical materials for learning together in migration societies.

Fergal: Let me first say how much I'm looking forward to this discussion. I have found what you have said about your research with migrants on various occasions we have met in recent years really fascinating. So... the plan is to explore together migration and education based on critical auto/biographical research and puzzle out what we have learnt and how this might be built upon educationally.

Migration is a 'big' political issue, but let's begin in a less grand way. After all, we are both biographical researchers who believe that in-depth accounts of personal experience are immensely rich sources of knowledge. Both of us believe that biographical interviews always have a context, and the particular shape the story takes depends on the relationship between the interviewer as well as the interviewee. This means we need to be reflexive and honest about our investments and interests in any research topic (see West, 1996). Maybe you can start by saying something about yourself and the topic of migration?

Auto/Biographies as A Source of Critical Knowledge on Migration

Silvia: Yes, I was born in Como (north-west of Italy, Lombardy) forty years ago. In my childhood, I learned from my maternal grandparents to love walking in the woods to collect firewood. They were poor farmers from Polesine (north-east of Italy, Veneto) that migrated to Como because a catastrophic flood hit their region

DOI: 10.4324/9781003124412-17

in 1951. They lost their home and everything else like the other 180,000 people that lived in a strip of land located between the lower courses of the Adige and Po rivers. Walking together in the woods they told me of their experience in Venetian dialect: in 1951 Paola, my grandmother, was pregnant with my mother, and they lived for a period in a reception center near Venice with their three children and other displaced people. Here, Gino, my grandfather, decided to move, looking for a job in Como where some relatives were hosted after the flood. In fact, in that period, several displaced people migrated from Veneto to north-west (Lombardy or Piedmont), because this part of Italy was becoming an industrial area of primary importance and needed workers.

This fragment of my autobiography (Merrill & West, 2009) shows how I became familiar with walking together and telling stories in my daily life. Let me expand a bit on how I see autobiographical research. My epistemological background is based on systemic thinking and constructionism (von Foerster, 1981; Gergen, 1999). Based on these perspectives, stories and meaning are only subjective because they are developed in a context with its own possibilities and constraints. So, radical constructivism and systemic perspectives require that we make explicit the researcher's own assumptions. As an autobiographical researcher this request concerns epistemological and biographical experiences intertwined with one another (Merrill & West, 2009).

I am aware that my interests in creating stories in movement are not separate from my daily life experiences where, like in my childhood, I continue walking through landscapes, and from my research's interest in walking as a method and methodology in qualitative research. In fact, during my last research (see chapter 9), I experimented with the sensobiographic walk (Järviluoma, 2017), a method of inquiry that creates, through rhythms of walking, a process of engaging with embodied and invisible stories. In this experience my autobiography participated on a plurality of levels in the co-construction of the narrative and embodied materials by building the interpretative frame.

Fergal: The story is really interesting. Even though we have discussed these topics before, I never knew all of this, and it helps me make sense of you and your research in a new way.

Paying attention to your own investments and commitments in research is a challenge but is rewarding. I am fascinated by the slow and subtle way we become visible to ourselves, and how often through research I discover something about my own experience and assumptions that I had not fully acknowledged or thought through before. That is the case for me with this book. My main research focus is on equality and higher education. I have interviewed migrants as part of my work, but I would not say that I have great expertise on migration. Nonetheless, it is a deeply embodied and proximate interest: for my partner is a migrant; our child is Polish/Irish; and my father and grandparents had to seek a living in a life outside of Ireland. Besides these reasons, I have been what is, often disapprovingly, called in the media an 'economic migrant' for brief periods in my life, including doing construction in the 'shadow' economy.

Teaching migrants for many years, I regard this as one of the truly formative stages in my own education. They were mainly adults but also children who had arrived in Ireland without their families. The stories these students from all over the world told me about themselves and migration, their everyday concerns, the joys, tragedies, and confusions, have stayed with me at a deep level. It is something I think about a lot—the stories that lodge and become part of us, part of our sense of how the world is. I believe they have the power to shape our dispositions and influences our affinities, identifications, and disidentifications in social space...what Bourdieu (1990) calls habitus.

My interest in migration is storied but also historical, and I would like to say something about the ways historical memory can be brought to bear on critical biographical research in general, and the topic of migration in particular. My way of approaching migration is rooted in an interpretation of Ireland's rather peculiar history as a semi-peripheral colony (O'Hearn, 2001). On a basic level, the effects of famine and economic underdevelopment in the 19th and 20th century mean that every Irish family has friends and family who migrated abroad. It is tied into widely available repertoires of meanings and symbols through story, song, and film (Cleary, 2006). We are a migrant people, 'Thousands are sailing' as a punk folk band I like a lot—the Pogues—put it. On a deeper level within Irish culture, and even in many strands of Irish nationalism, there is a deep knowledge that migration is an often forced, frequently difficult experience, and most Irish people have some understanding of what it means to be viewed as lesser and deficient in metropolitan cultures permeated by colonialist and imperialist ideas (Said, 1994). The periphery, or at least a history of being peripheral, casts things in a different light. It makes you aware of the arrogance of the powerful and how sure they are that their story, their history is 'the' history (Gopal, 2020). Have you ever seen any of those 19th century images of the animalistic and violent Irish "testing the patience and forbearance" of the British empire?[1]

I think the Irish story of colonial exploitation and misrecognition can help us read some of what is at stake in thinking about migration, in relation to power and the sources of racism. There is a picture of a boarding house in England in the 1950s which has been circulated widely, which says "No Irish, No blacks, No dogs." It is very well known in Ireland, a cipher and even a cliché of what we were once deemed, and a marker of what we have become.

We make journeys across land and sea as lone travelers with this or that talent and this or that idiosyncrasy, or we migrate in families or even larger groups, but regardless, we always feel the wind of history at our back. We are within a social space marked and defined by unequal access to the sources of social power (Bourdieu, 1984; Lefebvre, 1991). Without a grounding in history and an explicit theory of power, we miss a great deal—in fact I would say that migration cannot be really understood without these resources. So, the biographical interview is always in some sense autobiographical, but also sociological and historical.

Certainly, this has affected how I listen to migrants when I conduct interviews. It also bridges familial stories with wider histories. My father experienced a type of cultural dispossession, or at least displacement, as an Irish person in England. Despite the fact he moved there as a child, was educated there, and escaped poverty through measures taken by the British welfare state, he never felt England was his home—he returned to Ireland to marry my mother and never left. To add a layer to this story, some of his immediate family are proudly, even xenophobically English, and some even repeat anti-Irish slurs without a great deal of irony.

This is all a way of saying that migration is an evocative word for me—with a dense web of associations, which cannot be truthfully described as research 'out there' separate from my own experience, and perceptions which are not fully legible without an understanding of power.

Biographical Research and Reflecting on Migration

Silvia: These fragments from the Irish past remind me of the past of many Italians abroad: "Interdit aux chiens et aux Italiens" (No dogs or Italians allowed), a sign that Italian miners and their families found outside a café in Belgium in the 1950s. It is also what internal migrants (from the South or North-east of Italy) had experienced in the North-west where I was born. I was recently doing research in Lecco (see chapter 9), an industrial area in between the Lake of Como and Milan. In the past, it made use of workers from the South and North-east of Italy (Colli, 1999). Migration isn't a new phenomenon in Lecco—and more in general— internal migration from the South to North of Italy is a structural and evident reality (Colucci, 2018). One of the participants of the research, Cristina, created a biographical connection between her past experience of contact with migrants from the South and North-east, as my grandparents and her present attitude in front of migrants. Actually, Cristina was the mayor of a small village[2] on the shore of Lake Como. During an autobiographical interview in her home with her and her father (with whom she lives) sitting around a table together, she told me how she learned to be welcoming to migrants:

CRISTINA: I was born here in Abbadia Lariana, but my parents weren't from here. ... I know that seems strange, because their places of birth are very close to here, but in the past they were foreigners for the natives. ... My parents have always been very open with people who arrived here from the South of Italy. My father was a railway worker, and I saw the people who came looking for jobs. In the 1970s, there was a big migration of *Meridionali*. Silvia, do you have Southern origins?

SILVIA: I was born in Como, but my mother is from Veneto.

CRISTINA: Here too, there are many people from Veneto, and in general they were welcomed better than people from the South. A lot of families arrived here from the South by train, but they didn't have a house or simply a place to stay, so it was really hard for them at the beginning. So, my father saw them, and some families came to stay with us for a period.

SILVIA: What do you remember of that period?

CRISTINA: It was funny. We lived together in this flat that it isn't big enough for all, but nevertheless, we held each other. They slept in the living room, and I played a lot with the kids. Some of them are, even today, friends. ... After the migration from the South, it was started migration coming from foreign countries. The first were Vietnamese saved in the Gulf of Siam in 1979.

Cristina's point of view shows a historical process of migrations that create social stratifications where migrants are, generally, in a disadvantaged position—because natives recognize them as 'others.' Local identity seems based on division and dichotomy: separating 'us' from 'foreigners,' but at the same time, natives support migrants and make durable connections with them. Cristina's words describe a different perception of migrants in the North-west: there are people from the East that, "were welcomed better than people from the South," because Veneti have historically been considered as strong workers in comparison to people from the South, who are considered just lazy. This idea of division between a backward South, and an advanced West and North is the effect of 'The Southern Question' that has never been resolved from the end of the 19th Century (Gramsci, 1995). It is still present and invisible at the same time, which is difficult to explore because for many Italians, it is a painful past. Do you think the Irish experience can help me to understand better what Italians, including me, think about migration?

Fergal: Not Irish experience as such, there are peculiarities and points of interest in Irish history for sure, but it is hardly exceptional and certainly not useful if we treat the Irish state as some sort of undifferentiated, unified whole with a clear boundary between what is internal and external. We need to methodologically and conceptually to make a break with the nation state, in analyzing migration, as Gramsci grasped so acutely, and also as your research in Lecco indicates. A critical understanding of colonial history can make us sensitive to the hidden stories, to the complex forms of economic and symbolic domination that get described as 'just how things are' of even the 'nature' of a given group or people.

Also, historical memories—even very painful ones—can easily be domesticated and romanticized. Some things in a culture get passed around so often, they become smooth as stone—these made bright and simple like the touched part of a bronze statue. In the Irish case here, there are many complexities and contradictions in this colonial story. We know that the Irish served as stewards of Empire, learned to become white, and used that power to their advantage in the U.S. (Ignatiev, 1995). Now Ireland is very wealthy, if unequal, and for a small country quite influential in international economics and politics.

Besides, I am wary of how some committed researchers simplify in order to denounce injustice. I think that if we only search for oppression, we can inadvertently treat migrants as abject. To my mind, biographical research discloses the extent to which migrants are agentic and adaptive, as well as subject to social forces and historical legacies (see also Alheit & Dausien, 2000). Critical research has to seek and work through the tensions and contradictions in both history and individual biographies. For me, the crucial thing is to be personally and socially reflexive by becoming aware of how perceived affinities or differences feed into critical research, teaching, and activism. What do you think?

Silvia: I considered perceived affinities and differences as strategic sources to develop a critical reflection in research and teaching. For example, when I listened to the story of Cristina, I'm aware that her point of view about the welcome given to people from Veneto, evoked memories of my grandmother's tears when she told me her first difficult period in Como. Cristina said that natives were welcoming with the Venetians, but my grandmother, who was a migrant from Veneto, told me an opposed experience. My grandmother worked as a cleaner in a hospice, and she had to leave her three children alone because her husband was working in construction sites out of their home for weeks. Unlike Cristina's point of view, my grandmother felt lonely and unsupported by locals. In fact, her kids were brought up by themselves and were bullied in school. I think that we can find affinities from these past difficulties of my family and the present conditions, as inequalities of a large part of migrants in Italy. In fact, we know that many migrant women are care workers (Azzurra et al., 2019), especially for elder people, and many foreign children have difficulty in school learning and socializing with their teachers and classmates—because the Italian school system generates inequalities in education (ISMU, 2020). Narratives that position migration as a problem and migrants as vulnerable people are dominant now in Italy. I think that critical, good quality research can create divergent stories that challenge these linear and one-sided ways of thinking. We must be careful when we listen to stories about migration or when we remember our family stories, because we need to know that the dominant discourse is embedded in those stories. According to Mezzadra and Neilson (2013), in our post-colonial and global contemporary society, borders have become an apparatus to defining collective identities, which are continuing to generate a multiplication of divisions.

Fergal: I agree strongly with what you say about the importance of listening, as Paulo Freire (1970) says it is those who experience a particular oppression who know best what it means. So, what have you learnt from the people you have worked with about migration and about Italy?

Silvia: I honestly feel that I need to learn much more than I have already learned. In particular, I would like to do more research with transnational migrations to understand the complex transformation of the self, and the family relationships for building the 'Here' and 'There' (see chapter 9). But to try to answer your question, I would like to come back to the interview with Cristina, which as you underlined before, bridges familial stories with wider histories. I consider this an opportunity to bring to light the wider histories in a single story, and this is my biggest learning about the context of migration in Italy. I'm learning a lot about the contemporary history of my country from this field of research. For example, it was important to discover that the citizens of the small village where Cristina has always lived, had taken an active part to welcome refugees in 1979. This episode is significant in the history of migration in Italy because it was the first time that an Italian Navy vessel rescued refugees, and certainly it remains the intervention that reached the furthest sites; the Navy vessel travelled from Italy to the Gulf of Siam. Forty years later, Italian journals mention this fact, focusing on the solidarity of Italian people for welcoming refugees in contrast with the current situation "where the risk of migrants and refugees becoming shipwrecked in the Mediterranean and dying at sea is the highest it has ever been due to a lack of NGO rescue ships" (Tondo, 2019). Cristina's experiences permit us to look beyond dominant discourses that describe Italy as a decadent country, where solidarity is a value belonging to the past that was replaced by a national resentment towards migrants. Her words describe a community where two opposed forces are present at the same time. In fact, her family—as several others—was involved in different experiences of cohabitation with migrants in a community, where—at the same time—people have perceived migration as a threat. My hypothesis is that attitudes and habits can be learned subconsciously in everyday life, as Cristina learned from her family to take care of others. Actually, Cristina continued to be sensible to the matter of migration. So, during the interview, she remembers what happened in her town during the last refugee crisis (2016):

CRISTINA: All reception centers were full ..., so I found a place for a group of women from Somalia in a vacant apartment. Here, a group of voluntary women, including myself, were very active for supporting them. It isn't easy! Cultural and linguistic barriers seem to divide us. For the housewarming day, they wore Islamic dresses completely black, and natives were shocked to see them because it was the first time that Muslin women totally veiled walked on the streets. It was a huge misunderstanding! Women dressed in elegant clothes: black is the color for the party, but natives didn't understand, so didn't speak with them.

Once again, Cristina's experience is relevant. In that period, the historically high number of refugees coming to Italy was challenged in terms of 'social inclusion.' Zooming in specifically at the province of Lecco, we can see a visible number of young black men in the streets and, for the first time, a few women with Islamic dresses next to reception centers.

Looking at social inclusion from a micro-level, the everyday point of view takes into consideration a new perception of the migrant's presence in the territory, the manifold ways people try to get along with the people around them, and the environment they live in (Flick et al., 2019). The dominant discourse is that there is a crisis, and people such as Cristina responded to the emergency. This generated a deep and invisible misunderstanding in the Italian perception, which over-estimates the presence of migrants. There is a positive correlation between this mistaken perception and the attitudes toward the migration phenomenon.

Mbembe (2019) creates the neologism 'nanoracism' to define a specific and invisible form of prejudice. For Mbembe, 'nanoracism' is a narcotic form of prejudice based on race that expresses itself in daily life gestures, such as allusions, *lapsus*, jokes, funny stories with a subtext, until arriving to malevolence in public.

Nanoracism is not a prejudice intuitively understandable because it is a concrete posture in daily life. It is a habit, so it appears as a neutral gesture that we are not aware of. I think this is a big challenge for adult education, and I'm worried that adult education cannot handle this in the near future. On the other hand, as Gramsci said, we need pessimism of reason and optimism of spirit to move forward. In Lecco, something impressive happened this last summer after George Floyd was killed in the U.S., triggering a demonstration in the city where young Italian activists created a colorful writing on a square of the city town. They wrote 'Black Lives Matter' and added 'Human' and 'migrant'.[3] I feel that research in adult education should explore the ongoing transformation in the daily lives of young adults. What do you think?

Fergal: Well, let me say first that I think the response to police brutality in the U.S. and internationally has been remarkable, and a beacon of hope in a fairly bleak period. It demonstrates yet again just how powerful egalitarian movements are, not least in terms of what might be called public pedagogy. It is essentially part of a global learning process about power, history, and social structures.

To answer your question about the role of adult education in this, yes, I think the whole purpose of adult education is to support reflexive agency by individuals, communities, and societies in pursuit of human flourishing. I think this means grasping how we are transformed (and how and why we might seek to transform our assumptions, practices, institutions and social relations) is relevant to adults of all ages.

If we are interested in transformative education for migrants and post-migration societies, we have to be cognizant that this does not happen on a level playing field. One of the things I have learned from interviewing and teaching migrants from various places is the need to take into account the various and conflicting ways societies and parts of society make sense of *particular migrant groups*. We need to bear in mind who exactly is rendered invisible or too visible and why. Not everyone becomes an object of scrutiny, charity, or loathing—in Ireland, black Africans and Muslim women wearing a hijab are marked out as 'different,' and rich migrants are treated as emigres and expats. At the same time, all sorts of work and activities done by migrants are overlooked. So, I think part of critical research is to make sense of how this relates to hierarchies, moral economies, and resources.

I should also say that I am very interested in the related but distinct way that migratory flows are discursively framed. In your stories, you mentioned 'internal' migrants, Vietnamese boat people, and the recent migrant 'crisis' are discursively mediated in distinct ways. For me, it is well worth asking why one of the biggest migrations in human history with major global consequences—the movement from rural to urban areas in China in the past twenty years—is discussed so little in Europe. Or, we can reflect on the way events are forgotten or normalized through time. To pick some historical examples, we could talk about the half million people who fled the Falange as the Spanish Republic fell in the 1930s, or the millions of German speakers leaving newly gained Polish territories in 1945–1950, or mass migration to Portugal in the 1970s following the revolution there in 1974, and the subsequent rapid decolonization of Portuguese colonies in Africa. I wonder why these are not remembered as crises, or how this might position us in relation to contemporary movements of people. I think we need to actively foster a type of active, radical, historically informed type of awareness that bears witness to the complexities of migratory flows with especial focus on power and inequalities in education (Mayo, 2013).

Silvia: Yes, speaking about migration solely in terms of crisis reinforces negative prejudices toward migrants—in particular black and/or Muslim people—and discourages migrants' participation in democratic life, feeding an instrumental utilization of immigrants for the labor market that emphasizes the distance between 'us' and 'them' and remains a dualist vision of our society. To further explore these dimensions, during my last research I decided with Laura[4] to organize a seminar for high school students in Lecco. We held a seminar with 250 young students who are social workers with migrant backgrounds and researchers on migration. We tried to generate a space for dialogue with students and spent time to reflect on their frames of reference (Mezirow, 2003) in a public auditorium.

At the beginning of the seminar, we asked the students to write three words about migrants on their mobile phone and share those words by creating 'word clouds.' The question was: when you thought about migrants, what words came to your mind? And the answers were: words that evoke poverty, pain, and misery. At the end of the seminar, we asked the same question, but the answer was different. The words in our clouds were: hope, journey, courage, changes, and sharing. What happened during the seminar? Students listened to personal and professional stories of and about migration: Fanta describes how she has become an active member of the Burkinabe community in Lecco and her engagement in educational intervention with migrants and natives. Brizida, a lawyer, told her struggle with Italian bureaucracy and her work for promoting equalities of migrants in Lecco. Apart from them, Lidia, a sociologist, presented to the students her ongoing project about love in the age of globalization with multicultural families (Manzo, 2020). She considers love relationships a 'silent revolution' that permits us to challenge habits and beliefs in our daily life. The teenagers were very impressed—I saw their faces very focused from the first stage…what is your experience?

Fergal: I can well imagine that such a silent revolution is taking place. What you have said connects to my research. Interviews with migrants and other 'non-traditional' students prompted me to read about recognition and respect. Honneth (1995), the German critical theorist, makes the case that love and care in intimate relationships is a profound form of recognition. As an educator, I think it is worth linking this to institutional modes of (mis)recognition. Many migrants I have spoken to, see education as a space in which they can prove their worth to society. In some cases, this was described as a type of reconstruction of self. The experience of downward mobility, being locked into unrewarding work or a loss of status, can be profoundly wounding, a type of disrespect for migrants, and education is seen as a path to overcoming these challenges. There is a doubleness to this, though. It discloses just how much people feel they are at a disadvantage and have been made explicitly or tacitly to feel they somehow do not measure up to the 'norms' of Irish society, which is racialized as well as classed and gendered.

Reflections on the Need and Possibility for Transformative Education in Post-migration Societies

Fergal: Doing biographical interviews and teaching has taught me a valuable lesson that in our particular type of highly commodified, individualistic, and accelerated society, there is often very little space and time for people to consider the complexities of their own life in a critical and open way. Despite the fact that we spend more and more time in the education system, it still fails to provide a space for the exploration of the complex realities of everyday life. This open space is perhaps especially important for making sense of migration, both for migrants and for society as a whole. It sounded like there was some of this 'space' for dialogue and recognition with the teenagers you spoke with, and I would love to hear more from you about this.

Silvia: After the seminar, students completed a questionnaire. For most of them, this was an occasion to realize through the event that they do not have any contact with newcomers, and some expressed an interest to participate jointly with newly arrived migrants in future research. At the same time, they recognized that some friends and schoolmates are second generation and they have never talked about what it means for them. So, I decided to design a new educational project to involve high-school students and foreign students who study Italian in school for adults in Lecco. I hope to coordinate new sensobiographic walks soon...

Fergal: I think these sorts of initiatives designed for specific groups of migrants and for youth in a post migration society are very important, even vital. Before we finish, I also want to say how adult education might respond to people who feel left behind or marginalized in post-migration societies. I have spent the past six months analyzing far right YouTube and social media accounts in Ireland, and based on this I am convinced that a type of social disorientation—a certain type of mourning for lost or damaged life worlds—is quite widespread, and this is being actively manipulated by the far-right. I think this is also the case elsewhere, and is captured well in Eribon's memoir (2018) and in West's *Distress in the City* (2016). I think this is a very complex and delicate matter: if people feel they have lost their lifeworld—ways of being, ways of seeing, or aspects of this—then we need to find ways of doing research to speak to that. My impression is that this is above all a narrowing, a loss of hope, and a lack of futurability (Berardi, 2017)—this has become tied up with changes, which are easy to name. Fearfulness and anxious hostility are channeled at what is deemed 'unfamiliar,' but really marks the spread of a form of hopelessness. I think the only way that we can respond is by opening up space for hopeful and critical dialogues. I hope this does not sound obsessive, but in educational terms I think this can be best approached biographically by asking what we have learned from our lives (Dominicé, 2000) about continuity, change, and the sources of reflexive agency. I think community and popular education along with some course in higher education could help facilitate this. Sparking dialogue within and between communities who are badly disenfranchised and migrants seems necessary to me, but I have no time for political organizations and media outlets which purport to stand for the disenfranchised, and promote lies and half-truths. This political use of anxiety needs to be actively combated in adult education and beyond.

Let me say a bit more about what I mean by 'beyond.' I think we also need to avoid the educator's trap or myth that the best response to every situation is more education. It is crucial to develop new educational forms, but to know the limits of what this can do as well. Transformative learning in relation to migration and racism is simply too important to leave to academics or even solely adult education—this is a multistranded social learning process across diverse publics.

Silvia: What does 'beyond' mean to me? I think that transformative learning has to challenge the patriarchal conception of the world. In Italy, for example, education of the common sense is still very traditional. We categorize people in the category: 'good' or 'bad.' This process is automatic, and it also concerns me. Educating for a critical consciousness (Sanford et al., 2020) means deconstructing binary oppositions—as native/migrant, white/black, masculinity/femininity, etc.—to discuss and explore processes of discrimination, oppression, and racism like the ones we are writing about in this chapter. It is a long and complex journey where the patriarchal forms of adult education practices and studies are always around the corner! I think that *feminist pedagogies* show us the way: for a multistranded social learning process across diverse publics, to employ nonformal education and informal learning strategies aimed to encourage adult educators, researchers, and citizens to recognize how our social backgrounds and biography influence our perspective and our praxis.

Notes

1 https://en.wikipedia.org/wiki/Anti-Irish_sentiment#/media/File:Monkeyirishman.jpg
2 Abbadia Lariana, 3225 inhabitants at January 2019 when the interview took place.
3 https://www.leccofm.it/2020/08/08/in-piazza-garibaldi-la-scritta-black-human-migrant-lives-matter/
4 Laura Formenti, supervisor of the project 'Unexpected Subject' (see Chapter 9).

References

Alheit, P., & Dausien, B. (2000). Biographicity as a basic resource of lifelong learning. In J. B. P. Alheit, E. Kammler, R. Taylor, & H. S. Olesen (Eds.), *Lifelong Learning Inside and Outside Schools: Collected Papers of the European Conference on Lifelong Learning* (pp. 400–422). Roskilde University.

Azzurra, C., Bhattacharya, T., & Fraser, N. (2019). *Feminism for the 99 Percent*. Verso.

Berardi, F. (2017). *Futurability: The Age of Impotence and the Horizon of Possibility*. Verso.

Bourdieu, P. (1984). *Distinction: A Social Critique of the Judgement of Taste*. Routledge and Kegan Paul.

Bourdieu, P. (1990). *The Logic of Practice*. Polity.

Cleary, J. (2006). *Outrageous Fortune: Capital and Culture in Modern Ireland*. Field Day Publications in Association with the Keough-Naughton Institute for Irish Studies at the University of Notre Dame.

Colli, A. (1999). *Legami di Ferro. Storia del distretto metallurgico e meccanico lecchese tra Otto e Novecento*. Donizelli Editore.

Colucci, M. (2018). *Storia dell'immigrazione straniera in Italia. Dal 1945 ai giorni nostri*. Carocci Editore.

Dominicé, P. (2000). *Learning from our Lives: Using Educational Biographies with Adults*. Jossey-Bass.

Eribon, D. (2018). *Returning to Reims*. Allen Lane.

Flick, U., Hirseland, A., & Hans, B. (2019). Walking and talking integration: Triangulation of data from interviews and go-alongs for exploring immigrant welfare recipients' sense(s) of belonging. *Qualitative Inquiry*, 25(8), 799–810.

Formenti, L. (2018). Complexity, adult biographies and co-operative transformation. In M. Milana, S. Webb, J. Holford, R. Waller, & P. Jarvis (Eds.), *The Palgrave International Handbook on Adult and Lifelong Education and Learning* (pp. 191–209). Palgrave Macmillan.

Formenti, L., & West, L. (2016). *Stories that Make a Difference*. Pensa MultiMedia.

Freire, P. (1970). *Pedagogy of the Oppressed*. Seabury.

Gergen, K. J. (1999). Agency: Social Construction and Relational Action. *Theory & Psychology*, 9(1), 113–115. https://doi.org/10.1177/0959354399091007.

Gopal, O. (2020) *Insurgent Empire: Anticolonial Resistance and British Dissent*. Verso.

Gramsci, A. (1995). *The Southern Question*. Translated from Italian by P. Verdicchio. Guernica Editions Inc.

Honneth, A. (1995). *The Struggle for Recognition: The Moral Grammar of Social Conflict*. Polity Press.

Ignatiev, N. (1995). *How the Irish Became White*. Routledge.

ISMU Fondazione. (2020) *Venticinquesimo Rapporto sulle Migrazioni 2019*. Franco Angeli.

Järviluoma, H. (2017). The Art and Science of Sensory Memory Walking. In M. Cobussen, V. Meelberg, & B. Truax (Eds.), *The Routledge Companion to Sounding Art* (pp. 191–204), Routledge.

Lefebvre, H. (1991). *The Production of Space*. Basil Blackwell.

Manzo, L. K. C. (2020). Love in a diverse city. *The Sociological Review*, April 2020. https://www.thesociologicalreview.com/love-in-a-diverse-city/.

Mayo, P. (2013). *Echoes from Freire for a Critically Engaged Pedagogy*. Bloomsbury.

Mbembe, A. (2019). *Nanorazismo. Il corpo notturno della democrazia*. Laterza.

Merrill, B., & West, L. (2009). *Using Biographical Methods in Social Research*. Sage.

Mezirow, J. (1991). *Transformative Dimensions of Adult Learning*. Jossey-Bass.

Mezirow, J. (2003). Transformative learning as discourse. *Journal of Transformative Education*, 1, 58–63.

Mezzadra, S., & Neilson, B. (2013). *Border as Method, Or, The Multiplication of Labor*. Duke University Press.

O'Hearn, D. (2001). *The Atlantic Economy: Britain, the US and Ireland*. Manchester University Press.

Said, E. W. (1994). *Culture and Imperialism*. Vintage.

Sanford, K., Clover, D., Taber, N., & Williamson, S. (Eds.). (2020). *Feminist Critique and the Museum. Education for a Critical Consciousness*. Brill/Sense.

Tondo, L. (2019). Mediterranean will be "sea of blood" without rescue boats, UN warns. *The Guardian*, 9th June. https://www.theguardian.com/world/2019/jun/09/mediterranean-sea-of-blood-migrant-refugee-rescue-boats-un-unhcr.

von Foerster, H. (1981). *Observing Systems*. Intersystems Publications.

West, L. (1996). *Beyond Fragments: Adults, Motivation, and Higher Education: A Biographical Analysis*. Taylor & Francis.

West, L. (2016). *Distress in the City: Racism, Fundamentalism and a Democratic Education*. UCL Institute of Education Press.

ACKNOWLEDGEMENTS

As this book is the product of a symposium which brought together scholars from across Europe, we want to acknowledge and thank the Zentrum Flucht und Migration (Center for Flight and Migration) at the Katholische Universität Eichstätt-Ingolstadt for their financial support of this event. We also thank Janka Böhm for her handling of the many logistical tasks. After coordinating travel arrangements, hotel reservations, catering services, and other such necessities for our symposium, Janka had to turn around and undo all of her hard work when the Covid-19 pandemic forced us to convert the event to an online format. We also acknowledge Janka's help with preliminary literature research in preparation for this project.

Two graduate students of NC State University's Adult, Workforce, and Continuing Professional Education program, Somanita Kheang and Elizabeth Slagle, provided invaluable editing and proofreading assistance.

Lastly, we thank Dr. Michael Schirner for offering his photograph for use on the cover of this book. His commentary on the photo is perhaps the best way to explain its choice and significance.

> This bridge is located in eastern Poland, not far from the provincial towns of Drohiczyn and Siemiatycze, and is one of the few bridges over the Bug River. It reminds me of the short story by Andrzej Stasiuk '816' in which he describes the Bug and the parallel provincial road 816 as "the gap between the tectonic plates of history."
>
> Here along the Bug River, Europe's recent history has been relentless. A break of apocalyptic proportions. On the one hand there were horrific extermination camps, on the other hand in the vast expanses of the Soviet Union the bloody experiment of a better person.

DOI: 10.4324/9781003124412-18

Bridges are human structures that create connections between people; enable their movement across the boundaries of nature and history. There is something powerful and stable about this bridge. You can see the story on her. It leads far into the foreign land. It's like cast iron brackets that hold things together that would otherwise drift apart. The bridge in every form is a symbol that crises can be overcome.

INDEX

Page numbers in bold refer to tables. Page numbers followed by 'n' refer to notes.